LF

D1304872

DOING BUSINESS IN LESS DEVELOPED COUNTRIES

Financial Opportunities and Risks

Mashaalah Rahnama-Moghadam,
Hedayeh Samavati, and David A. Dilts

Q

Quorum Books
Westport, Connecticut • London

Library of Congress Cataloging-in-Publication Data

Rahnama-Moghadam, Mashaalah.
    Doing business in less developed countries : financial
opportunities & risks / Mashaalah Rahnama-Moghadam, Hedayeh
Samavati, David A. Dilts.
        p.   cm.
    Includes bibliographical references and index.
    ISBN 0–89930–854–6 (alk. paper)
    1. Developing countries—Foreign economic relations.
2. Developing countries—Commerce.   3. Investments, Foreign—
Developing countries.   I. Samavati, Hedayeh.   II. Dilts, David A.
III. Title.
HF1413.R34 1995
332.6'73'091724–dc20   94–24986

British Library Cataloguing in Publication Data is available.

Library of Congress Catalog Card Number: 94–24986
ISBN: 0–89930–854–6

First published in 1995

Quorum Books, 88 Post Road West, Westport, CT 06881
An imprint of Greenwood Publishing Group, Inc.

Printed in the United States of America

The paper used in this book complies with the
Permanent Paper Standard issued by the National
Information Standards Organization (Z39.48—1984).

10   9   8   7   6   5   4   3   2   1

Contents

Tables and Figures

Preface

This book is a natural extension of the authors' academic research programs. Two of the authors have been involved in examining the rescheduling of debt in less developed countries (LDCs) and the third in examining the impact of the North American Free Trade Agreement (NAFTA) on U.S. labor markets. In conducting their academic research programs, it became painfully clear that there was very little written for the practitioner that dealt specifically with the part that debt played in international business relations with LDCs. The purpose of this book is to synthesize the available academic research, particularly in finance and economics, and make it accessible to practitioners.

No previous academic training or experience in international business is necessary for the reader to gain full advantage from this book. Sufficient background is developed throughout the book for the reader to fully appreciate the concepts and information presented.

The authors have focused specifically on indebted LDCs. The reason for this relatively narrow focus, as discussed in Chapter 1, is that there has been adequate treatment of many of the issues facing businesses in international markets. Rather than burdening this book with volumes of discussion concerning more general topics, the reader is simply referred to the existing literature.

Acknowledgments

As with any undertaking of this size, the authors are indebted to several persons. The families of the authors of any book always sacrifice quality time. Thanks go to Sahand, Christina, Ariana, Jordan, and Ross for their patience and sacrifices. Thanks also go to June Hungerford, a work-study student who devoted her talents and energies to typing some of the tables for this book for which the authors are indebted. We are also grateful to Jim Whitcraft for all his patience and good work.

Eric Valentine, as always, was patient to a fault and gave valued encouragement. The editorial and production staff at Greenwood Publishing Group also provided expertise and substantial support to us in completing this project. To them go our thanks.

Several colleagues were involved in previous research projects that helped to shape this book. Larry Haber, in particular, provided input through portions of this project. Ahmad Karim was also a useful source of information and guidance. To both these colleagues go our thanks. Any errors of omission or commission belong to the authors.

Part I

INTRODUCTION TO LESS DEVELOPED COUNTRIES

Every definition is dangerous.   —Erasmus, *Adagia* (1500)

Chapter 1

Economic Globalization, Developing Economies, and Business

> The whole of science is nothing more than the refinement of everyday thinking.   —Albert Einstein

Just a couple of decades ago international business was considered by most academics and business people alike to be rather glamorous but still not very important to the well-being of the United States. The first Arab oil crisis in 1973 brought home the message that the American and European economies were dependent on other countries. Since that time the study and practice of international business has grown dramatically in the industrialized world.

Because most of the world's nations are less developed countries (LDCs) any discussion of international business will involve LDCs. The U.S. Department of Commerce reports that during the first half of 1994 the second largest customer of U.S. products in the world (i.e., Mexico) is an LDC. With the passage of the North American Free Trade Agreement (NAFTA) and continued expansion of economic interdependence, Mexico will continue to be a very important trading partner and potential location for American businesses. Most of the world's oil, latex, and mineral wealth is found in LDCs, and perhaps more important still is the fact the preponderance of the world's population (hence consumers and laborers) are also residents of LDCs.

There have been numerous textbooks, reference books, and articles written about international business.[1] There is also a large subset of this literature that is specifically concerned with business in LDCs.[2] Since the early 1970s, there has also been a growing literature concerning sovereign debt in LDCs.[3] However, there has been little attempt to synthesize and integrate the literature on international business, LDCs, and LDC debt in a practical guide to understanding and doing business in indebted LDCs.

The purpose of this chapter is twofold. First, this chapter will present a brief introduction to the increasing importance of international business in indebted LDCs. Second, the organization of this book will be presented.

IMPORTANCE OF INTERNATIONAL BUSINESS IN INDEBTED LDCS

International trade has always been an important aspect of national economies. Since the beginning of recorded history, there have been records of trade among nations. In fact, several nations were known mostly for their roles as merchants in international markets (e.g., Venice of the fifteenth century). In today's community of nations, there has been substantial reliance on imports and exports. Since the end of World War II, there has also been the development of international organizations designed to facilitate economic growth, political stability and peaceful resolution of disputes between nations. It is, therefore, unlikely that international trade and business will decline.

In the years since World War II, there has been increasing attention paid to the world's less developed regions. In part, this is a result of the demise of colonialism and the rise of independent nations in these regions. The importance of the developing regions of the world as sources of natural and human resources and for potential markets has also become recognized. The result is that international operations and trade in these regions of the world will become increasingly important to businesses in the developed regions of the world. Unless the governments and private enterprises in the developed world recognize the potential of the developing regions and plan for meaningful economic relations with these areas, substantial opportunities may be missed and economic well-being harmed.

In 1957, the United States was the largest supplier of goods and services in international markets, accounting for just over 18 percent of all the world's exports. In the same year, 14 percent of all goods and services imported into a country were imported into the United States.[4]

By 1991, exports from other nations had increased to such an extent that the U.S. share had declined to about 12 percent (even though U.S. exports increased by over 9 percent per year).[5] On the other hand, the United States maintained its leadership position as the largest importer of goods and services in the world.[6]

In 1960, just over 10 percent of all exports from LDCs went to the United States, with another 23 percent going to the European Economic Community (EEC) countries. By 1990, LDCs' exports to the United States increased to over 26 percent, and to the European community to nearly 24 percent.[7] Over one-half of all exports from LDCs go to industrialized countries. On the other hand, in 1960 about 34 percent of LDCs' imports were from the United States and another 22.4 percent were from the EEC. By 1990, the proportion of American commodities imported by LDCs fell to about 31 percent, and imports from the EEC fell to 12 percent.[8]

Part of the decline in imports is a result of trade among the LDCs growing significantly during the same period. In 1960, only about 22 percent of all imports in LDCs came from other LDCs. By 1990, imports between LDCs grew to just over 26 percent of the total.[9] This observed increase in LDC interdependence and proportional reduction in dependence on developed countries arises for two reasons. First, there has been a significant growth in free trade arrangements among LDCs.[10] Second, there has also been real economic growth in many LDCs that permit them to be competitive in international markets.[11]

The majority of the world's LDCs are indebted.[12] This indebtedness has a substantial influence on the risk of doing business in and trading with these LDCs. As is discussed in greater detail in Part III of this book, the debt burdens of LDCs affect the social and political environments of these countries and may create substantial burdens on the economies of these countries.

Because the majority of the world's potential consumers and work force lives in LDCs, economic growth in LDCs has the potential of creating vast markets for goods and services from developed countries. As many companies have already discovered, the relatively low wages in many of these LDCs create a significant incentive to locate operations in these countries.

Changes in technology, particularly in communications and transportation have caused the nations of the world to have more ready access to one another. Globalization of the economic systems of all countries is a natural consequence of this improvement in technology. There is simply no reason to believe that this trend will not continue to accelerate, making it imperative for developed nations' businesses to position themselves to compete in the developing world's economies. Thus, a better understanding of economic and political environments in these countries is imperative.

ORGANIZATION OF THE BOOK

The focus of this book is on providing the practitioner with the information necessary to be able to understand and deal with the various opportunities and constraints of doing business in indebted LDCs. Most professional books and college textbooks devote a chapter or two concerning LDCs. The cultural, political, legal, and institutional differences across nations have been examined at length elsewhere in the literature.[13] Therefore, this book will focus specifically on LDCs and the role their debt plays in international business.

Organization of Chapters

This book is divided into four parts. Part I introduces LDCs. Part II of the book gives theoretical and historical background upon which the remainder of the book is based. Part III is concerned with LDC debt, how it was acquired, for what purposes, and what determines a country's inability to meet its debt obligations. Part IV deals with the business practices necessary to survive operations in or trade with an indebted LDC.

Part I contains two other chapters. Chapter 2 is concerned with definitional issues and a general description of LDCs. Chapter 3 describes specific characteristics of LDCs.

Part II provides the theoretical and historical framework in which to understand how LDCs became less developed, how they became indebted, and why trade with these countries may be beneficial. Chapter 4 is an economic history. It examines the rise of the mercantilist school of thought and colonialism that gave impetus to many regions of the world becoming less developed. Chapter 5 is an examination of the economic theories that motivate international trade and business activities.

Part III of this book examines LDC debt and rescheduling. Chapter 6 examines the financial history of the current world debt crisis. Chapter 7 examines the economic causes for LDCs becoming debtor nations. Chapter 8 discusses what LDCs used the loans for and how these uses predict the viability of growth paths for LDCs. Chapter 9 examines debt rescheduling by LDCs and the general implications for LDCs' inability to service their debt. Chapter 10 is a regional examination of debt rescheduling and the regional differences in risk.

Part IV is concerned with business practices in less developed regions of the world. Appropriate strategic management is the key to success in operations in and trade with indebted LDCs. Chapter 11 introduces the peculiarities in dealing with the business environments in indebted LDCs. Chapter 12 examines the unique strategic planning requirements of doing business in indebted LDCs. Chapter 13 is a description of how strategic plans can be implemented in developing regions of the world. Last, Chapter 14 is a discussion of political issues impacting businesses in a free trade environment.

Appendixes and Bibliography

Also contained in this book are two appendixes and a selected, annotated bibliography. Appendix A contains specific economic and financial information concerning the world's indebted LDCs, as a reference.

Appendix B contains an index developed by the authors for the purpose of assessing the infrastructures of LDCs. There are numerous sources of information concerning finances, risk and other important variables concerning international trade. One rather obvious deficiency in the practitioner reporting services has been a consistent and reliable measure of infrastructure. The authors created an index from published data sources to provide a general guide to the relative quality and quantity of infrastructure among the world's countries.

Last is a selected, annotated bibliography. Knowledge comes in two varieties. A person can know something themselves, or, alternatively, a person can know where to find what he or she seeks. The selected, annotated bibliography is intended to provide knowledge of the second kind.

Philosophy

Any work of the size of this book will have a particular philosophical orientation. The authors are economists by training and profession. The economic paradigms used to analyze international trade issues are not value free. Economists' assumptions do much to determine what results will be obtained, and it is these assumptions that contain the key to values built into the analysis. Where assumptions are made in this book, they are identified. It is left to the reader to decide whether the values embodied in these assumptions bias the results.

As discussed in the Preface, the book is intended to be a useful guide to academics and practitioners. Two of the three authors are from an LDC; the third is from the United States. The authors have taken great pains to steer a neutralist course. Both the proponents and opponents of free trade will find things in this book they may believe demonstrate a bias. No work of this nature can be value free; however, there is a conscious attempt not to take sides on the issue of free trade. The authors simply present the information and theories as they saw them, and much of this information supports free trade, based on comparative advantage. However, institutional and political considerations can be harmful to achieving positive results from free trade, and these constraints have also been examined in this book.

SUMMARY AND CONCLUSION

The United States and other developing countries in the world already have substantial economic relations with LDCs. The increasing globalization of the world's economy has reduced the overall importance of the United States in international trade. However, imports and exports still account for a significant proportion of the U.S. gross domestic product (GDP). The recent trend of increased globalization will continue. Because LDCs have the majority of the world's population and resources, it would be wise for businesses in industrialized countries to give consideration to the impact of this trend on their operations.

The authors recognize that there are likely biases in analyses based on assumptions. The authors have generally attempted to steer a neutralist path through the issues presented in this book, but no work of this kind can be value free.

NOTES

1. For example, see Donald A. Ball and Wendell H. McCulloch, Jr., *International Business: Introduction and Essentials*, 4th ed. (Homewood, Ill.: BPI/Irwin, 1990); Michael R. Czinkota, Ilkka A. Ronkainen, and Michael H. Moffet, *International Business*, 3rd ed. (New York: Dryden Press, 1994); and Robert Grosse and Duane Kujawa, *International Business: Theory and Managerial Applications* (Homewood, Ill.: Richard D. Irwin, 1988).

2. See the Selected, Annotated Bibliography for many of the more significant recent publications concerning international business in LDCs and for LDC debt problems.

3. Ibid.

4. International Monetary Fund, "International Financial Statistics," Washington, D.C.: World Bank, February 1992, various tables.

5. Ibid.

6. Ibid.

7. United Nations, *Monthly Bulletin of Statistics*, various issues.

8. Ibid.

9. Ibid.

10. Ball and McCulloch, *International Business*, Chapter 2.

11. Ibid.

12. See Chapters 8 and 9 of this volume for further discussion.

13. See note 1 for college textbooks discussing these issues.

Chapter 2

An Introduction to Less Developed Countries and Their Debt

I asked Tom if countries always apologized when they had done wrong, and he says: "Yes; the little ones does."
—Mark Twain, *Tom Sawyer Abroad* (1894)

The purpose of this chapter is to introduce the reader to less developed countries and the basic definitions of terms used throughout this book. The examination of all social, economic, and political phenomena occurs within an analytical framework. Analytical methods in the social sciences are typically founded on assumptions and definitions of terms. Assumptions are used to simplify, and definitions are used to provide common understandings so that meaningful discourse can occur. The purpose of this chapter is to lay the foundation for discussion of less developed countries, their indebtedness, and their business environments.

The term *less developed country* is frequently used in technical and academic discussions and has even found its way into the popular press. Most people have some vague idea of what the term *less developed country* means, but few can offer a precise definition. In general, LDC refers to a country that is experiencing a low stage of economic development. The first section of this chapter will focus on developing a more precise definition of LDCs. However, the formal definition of LDC uses aggregate economic measures as the standard by which the various stages of economic development are identified. Therefore, some definitions of the measures of aggregate economic activity must be presented before the stages of development can be meaningfully defined.

The second section of this chapter focuses on definitional issues concerning national indebtedness. Definitions of the various types of debt observed in LDCs will be examined. The third section of this chapter examines why policymakers, economists, and private decision makers from developed countries should be concerned about the stage of development and the levels of indebtedness in LDCs. The final section of this chapter presents a summary and conclusion.

AGGREGATE ECONOMIC ACTIVITY
AND STAGES OF ECONOMIC DEVELOPMENT

Definition

The term *less developed country* fosters images of poverty, backwardness, and low levels of technological sophistication. In fact, there is some truth in these images. However, there is a large range of nations in the world that are properly described as being less developed. The operable word in the term *less developed country* is *less*. The word *less* undoubtedly conveys a relation. In this sense, that certain country has not reached the levels of economic well-being that *industrialized* nations have. The stages of development are defined purely as a function of the size of the aggregate economic activity of a country. The general economic welfare of the inhabitants, technological sophistication, and other economic characteristics of a country, in turn, are also a function of the size of the nation's total economy. The first step to understanding the stages of development is to determine how aggregate economic activity is measured.

The measurement of the well-being of nations is typically accomplished through devices such as gross national product (GNP), the total market value of all final goods and services produced (or income generated) in a specific nation's economy in one year. The World Bank relies on this definition of economic well-being to define the stages of economic development. To control for the total number of persons who share in a country's GNP, the GNP is divided by the total population of the country. This is called per capita GNP.

The World Bank specifically defines LDCs using per capita GNP as a measure of economic development (well-being).[1] Because per capita GNP is relied upon as the qualifying standard for determining stage of development, the threshold per capita GNP that qualifies a country for LDC status changes each year. In other words, the definition of LDC changes each year because the dollar value of per capita GNP, below which a country is classified as an LDC, changes each year. For example, in 1990, per capita GNP of $7,619 or less placed a country in the LDC category.[2] In 1991, this qualifying per capita GNP rose to $7,910.[3] However, the World Bank also classifies nations in the LDC category as medium-income or low-income nations. In 1991, the World Bank classified LDCs as low-income countries if their per capita GNP was $635 or less.[4] Middle-income countries are those that did not qualify as high-income countries, with a per capita GNP in excess of $7,910, or as a low-income country, requiring a per capita GNP of $635 or less.

In 1991, countries such as the United Kingdom ($16,550 per capita GNP), the United States ($22,240 per capita GNP), Ireland ($11,120 per capita GNP), and Japan ($26,930 per capita GNP) were all high-income countries and hence developed (or industrialized) countries. Middle-income countries, according to the World Bank's classification scheme, included countries such as Saudi Arabia ($7,820 per capita GNP), Greece ($6,340 per capita GNP), Iran ($2,170 per capita GNP), Bolivia ($650 per capita GNP), and Brazil ($2,940 per capita GNP). Low-income countries included Indonesia ($610 per capita GNP), Honduras ($580 per capita GNP), China ($370 per capita GNP), Mozambique ($80 per capita GNP), and Guinea-Bissau ($180 per capita GNP). As can be readily observed, there is a substantial amount of variation in per capita GNP within each classification, suggesting that there are significant differences in the stages of development even within high-, middle-, and low-income classifications.

In 1991, the World Bank classified 116 countries as LDCs, 51 as low income and 65 as middle income.[5] There is a certain arbitrariness in the World Bank's classification scheme. The difference between a country with a per capita GNP of $610 (Indonesia) and one with a per capita GNP of $650 (Bolivia) may not be a sound basis to determine that one or the other country is more or less developed. Under the World Bank's classification scheme the one with $610 is placed in the low-income group, while the $650 per capita GNP is in the middle-income group. Whether there are significant differences in the economic development of Bolivia and Indonesia is subject to debate. What is most important in the World Bank's definition are two things. First, if a country is in the middle- or low-income group, it is classified as an LDC. Second, it is impossible to infer much about the stages of development between countries in either LDC category. The World Bank simply claims that the use of the categories and the label LDC is "convenient."[6]

The World Bank also defines nations with incomes above the $7,910 for 1991 as high-income countries or, in other words, developed economies. These countries are also those that are members of the Organization for Economic Cooperation and Development (OECD). However, three middle-income countries were accorded membership in OECD: Greece, Portugal, and Turkey.[7] Again, countries that are not members of OECD (with the noted three exceptions) may also be classified as LDCs. The income classification is one determinant used to confer membership in OECD.

Exchange Rates

One of the reasons the definition of an LDC changes over time is because of the changing value of the U.S. dollar (which is used as the standard upon which the value of other currencies are determined through exchange rates). The value of the dollar with respect to other nations' currencies is determined in the marketplace; and it is the dollar value of goods and services within each country that the World Bank uses as a gauge to determine each countries' economic well-being (GNP). Therefore, as the value of the dollar changes with respect to the value of other nations' currencies, the threshold requirements to qualify for high-, middle- or low-income classifications will change, even though there may have been no change in real economic activity. For example, assume that Kenya has a current per capita GNP of $400. Should the U.S. dollar lose 10 percent of its value relative to the Kenyan dollar next year, then Kenya's GNP in U.S. dollars will be $440, even if there was no change in aggregate economic activity in Kenya. The same problem applies to the World Bank's definitions of income classifications. As the value of the U.S. dollar changes with respect to the value of countries' currencies, so will the dollar value of other countries' GNPs. The World Bank will then determine what per capita GNP is necessary to be classified into each category. This can be a significant problem with the U.S. dollar losing value with respect to some currencies and gaining value with respect to others.

During the summer of 1994, the U.S. dollar lost substantial value relative to some other currencies—such as the German mark, British pound and Japanese yen—which, in turn, will cause the GNP of these countries measured in U.S. dollars to increase by the amount of the relative change in the value of the currencies. However, the change in the dollar value of GNP in Japan, England, and Germany resulting from the relative change in the values of the currencies does not represent economic growth but only represents the increased value of the yen, pound and mark.

GNP as a Measure of Economic Welfare and Activity

There are several problems associated with using per capita GNP as a measure of welfare. These problems also apply in differentiating between stages of development. Economists recognize that the measurement of GNP has several serious imperfections as measures of welfare or aggregate economic activity. Among these imperfections are: (1) externalities, (2) nonmarket transactions, (3) distribution of income, (4) underground economic activities, and (5) global markets. Each of these will be reviewed, in turn, in the following paragraphs.

It is also important to note that there are data gathering problems involved with aggregate economic information. The World Bank relies on individual nations to report their aggregate economic data. Unfortunately, there are variations in the abilities of these nations to gather such economic information. The United States, for example, has relatively more sophisticated surveying abilities and routinely tracks economic activity. Even in the United States, the statistical discrepancy in measuring GNP is several dozens of millions of dollars per year. In countries such as Colombia, investigators risk physical harm for asking questions about economic activity in certain parts of the country. In short, we know that GNP measurements are imperfect but that the errors in measurement also vary significantly from one country to another.

Externalities

An externality is either a cost (external diseconomy) or a benefit (external economy) that is imposed on society in general or another person by the actions of a specific producer but is not reflected in GNP. For example, steel mills that produce air pollution along with the steel cause harm to those individuals living in close proximity to the steel mill. The market value of the steel is included in GNP, but the GNP does not account for the damage to the environment caused by the production of steel. The market price of steel fails to reflect all the costs of production because the steel mill can impose the cost of cleaning up its environmental damage on others. In fact, the cost of replacing damaged property or the medical costs associated with such pollution will be included in GNP and hence overstate the well-being of that economy.

External economies and diseconomies provide economic benefits and costs that may not be measured and included in GNP. For example, vaccinating a child against a communicable disease is included in GNP, but the reduction of a potential carrier of the disease has positive benefits to other children that are neither measured nor included in GNP. On balance, it is difficult, if not impossible, to determine the net effects (positive or negative) of externalities on a country's GNP.

Nonmarket Activities

In barter economies, people directly exchange goods and there is no measurable monetary transaction. In other words, people trade commodities with one another and do not make money payments for goods. This same barter system also results in the exchange of services. For example, one farmer will help another harvest his rice if the other farmer will help build an irrigation channel. An economic activity is included in GNP only if there is a monetary transaction.

The barter economy in relatively small agrarian societies extends to the village. However, in most LDCs there is substantial reliance on resources found within the household that may be market transactions in industrialized countries. For example, in LDCs the value of agricultural goods produced by subsistence farmers for their own consumption is not included in GNP, but in industrialized economies the farmers will purchase their groceries in the same store as the steelworker. In developed economies, the value of a housewife's services certainly contributes to social well-being, but because they are nonmarket transactions, the value of these services is not included in GNP. Household services in industrialized countries probably are substantially less than in LDCs. The reliance on the market for laundry services, housecleaning, and restaurants is reserved only for the wealthy in most LDCs, while they are commonplace in developed countries. If the proportion of nonmarket activities is similar across all income categories of countries, there is no problem. However, in general, the lower the stage of economic development, the higher the proportion of nonmarket economic activities and the more GNP will underestimate total welfare in LDCs. However, even within LDC categories there may be significant variations because of culture, traditions, and even religion in the extent of nonmarket transactions.

Distribution of Income

Per capita GNP is simply a country's GNP divided by its population. There is no problem with this measure if the distribution of income is rather uniform. There are often significant variations across the population of any country in the amount of income received. However, there are few generalizations that can be made concerning the distribution of income by stage of development. There are several LDCs that have highly skewed distributions of income where the top 10 percent of the population have in excess of one-third of the total income of that country. In the developed countries, the top 10 percent generally receive about one-fourth of the income.[8]

The Underground Economy

The underground economy refers to economic activity that is hidden from measurement. In the United States, there is a significant amount of criminal activity. This criminal activity is hidden and, therefore, not included in GNP. Many industrialized and less developed countries have a significant illegal drug industry that is simply not included in GNP, even though it creates substantial amounts of income and involves market transactions.

There are numerous hidden activities that contribute to the underground economy in most nations. Smuggling, drug trafficking, arms sales, government corruption, and even slavery exist in the world and are generally illegal activities. The illegality of these activities results in their being hidden and, hence, not measured as a portion of GNP, even though they may be the source of substantial amounts of income to the population of that country. In industrialized countries—such as the United States—and LDCs—such as Colombia—there are very significant underground economies that result in GNP in these countries being substantially understated.

Globalization

The increasing globalization of the economy also creates problems in drawing inference from GNP data. GNP measures all market activities in an economy regardless of the sources of production. For example, the value of all production by American factors of production are included in U.S. GNP regardless of whether the production actually occurred in the United States. If General Motors (GM) operates a plant in Mexico, using U.S. capital and labor, the output of that Mexican plant is included in U.S. GNP. To eliminate this problem with the accounts, gross domestic product is increasingly becoming the most important aggregate economic measure. GDP focuses on where production occurred and not on the nationality of ownership of assets or the nationality of who receives the income. In other words, the output of the GM plant in Mexico will be included in Mexico's GDP because the production occurred in Mexico, not in the United States.

GNP Does Not Measure Intangibles

The discussion here focuses exclusively on GNP or aggregate economic activity as a measure of development. GNP is the operable filtering mechanism for the World Bank to determine the stage of economic development of a country. However, in a practical sense, there is much more to determining the stage of development that a country has reached. The imperfections in GNP may cause important elements of economic activity to be ignored because the GNP measure says nothing about the social and institutional development of countries. In nations with well-developed institutions and culture such as India, the use of GNP as a sole measure of development is misleading: India is a low-income country. At the other extreme, the former Yugoslavia is a middle-income country. At present, the institutional arrangements in that country seem incapable of even peaceful resolution of internal disputes about where people can live.

BORROWING AND INDEBTEDNESS

To understand the debt crisis and what it means within the context of the global economy, one must first understand the nature of indebtedness. There are two categories of debt acquired. First, *sovereign* debt is the borrowing of the governments of LDCs or developed countries. Second, *private* debt is borrowing by private individuals or firms residing within the jurisdiction of a country.

As crisp as this categorization scheme of indebtedness may seem, it is confounded by government guarantees of private loans. In both developed and developing economies it is not uncommon for a government to guarantee loans obtained by private entities when it is perceived to be in the public interest. Witness, for example, the U.S. government guarantees of loans to Chrysler Corporation in the 1980s to assure the continued viability of the private company and, hence, the minimization of the loss of jobs that might otherwise have occurred had the government not interceded on Chrysler's behalf. Therefore, there is an intermediate category of indebtedness that involves both the public and the private sector.

In this context, sovereign loans can be classified into two categories. *Public loans* are indebtedness of a national government, its agencies, or autonomous public bodies within the country. *Publicly guaranteed loans* are obligations of private debtors that are assured for repayment by either the national government or some other public body. Borrowing by nongovernment entities within the country for which no government repayment assurances have been negotiated is classified as *private loans*.

Again, the indebtedness can be classified into two more categories: *internal* and *external*. Internal indebtedness is borrowing that involves a domestic borrower and a domestic lender. The availability of domestic sources of loanable funds depends primarily on the economy's total income (GNP) and the rate of savings within that economy. Nations with low and middle incomes historically have experienced low rates of savings. This creates two problems for the availability of internal credit. First, if the total resources of an economy are relatively small, all other things equal, there will be a small economic base from which to draw credit. Second, the low resource availability will cause consumers to spend a relatively large proportion of their incomes on the necessities of life, hence substantially reducing their savings rates, ceteris paribus. As should be obvious, LDCs are more likely to require external funding of indebtedness than developed economies. In other words, LDC debtors borrow from creditors abroad (normally from developed economies where there are more resources and higher savings rates).[9]

The stage of development (hence the size of the economy) and the savings rate only explain how the debt is acquired (internal or external, public or private); they do not explain why debt is acquired. The motivations of LDCs for borrowing are relatively simple and straightforward. Both forms of sovereign indebtedness stem basically from the LDCs' attempts to progress up the continuum of the stages of development.[10] For economies to develop, several conditions must be satisfied. Certain elements of a nation's infrastructure are critical to economic development. Elements such as communications, education, health care, sanitation, and transportation networks must be established to permit the improvement and growth of production and exchange. Even during ancient times, the Chinese recognized the importance of harbors and highways to conducting trade. The Romans constructed elaborate canal systems to provide water to their production centers.

The establishment of appropriate infrastructures for economic development is necessary, but it is simply not enough to assure an economic climate in which growth can occur. It has become increasingly recognized that political stability is one of the critical components of the foundations for economic growth.[11] Creditors and investors will not risk placing their resources in a country with substantial political instability. The destruction of property, possible nationalization, the demise of debtor governments, and the uncertainty associated with political instability reduce the creditworthiness of both public and private entities within LDCs. Therefore, the governments of LDCs must provide for the requisite political stability if credit and investment are to be attracted to their country.

There are prerequisites to economic growth, most of which can be provided for by the private sector. However, the private sectors of most LDCs are unable to provide for many of the requisite elements of infrastructure necessary for economic growth. It is commonly left to LDCs' governments to provide for these prerequisites. Again, because of the relatively weak private sectors, LDCs' public sectors typically provide infrastructure through borrowing. Once the prerequisites are satisfied, LDCs' governments and private entities may borrow to more directly foster economic growth. Public debt has been acquired to subsidize industries and consumption. This facilitates the demand for and the production of commodities.[12] The motivations for acquiring a debt are relatively straightforward; it is simply the LDCs' collective desire to have an increased standard of living. How all these elements of infrastructure, private-sector growth, and institutional development produce an increased standard of living comprises the body of theory and evidence commonly called economic development. The subtleties of this body of economic literature and its implications for LDCs and businesses contemplating investments or loans to LDCs will be examined in greater detail later in the book. Further discussion of this topic is reserved for the final four chapters.

DEBT CRISIS AND THE AMERICAN ECONOMY

The indebtedness of LDCs reached $1.418 trillion by the end of 1991. The 116 countries that comprise the low- and middle-income groups had a total GNP for 1991 of almost $3.8 trillion.[13] In other words, the debt to GNP ratio for LDCs in 1991 was about 37.4.[14] This heavy debt burden resulted in several of the debtor LDCs being unable to meet the obligations to service their debt. During the previous decade, several LDCs were forced to reschedule their debt to prevent defaulting. From 1980 through 1992, LDCs rescheduled 334 of their sovereign loans, amounting to over $616.5 billion.[15] There were 144 of these reschedulings that were with commercial banks abroad, mostly in the United States and totaling more than $418 billion.[16]

The LDCs' private debt rescheduling was significantly less than their public rescheduling. Loans to private debtors in LDCs totaled $314.7 billion by the end of 1991. However, this still creates a burden for the LDCs' governments. Normally, loans to private businesses in LDCs are guaranteed by the government of those countries. The data concerning the rescheduling of private loans are generally regarded as proprietary information and, therefore, not reported in the *World Debt Tables*. However, the fact that total private LDC debt is less than 25 percent of the sovereign debt of LDCs suggests that the total rescheduling of private loans is significantly less than that observed for public loans.

The size of total indebtedness of LDCs relative to their GNPs demonstrates the importance of credit to these countries. If growth is to occur in LDCs, it is imperative for them to have access to the world credit markets. If LDCs are to enter the ranks of the consumer economies, they need to have access to international credit markets. Therefore, the creditworthiness of these countries must be maintained.

The almost $1.5 trillion of LDC debt has absorbed a significant portion of the world credit resources. The data also demonstrate that more than two-thirds of the value of LDC debt rescheduled to date have been loans held by U.S. commercial banks. To put this into perspective, the amount of loans rescheduled by LDCs with U.S. commercial banks is about 140 percent of the 1991 U.S. government budget deficit. As the reader may recall, the federal budget deficit was no mean political issue in the 1991 presidential campaign.

The LDC debt crisis contributed significantly to recent bank failures in the United States, particularly in the southwestern region.[17] This substantially increased exposure to risk, especially from the loans to Latin American governments, and resulted in several commercial banks acting to limit their exposure to losses from these types of loans. The U.S. creditors acted by refusing to extend additional credit to LDC debtors with a history of rescheduling.[18] These direct and obvious implications of the world debt crisis for the creditworthiness of LDCs and their access to world credit markets are serious.

The loss of creditworthiness has significantly impaired LDCs' access to foreign capital markets, and this has resulted in slowed economic growth in many LDCs, especially in Latin America. The slowing of economic growth continues to result in lower wages in Latin America which, in turn, gives a comparative advantage to Latin American enterprises that rely heavily upon unskilled labor. This comparative advantage results in the loss of jobs in the industrialized nations (particularly the United States and Canada). The comparative low wages in Latin America for unskilled labor cause the movement of labor-intensive, low-skill industries from the industrialized nations of North America to the developing Latin countries. This is particularly harmful to the working poor in the industrialized trading partners.[19] Complicating matters further is the fact that as growth has slowed in Latin America, illegal immigration to the United States has increased.[20] Again, the illegal immigrants compete primarily with the working poor in the United States, driving down wages and making employment more difficult to obtain.[21]

The difficulties associated with the reduced creditworthiness of debtor LDCs not only impacts the credit markets but also creates domestic economic difficulties in the creditor nation's labor markets. In turn, the worsened labor standards for the low-income segments of the U.S. labor force has at least the potential for placing increased demands on publicly provided social services in the United States. These demands result from increased unemployment insurance costs, welfare, retraining, health care, and even increased criminal activity. The political wisdom of permitting the least-able portions of society to shoulder the burden of the indirect costs of the world debt crisis is suspect. The indirect effects of the world debt crisis have not been reliably measured but have certainly contributed to many of the domestic problems currently suffered in the United States.

LDCS AS A POTENTIAL MARKET

Approximately two-thirds of the world's nations are classified as LDCs. The total population of LDCs is approximately 4.2 billion; the developed nations' population is about 820 million. In other words, for each person living in industrialized countries there are five persons to be found in LDCs. The LDCs have massive market potential for export goods from the developed countries. For example, U.S. exports to all LDCs in 1990 were $135 billion, or about 35 percent of total U.S. exports.[22] The United States has already taken advantage of trading opportunities with low- and middle-income countries. If the LDCs' effective demand for commodities could be significantly increased through economic growth, one of the potential beneficiaries is the export industry of developed countries.

With economic development comes increased labor earnings. The increase in labor standards in the LDCs, particularly Latin American countries, eliminates many of the indirect adverse effects of the world debt crisis in the developed countries, particularly the United States. In fact, the proponents of NAFTA argued that the economic development of U.S. trading partners in the western hemisphere will improve the standard of living of all involved. This result may, in fact, be realized if the indirect costs of the world debt crisis can be overcome, especially as they impact the low-income workers in the United States and other creditor countries.

The world is currently a dangerous place. Numerous wars rage across the face of this planet as this book is being written. Most of these conflicts arise in LDCs where the lack of economic development has given rise to disparate living conditions which, in turn, frequently result in the ultimate political instability—warfare. The development of LDCs has significant potential for mitigating the causes of political instability and, hence, increasing the chances of world peace.

Beyond the effects currently identified from the economic development of LDCs many possible and currently unidentified benefits may be realized in the future. For example, innovation and scientific advancement has been somewhat limited to roughly one-sixth of the world's population. It is the populations of the developed countries who, in the main, can afford education and have access to research facilities and have created a modern global economy with significant potential for good. If five times as many talented people were working toward the common good, it is a safe assumption that the pace of discovery and innovation would be dramatically increased. There are also several other sources for potential good resulting from economic development, not yet identified.

IMPLICATIONS FOR BUSINESS

The definition of LDC is somewhat misleading and not very informative, at least on its surface. Greece and Rwanda are both LDCs but with significant differences. Greece is a middle-income country, and Rwanda is a low-income country; but the differences in the infrastructure, availability of resources, and business climate are differences more properly compared to early twentieth-century Canada (Greece) with early nintenth-century Italy (Rwanda). Greece is a member of the European

Common Market with most of the modern conveniences. Rwanda, on the other hand, has few, if any, necessities of modern life (particularly since the civil war in 1994). The term *less developed country* must be conceptualized as a continuum of economies that have not yet reached the threshold of full industrialization.

The GNP information used to determine what classification best characterizes an economy is fraught with inaccuracies and is not generally comparable between countries because of nonmarket activities, underground economies, and similar problems. For the private decision maker considering an economic activity in an LDC, substantial time and effort will be required to ascertain whether the prospective enterprise can flourish in that country. Colombia has significant and well-publicized difficulties because of domestic criminal activity. Locating an enterprise in the rural mountain areas in Colombia may make sense because of natural resources, labor costs, and government incentives; but when one examines who may really be in charge of local government, the costs may substantially outweigh the benefits. Each region of the world, and each country within each region, has unique opportunities and constraints that are not at all obvious from being classified as a low- or middle-income country or that can be determined from the level of market activities.

One of the most common and often trying difficulties in doing business in LDCs is currency exchange. The U.S. dollar is accepted even more widely than the American Express card; however, the Kenyan dollar or the Indian rupee will not buy much in Chicago. In deciding to do business in an LDC, one must pay particular attention to how revenues can be converted into something of value outside of the LDC. For example, in 1990 a company exporting scrap paper from the United States to India found that at the then-current exchange rate, a substantial profit could be had; but they overlooked the fact that India regulates exchanges of rupees into dollars. Because the paper exporters had only rupees, they had to buy Indian goods to export back to the United States to convert their rupees into dollars. The export of Indian brass products and cloth to the United States was at a significant loss; thus, the return to their planning and hard work was zero.

These are not the only difficulties in doing business in LDCs. Cultural, religious, climatic, and value systems differ widely among nations. Saturday is the first business day of the week in most of the Middle East. Friday is the sabbath, and people do not work on Fridays. These human differences may take some adjustment, but there are several other differences (many more significant than these, e.g., differences in electric current) that will be given greater attention in the chapters that follow.

There are also significant differences between LDCs concerning their indebtedness. Sovereign debt results in exchange rate instability, credit unavailability, and the lack of infrastructure in many LDCs. LDCs without significant indebtedness may not suffer from any of these difficulties. Any business contemplating operations in an LDC must determine what indebtedness exists and how this debt effects various aspects of the business climate in that country.

SUMMARY AND CONCLUSION

The world debt crisis arises from the significant debt rescheduling of LDC debtor nations. The preponderance of this debt is sovereign indebtedness, and the U.S. commercial banking system has absorbed most of the losses that have resulted. LDC indebtedness to developed nations is how political stability and economic development are financed. The lack of viable credit markets in the LDCs stems from relatively small economies and low saving rates within the LDCs.

The costs of the world debt crisis include the direct costs of increased risk to developed countries' banking systems and the lack of economic development in the Third World. There are also substantial indirect costs of the world debt crisis that are difficult to measure with precision. Illegal immigration, and its associated problems for developed countries, and the comparative advantage created by near-starvation labor standards in LDCs harm unskilled, low-income workers in developed countries.

The potential benefits from economic development of nearly four-fifths of the world's population will be to create a massive export market for developed countries. Maybe more important the mitigation of global political instability and the increased innovativeness of the global economy have benefits that have not yet been identified.

There are significant considerations for businesses contemplating doing business in LDCs. The classification of a country as an LDC does not portray in detail the viability of the support mechanisms for any particular enterprise. Any contemplated move to an LDC must be preceded by substantial research concerning various aspects of the business climate in the specific country under consideration.

NOTES

1. World Bank, *World Development Report, 1992* (New York: Oxford University Press, 1992), 307.

2. Ibid.

3. World Bank, *World Debt Tables, 1992–93, Vol. 1* (Washington, D.C.: International Bank of Reconstruction and Development, 1992), 137.

4. Ibid.

5. Calculated from World Bank, *World Debt Tables, 1992–93,* p. 154.

6. World Bank,*World Development Report, 1992,* p. xi.

7. Ibid., p. xii.

8. See World Bank, *World Development Report, 1993* (New York: Oxford University Press, 1993), Table 30.

9. Richard N. Cooper, *Economic Stabilization and Debt in Developing Countries* (Cambridge, Mass.: MIT Press, 1992), 58.

10. A more detailed examination of economic development, in theory and practice, will follow in subsequent chapters. However, it is important to introduce the driving motivations behind economic development that affect borrowing.

11. For example, see Seamus O'Cleireacain, *Third World Debt and International Public Policy.* (Westport, CT: Praeger, 1990).

12. Ibid.

13. World Bank,*World Debt Tables, 1992–93,* p. 160.

14. Ibid.

15. Calculated from data in ibid., pp. 104–107.

16. Ibid.

17. Hedayeh Samavati, Mashaalah Rahnama-Moghadam, and Lawrence J. Haber, "Financial Characteristics Associated with Debt Rescheduling in Latin America," *Southwest Journal of Business and Economics* (2; 1991): 13.

18. Ibid.

19. Lester Thurow, *Head to Head: The Coming Economic Battle among Japan, Europe, and America* (New York: William Morrow, 1992), 52.

20. Gary Clyde Hufbauer and Jeffery J. Schott, *North American Free Trade: Issue and Recommendations* (Washington, D.C.: Institute for International Economics, 1992), Chapter 6.

21. Ibid., pp. 13–14.

22. *Survey of Current Business* (Washington, D.C.: U.S. Department of Commerce, 1991).

Chapter 3

The Characteristics of Less Developed Countries: Further Refinements on Definitions

> All of us do not have equal talent, but all of us should have an equal opportunity to develop our talents.
>
> —John F. Kennedy
> *Address at San Diego State University,* June 6, 1963

In Chapter 2, a discussion of the World Bank's definition of LDCs was offered. The importance of LDCs as potential trading partners and the implications of LDC debt were introduced. However, the overview of LDCs offered in Chapter 2 provides only an arbitrary standard by which LDCs are defined for the specific purposes of the World Bank and other international organizations. As discussed in the final section of that chapter, this definition only scratches the surface.

For the purposes of the analysis and prescriptions offered in this book, more is needed. Each country in the world has its own unique cultural, economic, and political characteristics. However, this is true of developed countries as well as LDCs. As was mentioned earlier, LDCs must be thought of as a continuum of economies that have not reached the threshold to be classified as industrialized. Therefore, there is significant variation in the characteristics of the countries labeled LDCs. For the present purposes, it is important to gain some insight into what it means, in a practical sense, for a country to be included in the LDC category.

The purpose of this chapter is to extend the discussion contained in Chapter 2 and to provide a general overview of some of the more important characteristics of LDCs. Perceptions of abject poverty, impenetrable jungles, endless deserts, and unfathomable corruption are common among the uninitiated. In fact, some of the initiated have been acquainted with one or more of these characteristics when doing business in LDCs. The term *less developed country* is applied to a broad range of the world's nations; however, this array of countries that have been labeled LDCs differs from one end of the spectrum to the other with respect to several national characteristics. The poorest of the LDCs is far different in its economic characteristics from the richest of the LDCs. In fact, several of the middle-income countries are tourist havens (e.g., Greece and Mexico). Greece is not perceived by many Europeans and Americans as being all that different from the developed countries of northern and southern Europe, but it falls into the World Bank's middle-income classification and is, therefore, less developed.

To gain a more useful perspective of LDCs, this chapter offers an examination of the most important economic and institutional characteristics of LDCs. A great deal of country-specific information is gathered and published regularly in reliable forms for readers interested in specific countries or regions of the world.[1] The following sections of this chapter offer a brief overview of some of the various economic and institutional characteristics of countries that fall into each of the World Bank's income classifications so that comparisons can be made.

Infrastructure is a prerequisite to economic development and is often the hardest variable to isolate and fully examine in determining whether an enterprise in an LDC will be profitable. There is much that must be thoroughly examined for each specific country; however, the general development of infrastructure will be examined in this chapter. Appendix B presents an index of critical elements of infrastructure constructed from data presented in this chapter. As discussed later in this book, the purpose of this index is to provide a heretofore unavailable ranking of the state of development of the infrastructure for each of the world's countries. The reader is referred to Appendix B for a complete description of how the index was constructed and what inferences can be drawn from it.

INSTITUTIONS AND LDCS

The institutional characteristics of LDCs vary substantially. Virtually every form of government, judicial structure, and private institutions can be found in LDCs. Democratic governments to military dictatorships to Islamic republics are counted among the ranks of LDCs. Each country's political evolution, former colonial ties, culture, and religion will heavily influence the nature and conduct of their institutions.

One striking characteristic of many LDCs is the rather substantial social and political instability observed. Political instability, to the extent that it results in civil war, is rarely observed in developed countries. In contrast, many LDCs are plagued with recurrent internal or external conflicts. Examples include the recent civil wars in El Salvador, Nicaragua, Cambodia, Rwanda, and the Sudan. Examples of regional disputes involving military action between LDCs are also not uncommon; witness the recent hostilities between Iraq and Iran and between Libya and Chad. The intensities of these conflicts also vary substantially. As of this writing (summer 1994), there is a relatively small number of rebels fighting against the Khartoum government in the Sudan. This is a very low-intensity conflict. The civil war in Ethiopia is slightly higher in intensity. Moderate- to high-intensity civil wars are also presently observed in Bosnia. The highest-intensity conflict in recent years was the Iran–Iraq conflict that resulted in hundreds of thousands of casualties on both sides and the loss of billions of dollars' worth of property and capital.

Civil wars and international conflicts have been observed mostly between and within LDCs. The wars that plague LDCs are extremely costly, and the resources that were wasted in warfare could have been otherwise used for economic development. Conflicts between and civil wars within industrialized nations are almost unheard of since the end of World War II. The major institutional difference between LDCs and the developed countries is the greater propensity to political and social instability among the LDCs. This political instability has important and obvious considerations for private decision making concerning business opportunities in LDCs.

ECONOMIC CHARACTERISTICS

Various international organizations gather and publish data concerning a wide range of economic factors. The available information includes various measures of health care, labor force characteristics, infrastructure, and aggregate measures of economic activity. Comparisons of the major characteristics of LDCs and developed countries provide some useful insights concerning what can be expected as development occurs.[2] Unlike the World Bank's convenient definition of an LDC, the observed characteristics of nations at various stages of development cannot be neatly classified into three neat packages. Many national characteristics have significant degrees of overlap between income categories, while other characteristics are not shared across income categories. An examination of the available data provides a basis for meaningful comparisons of LDCs with developed economies.

Health Statistics

Table 3.1 presents health statistics by World Bank income classifications for the year 1990. In examining the averages for each category of country, it is observed that there are significant differences in all three health statistics. The high-income or developed countries have almost five times as many physicians per capita as do middle-income countries (higher development stage LDCs), and the middle-income countries have over three times as many physicians as low-income countries (the lowest stage of development for LDCs). Infant mortality rates differ by the same multiple between the high- and middle-income categories, but low-income countries only suffer about twice the infant mortality rate that middle-income countries suffer. The life expectancy data show that people in developed countries live, on average, about nine years longer than people in the middle-income countries and about fifteen years longer than people in low-income countries. However, in recent years the differences in life expectancy seem to be narrowing between the countries in the three income categories.

Taken at face value, there are rather substantial differences in the basic health care statistics presented in Table 3.1. However, the averages presented in this table do not tell the whole story. There is little or no systematic information available concerning the distribution and availability of health care services and its effects within the populations

Table 3.1
Health Statistics, 1990

	High Income	Middle Income	Low Income
Population per physician	420	2060	6760
Infant mortality (per 1000 live births)	8	38	71
Life expectancy (at birth)	77	68	62

Source: World Bank, *World Development Report, 1993* (New York: Oxford University Press, 1993), Tables 1 and 28.

of each of these classes of countries. In the United States, the recent controversies concerning health care demonstrates that there is not equal access to health care across the population. In fact, health care is rationed in the United States by a market system, with some public provision of services for the elderly and the destitute. The differences by individual country become somewhat more illustrative. The range of life expectancy among low-income nations runs from a low of thirty-nine in Guinea-Bissau to a high of seventy-one in Sri Lanka. For middle-income countries, a low of forty-eight is observed for Senegal and a high of seventy-six is observed in Costa Rica. The variation for high income countries is very small. The high observed in Japan is seventy-nine, and the lowest life expectancy observed in Singapore is seventy-four.[3] At the high end of the middle-income countries, life expectancy exceeds the low end for high-income countries, but there is no common range between low- and high-income countries' life expectancies. What is striking about these data is the differences in the ranges of life expectancy. The range of national average life expectancy in the low-income countries is thirty-two years from the lowest to the highest. This range drops to twenty-eight years for middle-income countries, but for high-income countries the range is only five years. These data suggest that the wealthiest proportions of the populations in the LDCs have life expectancies that rival those in developed countries, but the wide variation clearly indicates that there are significant differences across LDCs. In the developed countries, however, there is almost no difference in national average life expectancies across countries. Infant mortality ranges follow essentially the same pattern across categories of countries except that there is no common range between high- and middle-income countries. The lack of overlap between infant mortality rates between income categories suggests that there are still serious deficiencies in prenatal care and specialized pediatric care in both of the lower-income categories of countries.

In the population per physician ratio, there is no common range between the low- and high-income countries. However, there are many middle-income countries that have population/physician ratios that are higher than the ratios observed in high-income countries. For example, the population/physician ratio of the United States is at the average for this ratio for high-income countries. However, there are only sixteen middle-income countries with lower population/physician ratios than that of the United States (which is the average for high-income countries).

The health care information suggests that there are significant differences between the low-income and the middle-income LDCs but that those differences are less pronounced when the middle-income LDCs are compared with the high-income countries. This suggests that countries at higher stages of development place a relatively high priority on health care and that LDCs are those countries that have substantial difficulties in providing health care for their populations at lower stages of development. In other words, the development of health care industries may be a good indicator of a country entering the latter stages of development leading to becoming a developed economy.

Education Statistics

Education is another area in which comparisons are often made to determine the potential level of economic development and thus well-being of a country. Education is the acquisition of human capital, that is, knowledge, skills, and abilities that can be translated into productivity. The available information does not control for *quality* of the educational experience within any particular country or category of countries. The available information includes adult illiteracy rates and primary student/teacher ratios; these statistics for the year 1990 are reported in Table 3.2.

The available education statistics indicate that the categories of countries have essentially the same ordering as observed for the health care data. The illiteracy rates for middle-income countries are about five times that of the high income countries and about one-half of those observed in the low-income countries. The primary student/teacher ratios for high-income countries indicate smaller class size and probably greater per capita expenditures for instruction than in either the middle- or low-income countries. The only data that can be compared country by country are for primary student/teacher ratios. For low-income countries, the low was in Haiti, with twenty-one students per teacher; and the high was observed in the Central African Republic,

Table 3.2
Education Statistics, 1990

	High Income	Middle Income	Low Income
Adult illiteracy (percentage)	4	21	40
Primary student/ teacher ratios	17	25	38

Source: World Bank, *World Development Report, 1993* (New York: Oxford University Press, 1993), Tables 1 and 29.

with ninety students per teacher. Unfortunately, the difficulties of the early 1990s in Haiti may account for the low student/teacher ratios rather than any significant commitment to education in that country. For the middle-income group, the lowest ratio was in the Ukraine, with eight; and the highest ratio was in the Congo, with sixty. The high-income group varied more narrowly, as with the health care statistics, with the highest student/teacher ratio in Ireland, with twenty-seven and Sweden and Norway tied for the lowest, with six.

Again, LDCs tend to have higher illiteracy rates and fewer teachers per capita than developed countries. As can be clearly seen, the overlap between all three income categories of countries suggests that there may be little difference between the high end of the LDCs and the low end of the developed countries in the education provided. Without specific controls for teacher and program quality, however, firm conclusions are not possible. The success of many graduate students from LDCs in U.S. and European graduate school programs is corroborative incidental evidence for the data presented here. It is not implausible to conclude that education is a leading indicator of reaching the industrialized stage in growth paths. As can be observed from the data in Table 3.2, the middle-income countries begin to approximate characteristics of their educational systems that are common to industrialized countries. In examining the more detailed information in *World Development Report* (published annually), it is clear that the more developed of the middle-income countries are generally comparable to industrialized countries and not to other LDCs.

Economic Infrastructure

Economic infrastructure refers to those items necessary to facilitate or support economic activities. There are several elements of the infrastructure of a country that are prerequisites to economic development. Among these items are such things as postal services, telecommunications, electrical production, highways, and railroads. Many of these items of infrastructure can be classified as public goods or can be very difficult for the private sector to provide. Often, even in some industrialized countries, transportation networks, telecommunications, and postal services are so central to the operation of economic systems that the public sector provides most, if not all, of the infrastructure.

Reliable postal delivery is a critically important prerequisite to economic development. The ability to communicate, send, and receive documents and the transportation of small parcels plays a significant role in most, if not all, business activities. The need for businesses to communicate across national boundaries provided a political incentive to facilitate postal cooperation between countries. For developed countries, the motivation was to facilitate existing enterprise; but for LDCs, the motivation was to participate in economic development. Treaty arrangements were made by most of the world's nations in the nineteenth century to assure reliable international delivery. This need in developed economies resulted in the development of postal capacities throughout the world and the creation of international agreements concerning mail delivery.

The Universal Postal Union (UPU) is now a specialized agency of the United Nations that promotes cooperation between the postal services of various countries. The original international agreements on postal delivery, standards, and the creation of the UPU were established on October 9, 1874. On November 15, 1947, the UPU became a part of the United Nations. At present, 168 nations are members of the UPU, all United Nations members except, the Baltic Republics, Antigua and Barbuda, Bosnia–Hercegovina, the former republics of the Soviet Union, several Pacific Island nations, and South Africa. However, most of these nations cooperate by unilaterally honoring most of the provisions of the treaty. There are also several members of the UPU that are not members of the United Nations. These include Kiribati, Monaco, Nauru, Netherlands Antilles, Switzerland, Tonga, Tuvalu, and Vatican City.[4]

Economic infrastructure is a term used herein to describe elements of the infrastructure that are direct support for production of goods and services (e.g., capital equipment). Health care and education only indirectly support production through direct support for the labor force. The reason for this is that labor is the factor of production, support for the labor through health care, and education only affects the quality of the labor that is, in turn, used to produce goods and services.

Table 3.3 presents data on transportation, telecommunications and electrical generating infrastructures. Table 3.3 shows that there are substantial differences in the infrastructures among categories of countries. The largest difference appears to be in telecommunications facilities. High-income countries have over ten times as many telephones per 1,000 persons as are found in the middle-income countries. The number of telephones per 1,000 people in the middle-income countries is about ten times that observed for low-income countries (i.e., high-income countries have 100 times as many telephone per capita as low-income countries).

In electric power generation, low-income countries produce about one-fifth the amount of electricity produced in middle-income countries per capita. Middle-income countries produce less than one-fifth of the power per capita than high-income countries do. In other words, there appears to be a rather smooth continuum of development of electric power generation from the low end to the high end of the stages of development. The lack of a significant overlap between the income cat-

Table 3.3
Infrastructure by Income Category, 1992

	High Income	Middle Income	Low Income
Kilometers of highways per 1000 people	16.00	4.90	1.50
Kilometers of railroads per 1000 people	8.00	0.30	0.06
Number of telephones per 1000 people	700.00	68.00	6.50
Kilowatts of electricity per hour per 1000 people	2230.00	400.00	90.00

Source: Central Intelligence Agency, *The World Factbook, 1992* (Washington, D.C.: U.S. Government Printing Office, 1992).

egories of countries also suggests that electric power generation may not be indicative of future development but is probably the result of economic development. In other words, if a consumer economy uses far more electricity to power air conditioning, computers, and household conveniences than it uses for industrial purposes, then electric-generating capacity is a symptom of growth rather than a cause. If electrical generation is required for industrial production, then it may be a precursor to economic development. Without data concerning the structure of demand across nations, it is impossible to draw any firm conclusions concerning the significance of electric-generating capacity.

In transportation networks there are also extreme variations. Railroads appear to be almost exclusively high-income country characteristics, with about 16 kilometers of railroads per 1,000 persons. Neither the middle-income nor low-income countries have a full kilometer of railroad per 1,000 persons. Even so, middle-income countries have about five times as many kilometers of railroads per person as low-income countries have. High-income countries have over three times as many kilometers of highways per 1,000 person as middle-income countries do, and approximately the same difference is observed between middle- and low-income countries.

It is striking how consistent the differences are between the three classifications of countries. In telecommunications and railroads in particular, the differences between the high-income and low-income countries are ratios in excess of 100. To the extent that telecommunications are necessary to the success of all forms of business enterprise, it is easy to see the type of resource limitations that are observed in the low-income countries. The amount of railways available suggests something of the availability and extent of the heavy transport system to support manufacturing and also something of the distribution of raw materials and finished products in an economy. The lack of this vital support system may impose serious constraints on the economic growth of a country. As the stage of development changes from low- to middle-income status, the stark difference fades into merely small variations from the high-income countries.

Airports, ocean ports, and pipelines are also important elements for the support of economic activity. There are data available from various sources concerning the availability of airports, ocean ports, pipelines, and so on, including the Central Intelligence Agency publications. The data for these elements of the infrastructure are consistent with what is reported in Table 3.3, demonstrating large differences between each of the income categories of countries.

GEOGRAPHY

The geographic dispersion of countries by income group is of some interest. The high-income groups are located in Western Europe, with the exceptions of the United States, Canada, Australia, Japan, New Zealand, Qatar, United Arab Emirates, Israel, and Kuwait. The concentration of the high-income countries outside of Europe and North America is predominately along the Pacific Rim and in the oil-rich areas of the Middle East.

The middle-income countries are a more widely dispersed group of countries. The remainder of the Middle Eastern countries, except for Kuwait, Qatar and United Arab Emirates (which are high income) and Yemen (which is low income), fall into the middle-income category. The remaining Western Hemisphere countries except for Honduras, Haiti, and Guyana, are middle-income countries. The middle-income countries in Africa are concentrated along the Mediterranean Sea and in southwest Africa. All the countries of Eastern Europe, including the former Soviet Union, are middle-income countries. Most of the Pacific Island nations are middle-income countries.

All the countries of central and east Africa, with the exception of Djibouti, are low-income countries. Mongolia, Korea, Thailand, Malaysia, the Philippines, and Papua New Guinea are middle-income countries of Asia; but the remaining countries are low income, with the exceptions of Singapore and Hong Kong, which are high-income countries. For a visual depiction of the dispersion of countries by income, see Figure 3.1. Population density is presented in Figure 3.2 for comparisons with the dispersion of nations by income category.

There is little observable correlation between population density and income classification. However, it is interesting to note that many of the low-income countries, particularly in Asia, have very high population densities. The population growth of LDCs is projected to be about 1.9 percent between 1989 and 2000, but for developed countries the estimated population growth rates will be approximately 0.5 percent.[5] If the projected growth rates are realized, then the population density of the LDCs will grow at a rate four times faster than that of the developed countries.

NATIONAL CHARACTERISTICS AND STAGE OF DEVELOPMENT

The arbitrariness of the use of GNP as a gauge of economic development is confirmed by a more detailed analysis of countries in each income category. The LDCs are defined by the World Bank as those falling into the middle- and low-income categories, and the high-income category includes only the developed countries.

Economic development can be gauged by using aggregate economic data such as GNP, but this tells only a part of the story. Because there are significant difficulties with the measurement of GNP, including nonmarket activities, externalities, income distribution, and the globalization of markets, GNP is not always a reliable method of comparing the economic output of nations. The overlap between the high- and middle-income countries concerning education and health care statistics suggests that there is little or no difference between several nations in these two categories with respect to these institutions. With respect to transportation, telecommunications, and electrical generation, there are clear differences between each of the income categories. Whether these latter characteristics are precursors to economic development or symptoms of economic development is subject to debate, especially in the case of electric generating capacity.

The fact that there are significant differences in most measures of infrastructure is an important determinant of what types of business can be supported in LDCs. Whether growth is to be expected is also an important variable in the decision to locate operations in an LDC. What the evidence presented here clearly demonstrates is that there are wide ranges of variation of the stages of development even within income categories. In other words, before any business decision is made concerning the location of business, specific information concerning the availability and quality of infrastructure in the proposed location must be gathered and thoroughly examined.

SUMMARY AND CONCLUSION

The institutional differences between all nations of the world make generalizations difficult. It must be recognized that there are also stages

Figure 3.1
World GDP per Capita

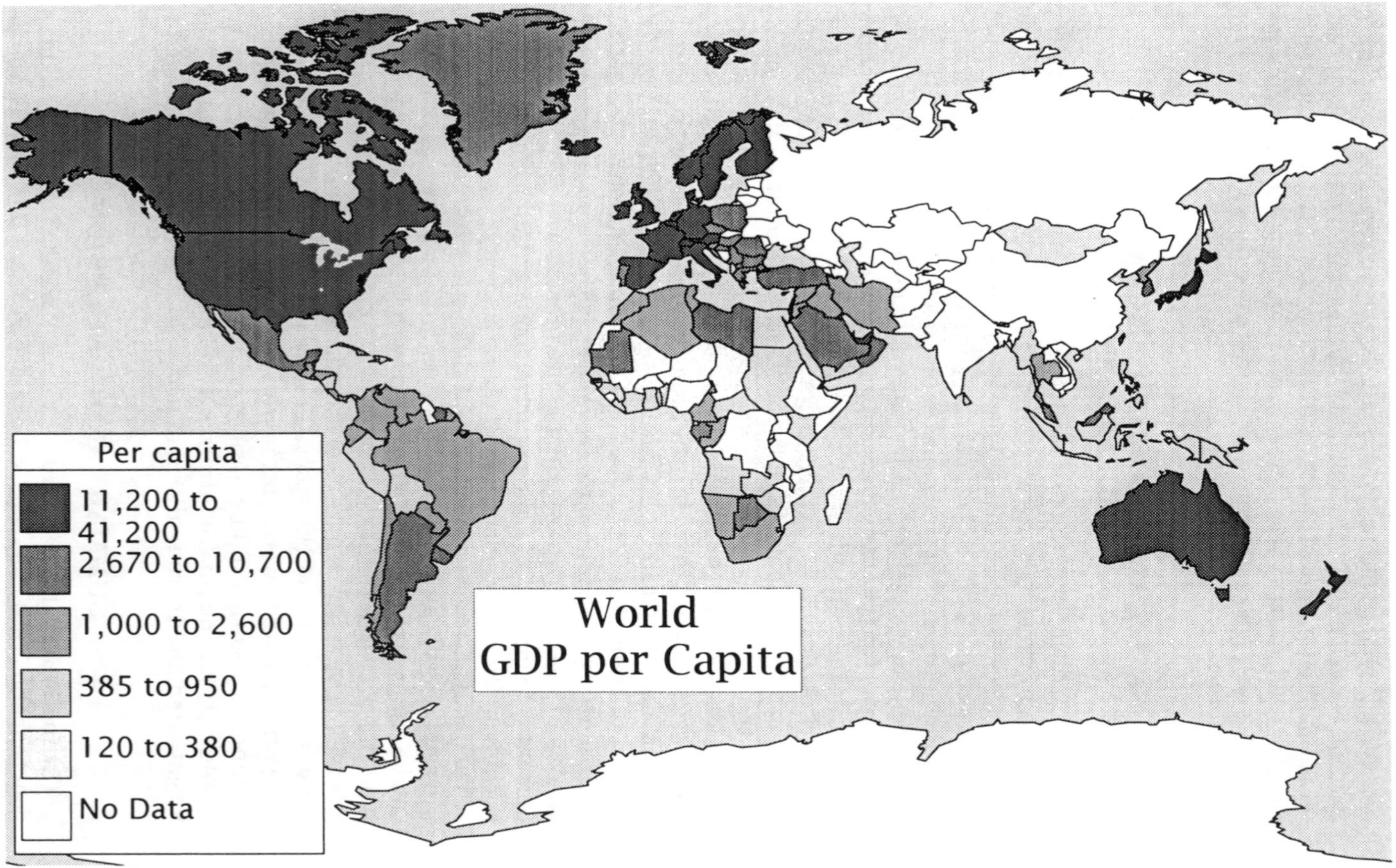

World
GDP per Capita

Per capita
11,200 to
41,200
2,670 to 10,700
1,000 to 2,600
385 to 950
120 to 380
No Data

Figure 3.2
World Population Density

World
Population Density

Per square kilometer

126.06 to
15,771
74.6 to 125.41
37.21 to 72.79
12.02 to 35.32
0.16 to 11.91
No Data

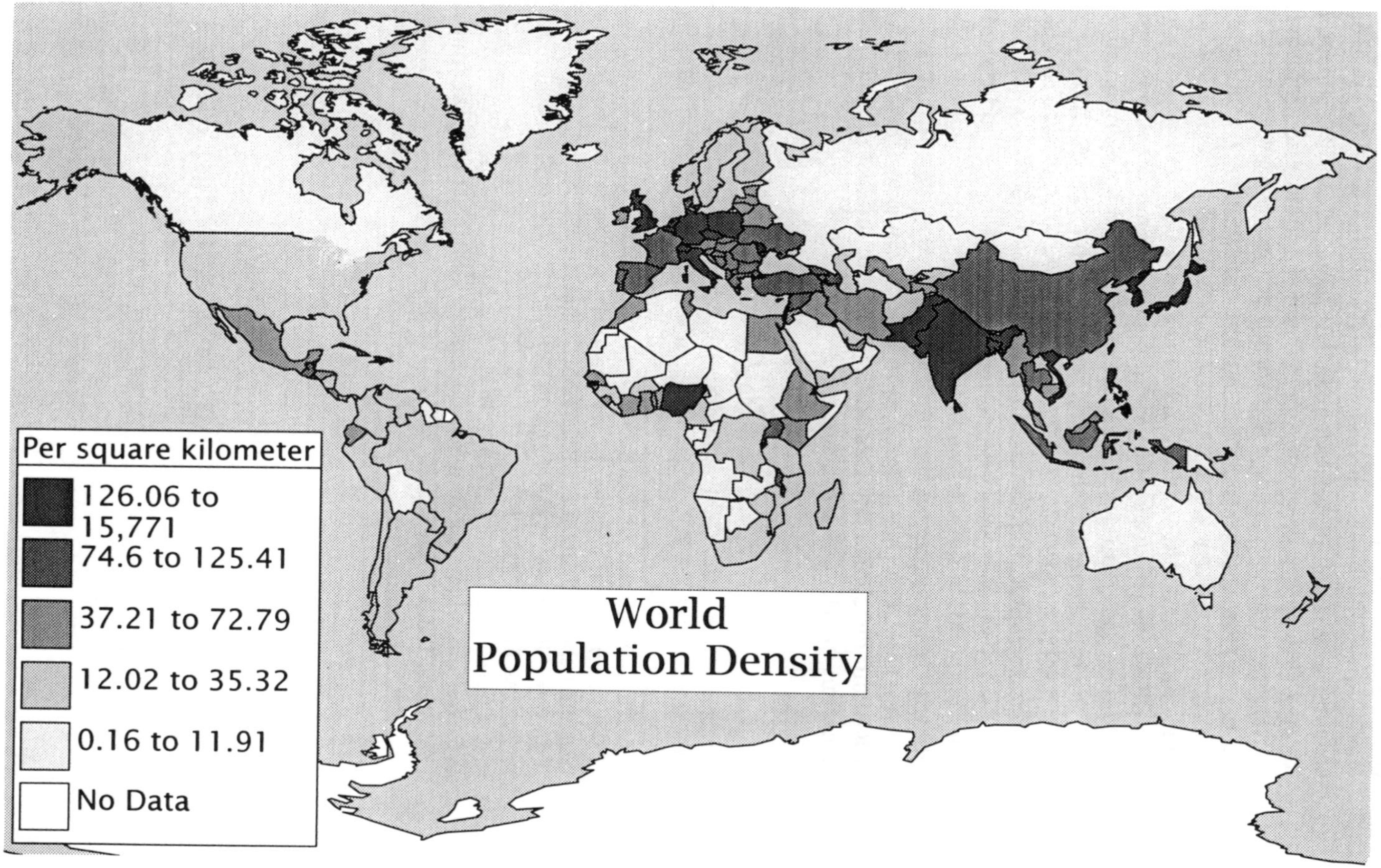

of development in the social, political, and institutional characteristics of countries. There is a "chicken or egg" dilemma present here. As the economies develop, so must their institutions; but unless the supporting institutions are present, economic development may be difficult.

The health statistics show significant differences between the high-income and low-income countries, but the middle-income countries have areas of overlap between both categories in most areas, except for per capita number of physicians. The educational data again show significant differences between high- and low-income countries, but the middle-income countries have some overlap with both groups. It is not until the infrastructure data are examined that the clear and marked differences between each income category of countries are revealed.

The geographic dispersion of LDCs appears to be concentrated outside the Pacific Rim, North America, Western Europe, and the oil-rich areas of the Middle East. Population density does not appear to correlate with geographic location of LDCs or the development stage of the country. However, the differences in population growth rates between LDCs and developed countries may result in an observed correlation sometime shortly after the turn of the century.

NOTES

1. For example, see Central Intelligence Agency, *The World Factbook, 1992* (Washington, D.C.: U.S. Government Printing Office, 1992)(published annually).

2. The authors cannot vouch for the reliability of the data published by most of the international organizations. The authors have found few inconsistencies and believe the data are reasonably accurate.

3. World Bank, *World Development Report, 1993* (New York: Oxford University Press, 1993), Table 1.

4. Central Intelligence Agency, *World Factbook, 1992*, p. 416.

5. World Bank, *World Development Report, 1992* (New York: Oxford University Press, 1992), Table 26.

PART II

HISTORY AND ECONOMICS OF LDCS

There is no fruit which is not bitter before it is ripe.
—Publilius Syrus, *Moral Sayings* (first century B.C.)

Chapter 4

History of the Relations between Industrialized and Less Developed Countries

International crises have their advantages. They frighten the weak but stir and inspire the strong.
—James Reston, *Sketches in the Sand* (1967)

Alliance, *n.* In international politics, the union of two thieves who have their hands so deeply inserted in each other's pocket that they cannot separately plunder a third.
—Ambrose Bierce, *The Devil's Dictionary* (1881–1911)

The relations between nations is what is popularly regarded as the bulk of history by the nonhistorian. That is because much of what is taught as history in the American public schools focuses on a survey of landmark events in military, political, and, to an extent, scientific history. Very little beyond Cyrus McCormick, Henry Ford, Thomas Edison, and Alexander Graham Bell is mentioned concerning the economic history of the United States. Virtually nothing of the history of economic thought and the economic systems that have evolved during modern times are taught, except to a few economics majors who comprise a captive audience for these classes. If one is to comprehend the conduct of modern economic systems, one must understand the historical development of the schools of thought that gave rise to the current economic wisdom.

The purpose of this chapter, in general terms, is to introduce the ideas upon which contemporary economic activities have been built. Most people are familiar with the broad conceptualizations of capitalism, and some even have a vague idea of what communists believe(d). Fewer still have any idea how these schools of thought arose, why they gained acceptance, and from what it was they emerged. However, many of the modern nations—developed and less developed alike—arose during times when far different ideologies reigned supreme. Maybe of even greater importance, the historical schools of thought were the cause for the retardation of the development of modern nations in many regions of the world.

This chapter is written as background to give the reader a formal reference point for the more pragmatic discussions that follow. Specifically, this chapter will introduce the precapitalist economic philosophies that guided both the economic and political policies of the day. The precapitalist philosophies were supplanted by capitalism, with little adventures into Marxism, Communism, Fascism, and sundry other less grand systems; but the world is shaped and reshaped by the philosophies that determine for people what is right or wrong, good or bad, and profitable and unprofitable. If politics and economics were separable, the authors would have written two chapters—one each on the politics and the economics. However, these systems are so entangled that separate presentations would be a fruitless academic exercise. In fact, the presentation of the economic background and political conditions that gave rise to the current world conditions is an equally hopeless task; but what we can do is to strip away all the trappings of practicality and deal only with the philosophy. As it happens, this is the most pragmatic and useful approach because it will give the reader an answer to why the world is the way that it is. This, in turn, can be used as a reference point in the following discussions.

The first section of this chapter offers a brief discussion on the evolution of economic thought. This section focuses on the premodern role of economics in society. The second section is an examination of mercantilism. The third section concerns modern economic philosophy, that is, capitalism. The final section of this chapter presents a summary and some conclusions.

ECONOMIC THOUGHT

Anthropology has demonstrated that simple tribal societies are not driven by sophisticated philosophical systems. In fact, the system of economic philosophy subscribed to by most primitive cultures is elegant but very simple: "no work, no eat." If an individual is self-reliant, then the very independence of that individual requires that he feeds and clothes himself. It is only when individuals seek the cooperation and association with other individuals that a true society begins to emerge. Interaction among individuals soon permits the discovery of the advantages of trade and cooperative production. Cooperative production soon gives rise to the specialization of labor and the need to determine how to allocate scarce resources among the unlimited wants of the individuals within that society. On the other hand, most primitive societies that experimented with cooperation found that groups could accomplish more in a cooperative venture than the sum of output of the various individuals that comprised the group. This discovery motivated cooperation, and it is this cooperation that meant economic progress for the members of the group and society as a whole.

With such economic progress comes difficulties. These difficulties arise because of competing interests within the society. These competing interests require an economic system capable of resolving the three basic economic questions:

1. What will be produced?
2. How will it be produced?
3. For whom will it be produced?

In the beginning, so to speak, the systems of solving economic questions were also rather straightforward and simple. These systems can be classified into two categories: tradition and command.

A traditional economic system is one based on a body of experience. In other words, this is the way we always did it, so this is the way we will continue to do it. Often these systems were based on religious precepts or, in more pragmatic cultures, on generations of trial and error. Today, pure traditional economic systems rarely exist outside of tribal cultures, but there are elements of most economic systems that are traditional. In the United States, for example, tipping waitresses and tithing in church are examples of traditional influences in the economic system. In many LDCs, tradition is far more important to the economic system than in most industrialized countries. In Islam, there are numerous economic obligations and traditions that are imposed on society as a matter of religion. For example, in Islam it is improper to charge interest on a loan; however, in most Islamic countries interest is not charged, but there are methods to receive payment for the making of a loan.

In command systems, brute force plays a far greater role than do morality, ethics, religion, or experience. Monarchs, generals, and other authorities (both secular and religious) are evident throughout history;

and in many cases their power was absolute. A command economy is simply a matter of an individual being in charge, making the decisions about production and distribution, and then being able to enforce those decisions through the use or threat of force. The twentieth century has many examples of command economies in both industrialized and developing countries. Nazi Germany was a command economy; but so too are Chile, Iraq, Saudi Arabia, and Kuwait (each with differing characteristics, traditions, and degree of control).

Command and traditional economic systems are not typically philosophically sophisticated systems; their underpinnings are rather simple and straightforward. As these systems were practiced in the medieval period in Europe, the distinctions between command and tradition became blurred in Asia and Africa. Feudalism in Europe was based on the divine right of kings (hence tradition) but was perpetuated and supported by the military power of kings (hence command). Serfs were tied to the land, hence the land owner, and a regimented system of production produced poverty for the masses and affluence for the few. The impoverished masses became increasingly restless through the period, and an enlightened explanation for economic activities was sought.[1] Asia also experienced feudalism but with slightly different characteristics. Genghis Khan ruled, not through the divine right of kings but through the overwhelming force of his horsemen and archers.

From the beginning of the renaissance (about 1490 in southern Europe, Italy, and Spain) through the middle of the eighteenth century, scholarly attention to economic activity began to take form. There were two reasons that academic inquiry into economic systems became possible. These two reasons were that surplus production resulted in a crude market system that needed to be explained and that the surplus created sufficient excess resources that a scholarly class could be supported to pose and answer mundane questions (questions not requiring answers for survival).

During the early part of this period (fifteenth and sixteenth centuries), contact with Asia and Africa and the substantial increase in scientific knowledge in Europe gave rise to trade. Shipbuilding, navigation, and the thirst for heretofore unavailable commodities, such as silks and spices, gave rise to more extensive market systems. The relatively sparse markets of medieval Europe, where serfs were occasionally permitted to sell surpluses of wool, fish, or vegetables, provided little of interest in examining markets and their operations.[2] The rise of merchant activities in trade with exotic lands and commodities—many of which were rapidly becoming regarded as necessities rather than luxuries—gave rise to large markets for imported goods. Because silks and spices had to be transported from the orient and received by merchants in Europe, a large network of supporting markets also arose. Merchant fleets required building and outfitting, and domestic markets were required to distribute the wares brought home by those merchant fleets.[3]

As the more extensive and complex markets began to develop throughout the decades after the renaissance, so did the amount of scholarly literature seeking to describe and systematically analyze markets. The widespread reliance on the operation of markets provided contemporary observers plenty of opportunity to witness both the benefits and the costs of a market system. As the mysteries of the market system became the subjects of debate, merchants and philosophers began to describe what they observed and attempted to offer explanations for their observations. It is this collection of interested philosophers and merchants that first began a systematic analysis of the market that became the world's first academic economists. This body of literature comprises what is commonly known as mercantilism.

MERCANTILISM

The school of thought that has come to be known to economists as mercantilism is not a solidified and unified system of reason. What is known of the prevailing wisdom of the day comes down to us from many independent writings—some scholarly and some not so scholarly. It is only after the fact that some unity was recognized in the thinking that prevailed 300 years before the American Revolution and was dubbed mercantilism by economists studying the development of the discipline.

Mercantilism was based on the idea of opening and servicing markets. The writers of the day were convinced that the wealth of the world was a fixed sum and that one's gain had to be at the expense of another. Therefore, markets and trade were the only things that gave rise to economic activity and, hence, economic gain. Markets in the mercantilist traditions were fragile mechanisms that allocated domestic resources and, more important, exotic goods imported from the Orient.

The mercantilists' views of economic activity were scholarly views that were significantly different from today's concepts. Mercantilists were concerned only with the allocative function of markets. Production, capital, the division and specialization of labor and even efficiency were alien ideas to the mercantilists. It was not until the classical economists (the first of the capitalists) that these ideas became central to economic reasoning. In other words, it was only through trade that the mercantilist system was thought to exist.[4]

In the centuries before the American Revolution, trade was a dangerous proposition. Sea routes and overland routes were the technologically feasible modes of travel. Travel by sea was a dangerous undertaking because of the relatively small and flimsy ships then available. The land routes were controlled by the Mongols, then by the Ottoman Turks, both well known for the hospitality for Christians and Europeans. Not only adventurous men but also stout ships for safe passage through the steppes and mountains of Asia Minor and Asia were needed. The hazards of the overland trade routes and the increase in navigation and shipbuilding permitted sea routes to be substituted for paying tolls and tributes to those who controlled the overland routes. Of even greater importance was the simple fact that a ship could carry a relatively larger cargo at a greater speed than the same size crew herding pack animals.

The fundamental elements of the mercantilist system can now be explained. The underlying assumption of a fixed sum of wealth and the transportation of goods to support a market being a rather hazardous calling, gave rise to a simple and often brutal economic philosophy. As Clive Day observed, "The prize in distant commerce went not to the best producers and merchants, but to the group of the best fighters; not size and resources, but ability to organize and willingness to risk resources in conflict determined the question of success."[5]

Day's view is not as radical as it may sound. Plainly, economic prowess was a function of relative naval and military strength. The Europeans had little of value to exchange with the relatively advanced cultures of east Asia between the fifteenth and seventeenth centuries. What was valued in the lands that were the sources of silks, porcelains, and spices was gold and silver. Gold and silver were the items from which currency was minted and could be stored, transported, and exchanged in almost all markets for economic goods and services.

The Europeans needed gold and silver to obtain those goods they had come to regard as necessary to their standard of living from China and India. It was also necessary that the Europeans obtain these commodities through peaceful trade. During the thirteenth century, the wrath of the Great Khans was demonstrated to the Europeans, and the Europeans of the day saw no potential advantage to scheduling a rematch.

The strategy for the Europeans was to obtain gold and silver to trade for silk and spices. As with many historically significant events, a great error provided the Europeans with the salvation of their emerging economic system. An Italian adventurer, rebuked by his own country's financiers, convinced the monarchy of Castile to fund a venture to East Asia for trade. As luck would have it, he failed and did so miserably. He missed Asia by more than 7,000 miles but instead bumped into islands off the coast of North America. What Christopher Columbus's folly provided Ferdinand and Isabella (his Spanish financiers) turned out to be the engine to drive mercantilism. Gold and silver were known among the societies of North America, and the ore was abundant. Even better, iron was rare and gunpowder unheard of among these trusting, primitive people. Without getting into the lengthy and bloody details, the

Europeans had a significant military advantage and could wrest from the Incas and the Aztecs the gold and silver they possessed and press the vanquished peoples into mining gold and silver. The European's accidental discovery of North America and brutal exploitation of the native people and their wealth permitted continued reliance on trade with Asia through mercantilist principles. Oddly enough, had Columbus not bumped into North America on his way to the Orient, the gold and silver necessary to fund the trading ventures of the Europeans would not have been available; and the mercantilist system would have collapsed in short order.

Mercantilism, contributed substantially to the modern understanding of the workings of an economic system. Probably the single greatest contribution was the illustration of what a monetary economy was and how it functioned. A popular oversimplification of mercantilism is a system in which the quantity of gold and silver amassed by a country determines its economic success.[6] The markets of the mercantilist period were viewed as barter economies, but this is only partially true. The Europeans had gold and silver, which was valued by the Asians as *money* (a concept that was well understood in China for centuries before European trade). The European gold and silver was money, the currency of the day. Maybe of even greater importance, the mercantilist experience gave rise to the more sophisticated modern understanding of the role of money in a market economy.

The experience of the mercantilists demonstrated that gold and silver had several uses. The exchange of gold and silver with Asians for spices and silk is the transactional value of money. Rather than having to establish terms of trade by establishing equivalency for dozens of different goods, the prices of goods could be easily stated as so much gold or so much silver. The use of precious metals permitted a standard by which value could be stated.

However, it was also discovered that gold and silver could be easily used as a store of value. For example, if the supply of silks and spices was sufficient for the immediate market period, there was no reason to risk spoilage or theft of these commodities in warehouses. The equivalent value of commodities could be stored in the safe as gold and silver. When the inventory of spices or silk became low, ships could be dispatched with gold and silver to exchange for these items.

IMPLICATIONS OF MERCANTILISM

Several interesting implications arise from the mercantilist view of the world that was founded upon international trade. The expansion of trade demonstrated how economic cooperation could be taken to an international level. The expansion of trade created a far higher standard of living in Europe for many which ultimately allowed the creation of a rudimentary middle class. However, there were other implications that had direct and profound effects on regions of the world. These implications would result in many regions being retarded in their economic development.

European interests in the Americas, Africa, and Asia were the result of their mercantilist views of wealth. It was necessary for the European trading partners to obtain gold and silver to exchange for silk and spices. The Europeans also relied upon sea routes as the mechanism for transporting the trade goods.

Gold and silver were obtained from regions of the world to which the Europeans could gain access to resources through bringing military might to bear (again, a holdover from the command economic systems with which Europeans were familiar). Primitive societies were easily dominated and their lands colonized so that the more advanced societies (militarily) could obtain those resources they valued. This explains much of the plight of early Latin America. The gold and silver from Mexico and Peru were the attraction of the earlier Spaniards, oddly enough called *conquistadors* and not the merchants of Seville.

This leaves much of the rest of the world unexplained. The sea routes to Asia from Europe were around the Cape of Good Hope (southernmost point in Africa). Sailing vessels of the pre–eighteenth-century variety were rather limited in their cargo capacity. Fresh water and other provisions needed to be obtained periodically throughout the journey. Therefore, Spanish, Portuguese, Dutch, French, and English merchants needed ports of call to obtain provisions for their vessels and crews. Africa, the Indian subcontinent, and much of south Asia provided these ports of call. Because of the frequent conflicts among European nations, each of the European trading nations found it necessary to have their own "ports of call" in order to assure adequate support for their merchants' trade routes. The almost ceaseless warfare among European nations and the forays of certain indigenous adventurers, such as the Djiboutis and other renown privateers, caused the major mercantile powers of Europe to seek protection of their merchant vessels. The introduction of naval power along the trade routes, required stable and secure ports, generally protected by the military and served by contractors from home.

The history of colonization of what is now called less developed countries is simply a by-product of the mechanics necessary to implement the mercantilists' views of trade with Asia. The European powers bore no grudge against the societies they encountered in their quest for trade with Asia. In fact, the Europeans readily shared their religion and diseases with the indigenous people they found in those regions. What the Europeans did not share was capital (either physical or human), the right to govern, or their income and wealth. Instead, the Europeans often sought gold and silver in and around the ports they established along the trade routes with Asia. The success of the Europeans in dominating the developing areas of the world, both militarily and economically, created not only colonies but also dependence on the Europeans.

The mercantile world was a rather simple place. Asia had the goods the Europeans wanted, Latin America had the gold and silver necessary to obtain the Asian goods, and the rest of the Third World was simply in the way. However, things changed in both the political and economic philosophies of the day and in the practical aspects of economic life. The observed, almost continuous expansion of trade was not consistent with the mercantilist assumptions of a fixed amount of wealth. Observers of the day began to question whether there was something wrong with the conventional wisdom. Most notably, there were those scholars who began to argue that wealth could be created and was not a fixed pool of assets. These scholars gave rise to the beginnings of modern economic thought.

In 1776, Adam Smith rewrote economic philosophy with the publication of his book, *An Inquiry into the Nature and Causes of the Wealth of Nations*. This book explained that the *production* of commodities was the cause of the wealth of nations and that trade, under the right circumstances, can enhance that wealth. Smith accounted for the deficiencies in the mercantilist school of thought by adding production to the model that explained the accumulation of wealth.

MODERN ECONOMIC THOUGHT

Modern capitalist economic philosophy still focuses on exchange in markets; however, there is more than simple exchange. The production of goods and services is incorporated into the explanation of wealth-accumulating economic behaviors. If producers are free to enter and exit markets and must compete with other producers serving the same market, the costs of production are of central importance to the competitiveness of any single supplier. Rather than the acquisition of gold and silver, the success of economy is measured by how efficiently it produces.

The seventeenth century in Europe saw the beginnings of manufacturing industries. Iron smelting, glass production, automated weaving, and numerous other technological innovations began to emerge. By the end of the eighteenth century, hydraulic power had been harnessed and massive machines were being used to replace animal or human power for production. In quick succession, steam power and standardized interchangeable parts for machinery made assembly line–type mass production possible. With these innovations came a burst of economic growth in Western Europe and North America based not on trade among nations but on the ability of a nation to produce manufactured goods. The production of manufactured goods also meant machinery—machinery to make agriculture more efficient, to weave cloth more efficiently, and to provide steam power for locomotion. The Industrial Revolution was simply the sudden ability to turn cottage industries (based on craftsmanship) into manufactories (based on mass production) to produce goods more efficiently.

In the early days of the Industrial Revolution, iron, brass, glass, and wood were the things of which manufactured goods were made; and charcoal (later coal) was all that was needed for transformation of raw materials into finished products. Competition among producers required innovation in both the design of products and the manufacturing processes used to produce products if dominant market positions were to be obtained and maintained. Tin, aluminum, chrome, zinc, and oil, among others, started to find their way into the production of European-manufactured goods. In Europe, just like gold and silver, these resources were available only in limited quantities (if at all). However, the Europeans had other sources of these raw materials—the places where they discovered gold and silver and where they had established their port of call along the original trade routes with Asia. Hence, a second wave of exploration, colonization, and the growth of material well-being in Europe and this time in North America started. This time, however, Asia did not share any increase in their advantages of trade with Europe. The problem for Asia was that the increase in economic well-being from the silk and spice trade was trivial compared with the economic growth spurred by the Industrial Revolution.

The divergence of industrialized from less developed countries had two causes. The first was the Europe–Asia trade activities of the fifteenth through the seventeenth centuries. European domination of enclaves along the trade routes and of the regions where gold and silver were sought resulted in subservient regions within colonial empires. The second was that the colonial empires realized that the lessons learned from the days of the silk trade could be easily reapplied in their quest for the raw materials needed to fuel the Industrial Revolution.

In other words, mercantilism taught the colonial powers how to colonize and gave them a taste of the benefits, but capitalism gave the mercantilists a broader understanding of opportunities that control of natural resources gave them in the marketplace. Capitalism is based on both the idea of production (absent in the mercantilist world) and trade. Capitalistic production generated the demand for natural resources that were readily available in the regions colonized during the mercantilist days.

As capitalism thrived, certain deficiencies were noted in the system that imposed external costs on individuals or society in general. The true strength of the capitalist system was based on freedom of enterprise, but this same freedom presented interesting dilemmas. Steel and chemical producers polluted the environment, textile manufacturers exploited child labor, agricultural interests turned the Great Plains of North America into deserts, and logging and coal-mining interests denuded vast expanses of land on both sides of the Mississippi River. These excesses occurred in countries with democratic governments and the public policies of these nations soon limited the harmful effects of the excesses of capitalism.

Slavery, child labor, and damaging the environment, among others, were identified as being socially unacceptable consequences of unbridled capitalism; and the deficiencies were either eliminated or constrained. These public policies reflect a certain evolving social conscience that also resulted in many of the colonial powers granting independence to their former colonies. However, the former colonies, just like the former slaves, were granted little or no part of the value they added to the wealth of their former masters.[7]

While this analysis may seem a harsh judgment of the Western industrialized world, this is precisely how most LDCs view their role in the evolution of the global economy. Objectively, the LDCs have a point. The industrialized powers of the eighteenth and nineteenth centuries exploited the resources of their former colonies, often without returning any significant benefits to their colonies. The exploitation of natural resources, manpower, and even taxation levied upon the colonies served to enrich the colonial power at the expense of the colony. Often, colonies revolted at this exploitation, sometimes successfully. The United States did not remain a colony of Great Britain because the colonists were getting such a good deal from the English. The very causes of the American Revolution contain important confirmation of the Europeans' propensities to exploit their colonies.[8]

IMPLICATIONS FOR BUSINESS IN LDCS

History may be a boring topic to some, but it provides valuable lessons. Mercantilism was accompanied by harsh military and political regimes. Often, Americans and Europeans take a great deal of pride in the dominance their nations have held over the rest of the world. This pride can be a source of constant grief when trying to do business in a part of the world that was once dominated by a European power. Much of the mistrust and hostility observed in LDCs towards Americans or Europeans is not without a sound historical foundation. The govern-

ments of these industrialized nations have had long histories of exploit-
ing the resources and people of these LDCs. Such exploitation can create substantial mistrust and hostility.

The rise of capitalism to replace mercantilism softened the government policies of the industrialized world toward LDCs only marginally.
Private interests supplanted sovereign interests with the suspicion and
mistrust of the LDCs' governments and people being extended to the
private interests of the industrialized nations.

Suspicion is a natural result of the history of the industrialized nations' contact with LDCs. However, with forewarning and a little sen-
sitivity, an American or European seeking trade or business relations
with government officials, workers, and businesspersons in LDCs can
be successful.

SUMMARY AND CONCLUSION

Tradition and command economies needed little or no guiding philosophical basis or much inquiry into why they worked. Feudalism was
only marginally more complex and still required little formal understanding. It was not until the development of the silk and spice trade
that scholarly attention became focused on economic matters. Mercantilism was the first attempt at any systematic discovery of economic
principles.

Mercantilist philosophy was rather simple and straightforward. Gain
was available only at the expense of a trading partner. The driving force
for Europeans became how to obtain gold and silver to trade with their
Asian trading partners. This Europe–Asia trade connection resulted in
the colonization of much of what is today called LDCs. The motivation
for the colonization came originally from the search for gold and silver
and to secure Europe's trade routes with Asia.

The mercantilist views, however, failed to explain how the observed
rise in economic well-being occurred in both Asia and Europe. Mercantilist philosophy simply failed to account for the benefits to be gained
from production. Capitalism was born out of the failures of the mercantilist school at about the same time as the Industrial Revolution was
heating up. Capitalism could explain the benefits of production. However, the European colonial powers' innovations in production required
fuel for the engines of economic progress. The natural resources that
were abundant in many of their colonial enclaves provided further
cause for LDCs to remain underdeveloped. However, most of the colonial powers were also democracies, with the inherent social consciences
and government structure that permitted change. Colonization disap-
peared for all practical purposes by the middle of the twentieth century,
only to be replaced by former colonies struggling to join the industrialized world.

NOTES

1. J. K. Beitscher and E. K. Hunt, "Insights into the Dissolution of the Feudal Mode of Production," *Science and Society* 40 (1976): 57–71.

2. For further discussion, see Lynn White, Jr., *Medieval Technology and Social Change* (Oxford: Clarendon Press, 1962).

3. For further discussion of the premercantilism period, see Robert Heilbroner, *The Worldly Philosophers,* 4th ed. (New York: Touchstone, 1972), Chapter 2.

4. Harry Landreth and David Colander, *History of Economic Theory,* 2nd ed. (Boston: Houghton Mifflin Company, 1989), 29.

5. Clive Day, *A History of Commerce* (New York: Longmans Green, 1938), 166.

6. Harry Magdoff, *Imperialism: From the Colonial Age to the Present* (New York: Monthly Review Press, 1978), 101.

7. Landreth and Colander, *History of Economic Theory,* pp. 45–47.

8. Heilbroner, *Worldly Philosophers,* pp. 303–304.

Chapter 5

Comparative and Absolute Advantage: Implications for Trade with LDCs

> What is prudeence in the conduct of every private family, can scarce be folly in that of a great kingdom. If a foreign country can supply us with a commodity cheaper than we ourselves can make it, better buy it of them with some part of the produce of our own industry, employed in a way in which we have some advantage.
>
> —Adam Smith, *An Inquiry into the Nature and Causes of the Wealth of Nations* (1776)

Markets are the mechanisms through which exchange occurs. The market provides the forum through which allocative decisions are made. In a global economy, the market system performs that allocative function but is complicated by the trade occurring between nations and not individuals. Individuals within a country use the same currency, or they barter. They probably live under the same laws and practice the same customs. When nations trade, they have none of these conveniences. Because the mercantilist school of economic thought held prominence for centuries in the Western World there lingers a blind faith in the efficacy of international trade.

The purpose of this chapter is to review some of the basic principles of economics concerning international trade and apply them to trade with LDCs. The modern theory of international trade is a powerful model that not only permits examination of why trade occurs between nations but also permits identification of the terms of trade and the likely monetary and real consequences of the trade within each country.

Trade between LDCs and developed countries has become a particularly controversial subject in most developed nations because of its consequences for domestic labor markets in the developed countries. For example, critics of NAFTA have been most vocal because of the perception that one of the economic consequences of the treaty will be exporting jobs to Mexico. Whether there will be adverse effects on the U.S. labor market because of NAFTA is an empirical question.

This chapter begins with a review of the theories of comparative advantage and absolute advantage. Comparative and absolute advantage are the driving mechanisms behind the modern theory of international trade (no previous exposure to economic theory is necessary to understand the materials in this chapter). A discussion of international trade and its effects on economic development will be built within the comparative and absolute advantage frameworks. The final section of the chapter is an examination of the motivations for American investment in LDCs and how the debt crisis may affect the decision by entrepreneurs in developed countries to invest in LDCs.

Economic activity between industrialized and developing economies can take many forms. Importing and exporting goods is what is commonly thought of as international trade. Manufacturing firms located in the United States outsource production to operations in Mexico and other LDCs. This form of trade is what is anticipated by NAFTA. Another view of economic activity is opening a facility or moving operations to an LDC to take advantage of cost savings. In either event, the principles of international trade are the underlying foundation upon which sound business decisions must be made. Capital, labor, and other resource markets within those LDCs will determine whether trade with or the location of operations to an LDC is a viable economic alternative. As will be seen in the following chapters, indebtedness is one of the major indicators of the viability of business in LDCs.

EXCHANGE, OPPORTUNITY COST, AND PRODUCTION: PRECURSORS TO COMPARATIVE ADVANTAGE

International trade is based on some simple but powerful economic concepts. Economics is a simple but powerful framework within which to examine human behavior. Trade among individuals and nations is an important human behavior. Several important concepts must be developed before attempting to bring them together in a coherent theory of international trade.

International trade, at its simplest, is the exchange of goods. Exchange occurs because it is to the advantage of the trading partners to do so. With exchange, however, there are costs. Once the simple exchange economy is developed and mastered, production can be added to the model. With production comes more costs (the costs of production). Production and exchange permit a more elaborate model of trade to be developed. The following paragraphs of this section will develop the basics necessary to describe the behavior of nations in international trade. The more economically sophisticated reader may already be familiar with the ideas of an exchange economy, opportunity cost, and absolute advantage and may wish to skip the rest of this section and move on to "Comparative Advantage and the Terms of Trade."

The Simple Exchange Economy

Just like between two people, transactions occur between nations because it is to the trading partners' mutual advantage to enter into contracts of exchange. For trade to occur, there must be what economists call a *coincidence of wants*. In a two-person, two-commodity world without the production of commodities, we have only an exchange economy (sounds suspiciously like mercantilism, doesn't it?).

In this exchange economy, if the initial endowment of resources (in our two-person economy) is that Groucho has two oranges and Harpo has two apples, there may be trade. Groucho decided he would like to have an apple and an orange, and Harpo is indifferent between apples and oranges. There may be an exchange. If both trading partners would like an apple and an orange, then there is no doubt a transaction will occur. The terms of trade are also easily identified—one apple is worth one orange. The coincidence of wants is that each of the trading partners has something that the other one wants.

Transactions become more complex if we add a third party to the simple economy we have assumed. If Harpo and Groucho have their original pieces of fruit, but Harpo hates oranges, Groucho will not get his apple. Enter the third party with two bananas. Harpo likes bananas, but Groucho hates them. The third party, Karl, does not like apples but will eat bananas and oranges. How does poor Groucho get his apple? Groucho can go to Karl and trade one of his oranges for one of Karl's bananas. Karl is satisfied, and Groucho now has that one commodity that he can exchange with Harpo to get an apple. This is a simple matter of coincidence of wants. This is precisely how trade occurs between nations. Unless there is an absolute or comparative advantage, the coincidence of wants is not sufficient to make the trading partners better off. Notice, if you will, in the fruit example, everyone still has two pieces of fruit.

Opportunity Costs

Every decision has an implicit cost. If you decide to read this book, you must forego something else that could have been done during the time you read. Sleeping, watching television, or whatever your next-best alternative allocation of time is the opportunity you gave up to read this book. In the exchange economy example above, Groucho's cost to obtain the apple in the two-person model was one of his oranges. This simple example demonstrates the idea of opportunity costs, but it also illustrates the terms of trade (e.g., one apple is worth one orange). The idea of terms of trade will become considerably more complicated as we move along in this section.

Costs of Production and Absolute Advantage

The advantages in the cost of production can come from several sources. The division and specialization of labor is one of the most common sources of advantage in the production of a specific commodity. There are also several other sources, such as endowments of natural resources, climate, and technological advantages. The division and specialization of labor was first described by Adam Smith in the *Wealth of Nations,* he described it as follows:

To take an example, . . . from a very trifling manufacture; but one in which the division of labour has been very often taken notice of, the trade of the pin-maker; a workman not educated to this business (which the division of labour had rendered a distinct trade), nor acquainted with the use of the machinery employed in it (to the invention of which the same division of labour has probably given occasion), could scarce, perhaps, with his utmost industry, make one pin in a day, and certainly could not make twenty. But in the way in which this business is now carried on, not only the whole work is a peculiar trade, but it is divided into a number of branches, of which the greater part are likewise peculiar trades. One man draws out the wire, another straights it, a third cuts it, a fourth points it, a fifth grinds it at the top for receiving the head; to make the head requires two or three distinct operations; to put it on, is a peculiar business, to whiten the pins is another; it is even a trade by itself to put them into the paper; and the important business of making a pin is, in this manner, divided into about eighteen distinct operations, which in some manufactories, are all performed by distinct hands, though in others the same man will sometimes perform two or three of them. I have seen a small manufactory of this kind where ten men only were employed, and where some of them consequently performed two or three distinct operations. But though they were poor, and therefore indifferently accommodated with the necessary machinery, they could, when they exerted themselves, make among them about twelve pounds of pins in a day. There are in a pound upwards of four thousand pins of middling size. Those ten persons, therefore, could make among them upwards of forty-eight thousand pins in a day. Each person, therefore making a tenth part of forty-eight thousand pins, might be considered as making four thousand eight hundred pins a day. But if they had all wrought separately and independently, and without any of them having been educated to this peculiar business, they certainly could not each of them have made twenty, perhaps not one pin in a day.[1]

Smith's description of the division of labor and its benefits has attained the status of economic principle. But notice carefully, not only is labor divided so that it may become specialized, but it is also educated to the specific skills (peculiar trade) necessary to its part in the production process. Naturally, several historical examples on an industrial scale come to mind. England of the sixteenth and seventeenth centuries was the dominate naval power and trade center because her craftsman had mastered, better than others elsewhere, the production of seaworthy ships of the merchant classes and of warships necessary to protect her trade routes. German craftsman a century later mastered the production of steel, with few rivals. These advantages came from the mastery of specific trades, through specialization that arose through the division of and the education of labor into, as Smith called them, "peculiar trades."

Before the production advantage can be fully translated into international trade, something of the concept of efficiency must be understood. Economic efficiency is defined alternatively in two interchangeable ways. To be efficient in production, one must produce a given amount of output and minimize the costs of production or, alternatively, for a given cost must maximize the amount of output. If a cost advantage is to occur in a competitive world, then it is a result of one producer being more efficient. However, there are problems with this analysis. Notice that we assumed a competitive world. That means there are no barriers to trade or entry into an industry, there is perfect knowledge, atomized competition (a very large number of buyers and sellers, such that no one or group can appreciably affect price or quantity in the market), and we produce a homogenous product. Unfortunately, most of these assumptions are not very descriptive of what really happens in economic endeavors. We have barriers to entry into industries, advertisers try to convince consumers that "Coca-Cola is the real thing" or whatever, and there is nothing approaching perfect knowledge (barring insider trading). The positive effects of efficiency can therefore be short-circuited because of intervening imperfections in the marketplace. In other words, we have simply taken the "con" out of economics.[2] In the real world, efficiency is sometimes overwhelmed by market imperfections and is rarely, if ever, attained but is simply the goal of the profit-maximizing firm. The pin factory example can be extended to demonstrate how efficient production can create advantages to international trade.

The principle of *absolute advantage* is perhaps the appropriate start-
ing point to understand the motives for international trade. In the eighteenth century, the British had invented the steam engine and had
mastered its production. Because the British had coal in Wales and
access to European iron ore, it was technically feasible for the British
to produce steam engines, but only if they could obtain the iron ore
necessary for the casting of boilers. Both the French and Germans had
the iron ore, but they did not have the technical expertise to build steam
engines. The principle of absolute advantage can be seen from this example. Because both the French and Germans have iron ore neither has
an absolute advantage in its production, assuming mining and refining costs are identical in the two countries. Even though both the Germans and French have all the raw materials, they did not have the skills
and the knowledge to build steam engines. In this case, because the
British had the knowledge and skills to build steam engines, they had
an absolute advantage in their production, even though iron ore had to
be imported. In fact, both the Germans and French obtained the technology by importing steam engines, tearing them apart, and examining the individual parts. Within a very few years, the Germans and
French educated themselves in the production of steam engines; and
the Germans eventually obtained an absolute advantage in their production.

Comparative Advantage and the
Terms of Trade

The idea of comparative advantage moves us away from the simple
exchange model into production cost advantages. The principle of *comparative advantage* is based on one trading partner being more efficient
in the production of one particular commodity and the second trading
partner being more efficient in the production of another. *Efficiency,* in
this case, refers to technical efficiency and means that the more efficient country can produce more for the same cost or, alternatively, can
produce the same amount but at a lower total cost. Lest the reader become confused about what is meant by cost, we will assume that all
countries use the same currency and that it has the same real value
across all countries.

Allocative efficiency can present a significant problem in this analysis and is therefore assumed not to be a problem. Allocative efficiency
is concerned with how goods and services are distributed within an
economic system. By assuming away distributional problems within the
trading-partner countries, there is not significant violence done to
analysis offered herein.

For technical efficiency to produce a comparative advantage, it cannot be overwhelmed by some market imperfection (i.e., monopoly

power). If a country has a cost advantage in production, that cost advantage can be mitigated by monopoly power in the market. In other words, efficiency in production reduces costs; but should the producer have a monopoly, it need not pass the cost savings on to customers (e.g., trading partners). In other words, the monopolist producer can retain the cost savings because there is no other source of the product where consumers can go to obtain the product at any price.

The international trade implications of this market power is substantial. A country can gain monopoly power by pricing its output below cost and driving competitors out of the business. By so doing, a country then can be the sole remaining producer and recover its losses (and monopoly profits) by pricing its product higher than what it could in the presence of competition. These market imperfections exist in the real world. In fact, the description of selling below cost to create a monopoly is why the General Agreement on Tariffs and Trade (GATT) prohibits "dumping." Dumping is selling something in international markets for a price below production costs. For present purposes, the authors assume a competitive international market without any distortions created by monopoly strategies.

To illustrate the principle of comparative advantage that motivates trade among countries, consider the following hypothetical example. Assume that both Colombia and Canada can produce only two goods each—coffee and whiskey. The production levels of whiskey and coffee are presented in Table 5.1. If Canada allocates all its resources to the production of coffee, it can produce 5,000 tons of coffee; but if all of Canada's resources are used to produce whiskey, Canada can produce 500,000 barrels of whiskey. Similarly, in Colombia if all resources are used for coffee production, then 100,000 tons of coffee can be produced; however, if Colombia specializes in whiskey, it can produce only 2,500 barrels.

In Colombia, for each barrel of whiskey that is made, the population must forego the production, hence the consumption of forty tons of coffee. In Canada things are different. For each ton of coffee that is produced, 100 barrels of whiskey must be foregone. If there was trade

Table 5.1
Production of Coffee and Whiskey

Country	Coffee (tons)	Whiskey (barrels)
Colombia	100000	2500
Canada	5000	500000

between these two countries, as things stand, then whiskey is more dear in Colombia than is coffee; but in Canada, coffee is more dear. For sake of this example, we will assume that both Colombia and Canada have the same endowments of resources and the same size economies (in reality, this is not the case). The two countries realize that it is their mutual best interests to specialize in the production of the commodities in which they have the comparative advantage and to trade. However, the problem is what terms of trade will be established, that is, what will be the rate of exchange of coffee and whiskey. If the trading partners have no currency and equal utility derived from each commodity in each country, then we would expect an exchange rate of something on the order of five barrels of whiskey for each ton of coffee. The terms of trade are based on specialization of Colombia in the production of 100,000 tons of coffee and Canada in 500,000 barrels of whiskey. Because we assumed equal utility in the consumption of both goods across both country and equal-sized economies, the terms of trade are simply the ratio of whiskey to coffee production.

If the equal utility assumption is supplemented with an assumption that resources can be transferred from one use to another consistent with the ratio of coffee to whiskey production for each country, then the positive effects of trade can be easily demonstrated. If both Colombia and Canada allocated one-half of their resources to the production of each commodity, then the world would have 52,500 tons of coffee and 251,250 barrels of whiskey. By specializing, Colombia would produce 100,000 tons of coffee (47,500 tons more than was previously available) and Canada would produce 500,000 barrels of whiskey (248,750 barrels more than was previously available).

As if by magic, both Colombia and Canada are clearly better off by specialization and trade. The only magic is that the division and specialization of labor (and other resources) permits greater productivity. The example is simplified, however. It is unlikely that the rates at which you can produce whiskey using labor and capital previously used in the production of coffee will continue to produce whiskey at a constant rate as you continue to increase production. In fact, the *law of diminishing marginal productivity* states that productivity gains will continue as you increase output but at a decreasing rate. There is another limiting principle: the *rate of technical substitution*. The rate of technical substitution is the rate of output that can be expected from substituting one factor of production for another. For example, a whiskey distiller may not be a good substitute for a coffee picker. However, if the trade of distilling is easily taught to a coffee roaster not much would be lost in the trade.

Comparative advantage is a powerful incentive to trade among people and among nations. Even if we have marginally less whiskey and coffee than presented in the previous example, because of the problems associated with the law of diminishing marginal productivity and the limits caused by the rate of technical substitution, both Canada and Colombia are clearly better off than if no specialization and trade occurred.

CURRENCY EXCHANGE RATES
AND ADVANTAGE

In the discussion of absolute and comparative advantage, both countries were assumed to use the same currency to measure costs, and barter was the mode of exchange. In the global markets, however, several currencies are used for transactions. *Hard currencies,* or fiat monies, are the media of exchange in these markets. The German mark, Japanese yen, British pound, and U.S. dollar are the most common, the U.S. dollar accounting for the largest proportion of foreign exchange. There are several reasons for this observation. When a country sells its output, the currency it receives in exchange determines where it can purchase things. If Kenya sells coffee and receives Danish krone in exchange, then it must buy things Danish or from a country that has a demand for Danish output. Because the Germans, Japanese, British, and Americans have the largest economies, and variety of desired commodities, then most countries prefer to exchange their goods for currencies that will enable them to purchase the things they want— typically from the major industrialized countries.

Often, in the international trade literature, the U.S. dollar is assumed to be the medium of exchange. In the real global economy, this assumption is not too far afield. The value of most countries' currencies are influenced by the supply of and demand for the U.S. dollar. The prominent positioning of the U.S. economy in the global marketplace is reflected in the trust that virtually all the world's nations have in the value of the U.S. dollar. The value of any nation's currency is a reflection of the viability of that nation's economy (and government) and the historical performance in maintaining that currency's real purchasing power.

Industrialized nations, therefore, have an advantage because of the attractiveness of their currencies in global money markets. For example, if one wishes to buy wheat in the United States, American farmers are not generally willing to take Mexican pesos but would prefer to have U.S. dollars because that is what they must use to buy fuel, seeds, and chemicals and to support their families. If Mexicans want American wheat, then they have to be able to convert pesos into dollars; and that is typically accomplished by selling something they produce in the world marketplace for U.S. dollars or by borrowing U.S. dollars, hence, one of the major motivations for trade and U.S. lending to LDCs. If

Americans wish to sell wheat to Mexicans, and the Mexicans do not have the dollars or something to sell to obtain dollars, then Mexicans will need to borrow dollars. If the Mexicans spend their borrowed dollars on wheat, make bread and eat it, then they will need to borrow more dollars next week. If, on the other hand, our Mexican friends borrow the dollars, drill oil wells, and sell Americans oil, then they eat bread next week that was bought with dollars that Americans spent to fuel their tractors in Kansas.

SO WHY TRADE WITH LDCS?

Trading with LDCs may make good economic sense. As can be readily seen from the discussion of comparative and absolute advantage, the motivation is that both trading partners are made better off. The industrialized world may have absolute advantages in the production of many commodities, but much of the world's natural resources are to be found in LDCs. As long as there is a comparative or an absolute advantage in raw materials or finished products there will be trade between the developed and less developed countries.

In general, natural resources have been mined from LDCs and shipped overseas for refining and fabrication. The reason for this is because of the high levels of infrastructure (particularly utilities and transportation), skilled labor, and capital that are available in the industrialized countries but are relatively scarce in LDCs. The occurrence of natural resources in LDCs may seem to suggest that economic growth had a base in those countries. However, because of the lack of requisite economic resources natural resources, have been little more than export commodities in most LDCs. This is particularly true of African countries south of the Sahara.

LOCATION OF ENTERPRISES OVERSEAS

As the debate concerning NAFTA illustrated, there is large pool of human resources in LDCs. In Mexico, the hourly wage is a small fraction of the hourly wage in either the United States or Canada. Mexico clearly has a comparative advantage in the production of labor-intensive commodities, but only if the required labor is not highly technical or skilled. Many such advantages can be found throughout the less developed regions of the world. In fact, the authors experienced an interesting example of this fact during the summer of 1994. One author's brother came to the United States for a visit. He produces stainless steel teapots in Iran. His name is Amjad.

Amjad is a highly skilled welder. He fabricates teapots using stainless steel, but the type of welding needed to join the parts into a whole teapot requires a high degree of skill. Amjad possesses this skill, but unfortunately his employees do not. Therefore, he spent the better part of his vacation searching for machinery to eliminate the need for skilled welders so that he could expand his output. The authors, much to their chagrin, learned a great deal about welding between chapters.

Comparative and absolute advantage are important not only in analyzing trade between countries but also in determining whether operations can be profitably located in another country. The abundance of resources and unskilled and skilled labor may make the location of certain operations very attractive in certain countries. For example, the production of Persian carpets requires substantial skill and time. Therefore, you need skilled labor, but cheap skilled labor. Because there is an embargo against Persian carpets coming into the United States, enterprising individuals exported Persian weavers to Egypt to make exactly the same product but from a country of origin that has normal trade relations with the United States.

After NAFTA, there has been some relocation of retail establishments from Canada and the United States in Mexico. There is a valuable lesson in this observed movement of retail trade south of the border. Because a country is classified as a low- or middle-income country, it does not mean that there are not substantial markets for goods in those countries. Mexico is a middle-income country with a per capita GNP of just $3,000 per year. Because of a large standard deviation, there is a large proportion of Mexico's population living at subsistence levels more common in low-income countries. In Mexico City, however, there is a large enough group of consumers with relatively high incomes to make it profitable for establishments such as Wal-Mart and others to locate stores in these areas.

SUMMARY AND CONCLUSION

Coincidence of wants exists when two or more people have something someone else wants and vice versa. Coincidence of wants is sufficient to motivate trade in a simple exchange economy. However, exchange is not the only thing accomplished in an economic system. Economic systems also determine what is to be produced and, in part, how it is to be valued. Comparative and absolute advantage provide the incentive for exchange when production is introduced into the system. Both concepts underpin the explanations for the existence of trade, and both motivate trade between LDCs and developed economies.

Comparative advantage is where a country experiences a cost advantage in the production of one commodity and its trading partner experiences a cost advantage in the production of another. It is to the advantage of the two countries to specialize in the production of their cost-advantaged commodities and trade. Absolute advantage is where a country has a cost advantage in the production of all commodities or is the sole producer of a commodity. In such cases, trade may still be mutually advantageous.

Money is also a commodity. Currency exchange rates and the value of money derives from the economy which backs that currency. The U.S. dollar has become the standard by which virtually all other currencies are measured because of its historic stability and the central role of the U.S. economy in the world marketplace.

NOTES

1. Adam Smith, *An Inquiry into the Nature and Causes of the Wealth of Nations,* ed. Edwin Cannan (New York: G. P. Putnam & Sons, 1877), 19. Original work first published under the same title in 1776.

2. For an elementary discussion of economic efficiency and purely competitive markets see Campbell R. McConnell and Stanley L. Brue, *Economics,* 12th ed. (New York: McGraw Hill, 1993), Chapters 2 and 23. For a more advanced treatment, see Heinz Kohler, *Intermediate Microeconomics: Theory and Applications* (Glenview, Ill.: Scott, Foresman, 1982), Chapters 7 and 14.

Part III

THE DEBT CRISIS

Creditors are a superstitious sect, great observers of set days and times.
—Benjamin Franklin, *Poor Richard's Almanack* (1732–1757)

Chapter 6

International Financial Foundations
of the World Debt Crisis

In every age "the good old days" were a myth. No one ever thought
they were good at the time. For every age has consisted of crises
that seemed intolerable to the people who lived through them.
—Brooks Atkinson, *Once Around the Sun* (1951)

Indebtedness is one measure of the viability of business enterprises and
of governments. Sovereign debt, whether in an industrialized or developing country, is almost always a controversial and emotional issue. One
of the most remarkable economic events of the 1980s and 1990s was the
inability of LDCs to meet their sovereign debt obligations. Because
LDCs had difficulties in meeting their debt obligations, there were
numerous reschedulings of sovereign debt during this period that came
to be called the *world debt crisis*.[1] The world debt crisis had profound
effects on the abilities of LDCs to sustain economic growth and political and social stability. Creditor governments and banks in industrialized countries began to recognize that the loans they made to LDCs
were riskier than they had first anticipated. Further, as the economic,
political, and social conditions within many LDCs seemed to worsen,
world organizations became concerned with policies to help alleviate
the crisis. Complicating matters even more, economic and sociopolitical
difficulties associated with the heavy debt burden made any business
relations with these LDCs more uncertain and, in many cases, more
difficult.

Conducting business in any LDC can be an adventure. The differences between industrialized and developing countries in their cultures, religions, and legal environments can be baffling to European and American business people. Because most industrialized nations are creditworthy and do not have significant instability in their currency values or their financial institutions, businesses have grown accustomed to a business environment with few uncertainties. In an indebted LDC, however, uncertainties are numerous and instability of the business environment is the norm. Again, the history of the debt crisis provides a useful benchmark for understanding the financial and currency limitations in conducting business in an indebted LDC.

The purpose of this chapter is to present the history of international financial markets relevant to the world debt crisis.

THE WORLD FINANCIAL MARKETS
PRIOR TO WORLD WAR II

The international financial markets prior to the Bretton Woods agreements were neither well organized nor very formal. The result was that the performance of these markets was not particularly impressive. In the early twentieth century, there had been a series of financial panics. These financial panics were particularly acute in countries that had not yet created a central regulating authority for their banking systems. The developed countries created their own central banking systems in a piecemeal fashion and through assigned regulatory responsibilities (more or less experimentation) to these systems. The inflation in Europe after World War II, particularly in Germany, demonstrated that international influences had significant potential for harm.

By 1929, the world was in the midst of the Great Depression. The Great Depression was accompanied by a financial panic in the fourth quarter of 1929 that demonstrated that there were serious problems in many industrialized countries' financial markets, which, unfortunately, had international implications. During this time, the United States had pegged the value of its currency to gold; and prior to 1934, the value of the dollar had been set at $21.65 per ounce.

In 1934, President Roosevelt devalued the U.S. dollar from $21.65 per ounce of gold to $35 per ounce. The real markets, however, reacted violently when President Roosevelt was seen as attempting to manipulate the dollar's value relative to gold.[2] Roosevelt's intention was to help stimulate the economy through making export goods more competitive in world markets. However, in 1934 most of the rest of the world was in the midst of the same Great Depression that the U.S. economy was suffering, and most of the industrialized world acted to protect the value of their currencies against the devaluation of the U.S. dollar. Roosevelt's actions were little more than a public admission of weakness in the U.S. economy. For the next forty years, the $35-per-ounce price of gold would remain the standard.

By 1934, the United States had become one of the preeminent economic and financial powers in the world. The 1934 U.S. dollar devaluation was particularly serious for the international currency exchange markets. Without international organizations and agreements to stabilize international monetary exchange, the unilateral devaluation of the U.S. dollar clearly demonstrated a need for more formal agreements and a more orderly international financial market. This need would be answered in the form of the financial provisions embodied in the Bretton Woods agreements.

A MONETARY HISTORY

As World War II drew to a close, the United States had become the dominant global economic power. The financial panics at the beginning of the twentieth century (e.g., 1908) and the Great Depression of the 1930s taught the world's great economic powers the value of stable global financial markets.[3] On July 22, 1944, the International Monetary Fund (IMF) and the International Bank for Reconstruction and Development (IBRD) or World Bank were created by agreement at Bretton Woods, New Hampshire. The IMF was created to facilitate the expansion and balanced growth of international trade and to contribute to the promotion of high rate of employment and real earnings. The World Bank was created to assist in the reconstruction and development of countries by facilitating the flow of capital for productive purposes. For the next twenty-five years, the world would experience a relatively stable global financial system based on the dollar and gold.

There were two specific purposes of the Bretton Woods agreements. The Bretton Woods agreement contained relatively short-lived agreements on international trade and the balance of payments. These agreements lasted about two years and were subsequently replaced by more detailed trade agreements later in the century. The best known and longest lived were the provisions that dealt with international financial markets.

The Short-Lived Trade Provisions of Bretton Woods

The vision the United Nations had for the post–World War II global economy included not only peace but also a new world economic order. The experience between the two world wars taught those who would learn some valuable lessons. The Treaty of Versailles that ended World War I imposed harsh terms on Germany, including severe reparations and loss of valuable territories that were heavily industrialized (i.e., the Rhineland). The inequities of the Treaty of Versailles created more problems than it resolved. Among the more serious of these problems were the financial instability and economic contraction that reparations could cause. Much of the post–World War I difficulties resulted from trade imbalances and inflation. Therefore, the United Nations addressed both issues in the Bretton Woods agreements; but because the agreements concerning the international financial markets survived into the 1970s, the trade agreements have been all but forgotten.

The Bretton Woods agreements created a program that effectively put checks on international balance of payments. The intent was to provide pressure on countries to correct both deficit and surplus trade balances. Countries that had persistent trade deficits were to increase exports and restrict imports, and countries with surplus were to restrict exports and increase imports. Compliance was to be voluntary, and only minimal provisions for discipline of wayward nations were made. The stability that such a plan brought to the world's financial markets, it was hoped, would prevent a repeat of the financial shocks of the early 1900s, the 1920s, and the depression of the 1930s.

The plan was also intended to assist in the economic recovery of several of the World War II belligerent nations. It appeared for a brief time that the world may experience a period of unprecedented prosperity. However, in 1946 the United States decided that it was not in its national interests to continue with the trade portions of the Bretton Woods agreement and effectively nullified the provisions designed to check trade imbalances.[4] As Makin observed:

> The result was a system biased toward thrusting the burden of [trade balance] adjustment on deficit countries. The corollary was the essentially *mercantilist* view that since they did not need to adjust, surplus countries were somehow doing the right thing. Asymmetry in the adjustment process was partially the result of an unfortunate lack of American sophistication in these matters, eventually it brought the Bretton Woods system down.[5] [emphasis added]

The United States perceived a need to rebuild many of its former allies' and enemies' economies after the end of World War II. The motivations for the Marshall Plan was to assure that there were healthy economic systems, based on free enterprise and democratic governments in the devastated belligerent nations and in parts of the world that were perceived to be in danger of falling into the Soviet sphere of influence. Direct economic aid to specific countries was how the United States approached the problem of reducing deficit trade balances of these countries with the United States and the providing for their economic development. Under the Marshall Plan, the United States provided more than $14.5 billion in grants and loans to Europe and Japan between 1948 and 1952 (in then-current dollars). To give the reader some idea of the magnitude of the Marshall Plan, Thurow described it as follows:

The next five years, however, are apt to a repetition of what happened in Western Europe after World War II. From 1945 to 1948 everyone waited for spontaneous capitalistic economic combustion to happen. It didn't. In 1948 the British economy was falling apart. When that reality became apparent, the Marshall Plan was initiated by the United States. For ten years, seventeen billion dollars per year (in today's dollars) was pumped into Western Europe and Japan to create the human and physical infrastructure of a market economy. Aid amounted to $410 per capita, or about 10 percent of the recipients' GNPs ("Book Ends for the Cold War," *Boston Globe,* July 8, 1990, p. 10).[6]

The dominate economic position the United States occupied in the world immediately after World War II made the Marshall Plan possible, but the motivation was political—the Cold War had already begun.

The forces were set into motion that ultimately assured indebtedness in LDCs. However, this indebtedness would not be predictably distributed by natural resources or former colonial status. The indebtedness of LDCs would be as much a function of global politics as it was of global markets.

Post–World War II Financial Markets

After World War II, the United States emerged as the dominant economic power and its currency was accepted in exchange for goods by virtually all nations in the world. The value of the U.S. dollar, as a stable and readily exchangeable currency, had become the standard upon which all other currencies were measured. The Bretton Woods agreements provided for setting the value of the U.S. dollar on a gold standard. All other currencies would be based on the U.S. dollar, and value of the dollar was tied to gold at $35 per ounce. The volatility of currency values prior to World War II was thus minimized. More appropriate banking and macroeconomic policies over the post–World War II period were other factors that contributed to global monetary stability.[7] In the United States, for example, the creation of the Federal Deposit Insurance Corporation (FDIC) to minimize depositor panics, and the automatic stabilizers of the New Deal era (i.e., unemployment insurance, Social Security, and more extensive public aid programs) made a recurrence of the Great Depression and the collapse of the financial system of the previous period far less likely.[8]

The Bretton Woods system promoted world trade and prosperity over the 1945–1971 period. The system, however, was plagued with problems that led to the November 1967 British financial crisis and the French financial crisis in May 1968 that led to the devaluation of French franc in August 1969. The international trade between the United States and other countries and the trade imbalances that developed between the United States and its trading partners, especially West Germany, were among other reasons that led to the demise of that system.

Beginning in 1958, the United States began to develop large trade deficits particularly as the U.S. economy entered the recession of 1958. Because of these mounting trade deficits, the U.S. trading partners had increasing dollar claims against the United States. According to the Bretton Woods agreements, the United States was obliged to buy and sell gold for $35 per ounce. Therefore, foreigners could exchange their surplus dollars for gold. The result was that between 1957 and 1968, the U.S. gold supply was depleted to the tune of $13 billion.

In addition, during the 1960s the United States pursued an inflationary policy in an attempt to reduce its domestic unemployment rate. The result was further reduction in the value of the dollar. In fact, the U.S. dollar lost approximately 80 percent of its purchasing power from 1934 to 1971.

By spring 1971, the exchange rate problems had become acute. This was true for Japan and especially for West Germany, who had large trade surpluses with the United States and held more dollars than they wanted. Under these conditions, the U.S. dollar was rapidly losing value against the German deutsche mark. From January to April of 1971, in keeping with the Bretton Woods agreements, the German Bundesbank had to acquire more than $5 billion of international reserves in order to defend the value of the dollar. To protect the value of the dollar and its exchange rate with the German mark, however, the German central bank was losing control over its domestic monetary policy. By May 5, 1971, the Bundesbank abandoned its efforts to protect the dollar and permitted the deutsche mark to seek its own value in the world's currency markets. The scenario was the same for all the countries that had trade surpluses with the United States. The excess supply of dollars was causing those countries to lose control over their money supplies. Given that the United States was rapidly losing its gold reserves, on August 15, 1971, by Richard Nixon's order, it was announced that the United States officially abandoned the Bretton Woods system and refuseed to exchange gold for U.S. dollars held by foreigners. For the first time in modern monetary history, the U.S. dollar was permitted to seek its value in open markets. The move to a flexible exchange rate system where the exchange rates are determined by the basic market forces was the official demise of the Bretton Woods system.

Once the dollar was permitted to seek its own value in the world's money markets, it was presumed that its increased value would permit Americans to enjoy the fruits of other countries' production at a reduced cost. However, the long-term trend in the value of the dollar against the German mark and British pound is quite different. While the dollar gained value relative to the British pound, it has been losing value relative to the Deutsche mark.

Another important development is the fact that there have been significant fluctuations in the exchange rates between the U.S. dollar and most LDCs' currencies. The loss of value of the dollar in the mid-1970s gave LDCs an ability, if not incentive, to borrow U.S. dollars; however, the increase in the value of the dollar by 1982 left LDCs in the position of being unable or unwilling to service their debts in the 1980s. In many respects, the genesis of the current debt crisis is a monetary one, but the monetary problems alone were not sufficient to cause a crisis. In fact, in 1982 the international financial markets hardly noticed Mexico's rescheduling. The banks were convinced that this was an aberration and not cause for panic. Had it only been the currency exchange rates that changed, there may have been reason for optimism; but much more occurred, particularly in the Middle East.

U.S. Commercial Banks Enter the Global Market

The stage is set for U.S. commercial banks to become active players in the global capital markets. The relaxation of lending restrictions and the disconnecting of the dollar to gold permitted U.S. banks to actively pursue perceived profitable investments and loans overseas. Two things happened at about the same time that gave impetus to American banks making loans to LDCs.

First, American participation in the Vietnam War slowed and then ended. In 1971, the United States began to Vietnamize the war in southeast Asia and reduce its troop commitments. By 1974, the U.S. participation in the Vietnam War had ended and the recession of 1975 began. The reduction in demand for military goods and the return of thousands of military personnel to civilian labor markets brought recession to the United States. As the American economy entered a recession, domestic demand for credit declined and thus loans to borrowers abroad became more attractive to U.S. bankers. The U.S. bankers were aware of the British experience with investment in LDCs earlier in the century and sought higher returns abroad than could be earned at home. In fact, U.S. commercial banks were actively pursuing foreign clients among the LDCs. Other industrialized nations were also sharing the American recessionary experience. Bankers in Europe pursued the same strategy followed by American Banks.

Second, in 1973 to 1974, the Organization of Petroleum Exporting Countries (OPEC) raised oil prices dramatically. In October 1973, the

Israeli–Arab war broke out, and the Arab countries found that the United States and Holland were supporting the Israelis. In protest of this support, the Arab members of OPEC imposed an embargo on these two countries. Anticipating further supply difficulties, the world's oil-consuming nations purchased large reserves of oil, driving the price of oil up from $3.00 to over $12.00 per barrel by March 1974.[9]

The increase in oil prices created substantial wealth in the OPEC countries, much of which found its way to American and European banks. The increased deposits from OPEC countries generated significant loanable reserves for banks in the industrialized countries. Relatively high rates of inflation in several industrialized countries, together with the increased supply of funds through new deposits from oil-rich depositors, began to drive real interest rates down. The lower domestic real interest rates provided an even greater incentive for bankers in the industrialized nations to seek borrowers outside of the industrialized world (where higher interest rates could be charged).

Further, because of the collapse of the Bretton Woods system in 1971, the value of the U.S. dollar relative to other industrialized countries' currencies had fallen. This made it attractive for LDCs to borrow the U.S. dollars which were in excess supply and, therefore, more accessible to these countries.

The first round of loans to LDCs during the early 1970s caused little reason for concern about possible default by LDC debtor countries. The inflation experienced in the developed countries resulted in the bankers asking for higher interest rates on loans to LDCs to protect themselves from losses due to inflation. At first, these inflation risk premiums caused little difficulty for LDCs in servicing their debts. However, as the inflation accelerated through the remainder of the 1970s, it began to drive real interest rates down into negative ranges.[10] The declining real interest rates made loans a relative bargain for LDCs. What was happening was that LDCs were now able to borrow U.S. dollars because there was an excess supply and because the U.S. dollar had lost substantial value during the first part of the decade of the 1970s. Banks anticipated the inflation and negotiated indexing systems to hedge against inflation or higher-risk premiums into loans going to LDCs. What was not anticipated by both parties was the effectiveness of the efforts at correcting the U.S. domestic inflation problems that would occur ten years later during Reagan's first term.

Reagan's Contribution

Ronald Reagan's conservative views of foreign policy resulted in unprecedented peace-time military expenditures in the United States. Reagan also believed that the burden of government on taxpayers had to be relieved. The regime of tax cuts and increased military expenditures that was instituted during the Reagan administration drastically increased the U.S. budget deficit and sovereign debt. Federal budget deficits grew from $60.1 billion in 1980 to a staggering $303 billion in 1993. The national debt tripled from $1 trillion to more than $3 trillion during the 1980s, thus draining U.S. dollars out of the hands of the OPEC nations and attracting the Japanese to fund this national debt. In the early 1980s, the loss of liquidity and the resultant higher world interest rates made the second round of loans to LDCs by banks in developed countries less than satisfactory.

Throughout the Reagan administration and at the beginning of George Bush's term, the U.S. national debt increased at accelerating rates. The U.S. balance of trade worsened, and the U.S. economy began to have trade deficits rather than the surpluses it enjoyed throughout most of the century prior to 1958.

In addition, in 1979 the downfall of the Shah of Iran sparked a second round of oil price increases resulting from a panic over disruption of oil exports from that country. The oil prices rose from $13 per barrel in 1978 to about $32 per barrel in 1980. This increase in the price of oil had a significant adverse effect on the inflation rate and the economic growth in the industrialized as well as the oil-importing LDCs. The increase in oil prices also caused a significant current account deficit for many of the oil-importing LDCs (as well as some industrialized countries). This current account deficit problem for the oil-importing LDCs provided a real (rather than monetary) cause for the debt crisis that began only a short few months after the fall of the Shah.

It is interesting to note that most U.S. commercial banks and the World Bank perceived the early round of reschedulings, beginning with Mexico in 1982, as a short-term liquidity problem. In fact, there is a monetary genesis to the problem, but the currency exchange rates alone could not account for most LDCs' inability to service their debt. Without the rather substantial increases in oil prices, there may have been no noticeable amount of rescheduling, at least in the first round. In other words, the monetary problems were substantial financial constraints, but the trigger for the initial rounds of rescheduling (for the oil-importing countries) was the sharp rise in oil prices in 1980 and 1981.

During the first Arab oil embargo the Federal Reserve had expanded the money supply to counter the recessionary forces generated by the increases in the price of oil. Much of the subsequent inflation in the United States was blamed on this expansionary monetary policy. With the 1980 oil shock, the Federal Reserve was determined not to repeat the mistakes of the earlier period. Paul Volcker had replaced Arthur Burns as Chairman of the Federal Reserve Board, and he was committed to fight inflation that was perceived to be the number-one problem in the U.S. economy.

At the same time that the U.S. government was borrowing heavily to support its rapidly accelerating deficits, the U.S. monetary authority was fighting the inflation battle to the fullest extent. The U.S. money supply actually contracted, driving up domestic interest rates and strengthening the dollar in world money markets, despite the large trade deficits (in fact, the U.S. dollar reached record heights in 1985). U.S. government obligations became steadily more attractive relative to direct investments, risky sovereign loans to LDCs, or increasingly risky deposits in financial institutions in the industrialized nations. The banks in the developed countries were experiencing a debt crisis of their own resulting from poor management (in the case of some savings and loans and thrifts, fraud), poor real estate investments, and rescheduled loans to LDCs.

The successful monetary policy in the United States during the first two years of the 1980s began to move the value of the dollar upward from its all-time lows of the fourth quarter of 1979 (some argue overvalued LDC currency in the countries that did not produce oil),[11] resulting in movement toward the first debt rescheduling by Mexico in 1982.

As the value of the dollar began to rise during 1981 and 1982, several LDCs began to experience significant domestic inflation that resulted in an ever-accelerating unfavorable exchange rate between the indebted LDCs' currencies and the U.S. dollar. Some LDCs argued that during the period of 1981 to 1985, the United States simply exported its debt problems overseas to LDCs that owed U.S. banks large sums. In fact, the LDCs were faced with the problem that they had borrowed dollars when they were "cheap" in the 1970s and were now expected to repay dollars that were worth considerably more in the early 1980s.

As complicated as this scenario may seem, it is quite simple. During the first round of LDC loans, the United States and other industrialized nations made loans to LDCs when the U.S. dollar was declining in value, from 1971 through 1979. Because the loans to LDCs in the early 1970s were profitable, bankers in the United States and Europe were willing to make a second round of loans in the mid-1970s. As the dollar approached a record low in the international money markets, LDCs leaped at the opportunity—not expecting the turnaround in the value of the dollar, accompanied by higher interest rates (because of U.S. monetary policy and possibly the increase in the U.S. national debt). In other words, LDCs borrowed dollars in the 1970s that were worth substantially less than the dollars they had to pay back in the 1980s. This simple fact resulted in the LDCs' inability to service their debt obligations and thus created the world debt crisis.

SUMMARY AND CONCLUSION

The financial and economic conditions in the post–World War II era created the financial motivations and the means necessary to provide an opportunity for LDCs to acquire relatively large loans from the banking community in the industrialized nations. The collapse of the Bretton Woods agreement and the abandonment of the gold standard created a world financial market where banks in industrialized countries were searching for foreign customers so as to earn higher rates than could be earned in their domestic economies.

The OPEC embargos of 1973 and 1974 created substantial wealth for the OPEC countries. Much of this wealth found its way to U.S. and European banks, creating excess reserves for these banks. With the reduction in the domestic demand for credit resulting from the slowdown in the U.S. economy or the recession of 1974, LDCs were being sought out as customers for these excess reserves of U.S. dollars. The end result was LDCs borrowing large amounts of U.S. dollars at relatively high interest rates, when the dollar was nearing record lows relative to other currencies.

The monetary policies after the second oil shock was far different than those of the 1970s. Also during the 1980s, the supply-side theories of the Reagan administration resulted in large U.S. budget deficits that substantially drew U.S. dollars out of the global markets to fund U.S. sovereign debt, much of which was funded by borrowing from other industrialized countries. The monetary policies of the first half of the 1980s resulted in the U.S. dollar gaining substantial value against other industrialized countries' currencies and against the currencies of LDCs, many of whom experienced very high rates of inflation during this period. LDCs found themselves in a position where they were paying relatively high interest rates on dollars they had borrowed when the U.S. dollar was worth significantly less than in the 1980s. Mexico started the rush to reschedule in 1982 and was quickly followed by the majority of the world's indebted LDCs.

NOTES

1. See Appendix A for detailed information concerning the indebtedness of LDCs.

2. Milton Friedman and Anna Schwartz, *A Monetary History of the United States* (Princeton: Princeton University Press, 1963).

3. For example, see "Gold Standard, Deflation and Financial Crisis in the Great Depression: An International Comparison," NBER Working Paper No. 3488, Washington, D.C., October 1990.

4. John H. Makin, *The Global Debt Crisis: America's Growing Involvement* (New York: Basic Books, 1984), 21.

5. Ibid.

6. Lester Thurow, *Head to Head: The Coming Economic Battle among Japan, Europe, and America* (New York: William Morrow, 1992), 94.

7. Charles Calomiris and Charles Kahn, "The Role of Demandable Debt in Structuring Optimal Banking Arrangements," *American Economic Review* (June 1991): 497–513.

8. For a more detailed discussion of the U.S. monetary aspects of the relevant financial history, see Friedman and Schwartz, *Monetary History.*

9. Paul R. Krugman and Maurice Obstfeld, International Economics: Theory and Policy. (Glenview, Ill.: Scott, Foresman, 1988), 548.

10. Kristin Hallberg, "International Debt, 1985: Origins and Issues for the Future," in *World Debt Crisis: International Lending on Trial*, ed. Michael P. Claudon (Cambridge, Mass.: Ballinger, 1986), 10–11.

11. Ibid.

Chapter 7

Why LDCs Acquired Debt

First payments is what made us think we were prosperous, and the
other nineteen is what showed us we were broke.
—Will Rogers, *The Autobiography of Will Rogers* (1949), p. 15

The most recent round of rescheduling of LDC debt began in the early
1980s. However, the seeds of the world debt crisis were not sown with
the sovereign loans made during the 1970s. In fact, the path to a world
debt crisis began decades before. A debt crisis of the magnitude observed
in the 1980s and 1990s does not arise over night. The underlying financial and economic reasons for the world debt crisis take years, sometimes decades, to result in the observed debt servicing problems.

The purpose of this chapter is to present the history of LDC indebtedness during modern times. The causes of the debt crisis differ significantly from the reasons that LDCs acquired debt. Chapter 6 focused
on the causes of the debt crisis; but unless there was debt, there could
not be debt repayment problems. Therefore, to fully understand the
implications for business of the debt crisis, one must gain an apprecia-
tion for why the debt occurred.

Even though sovereign debt was observed in earlier epochs, the debt
that is of interest for current business decision making has its beginnings in the decade following the American Civil War. The history of the
current debt crisis is informative for two specific reasons. First, the
history describes how LDCs came to be in a position that they were less
developed and required external financing for economic growth. Second, the history shows how such a problem can be persistent.

This chapter is divided into two major sections. The first section concerns the relationship between the financial history and the economic history of the debt crisis. The second section of this chapter presents the economic history of the World Debt Crisis.

FINANCIAL AND ECONOMIC HISTORIES

Macroeconomists have long differentiated between "real" and "monetary" phenomena. *Real* is an adjective typically used to describe economic variables or activities that involve real goods and services, including such things as factors of production, medical services, or baseball tickets. Money is only a convenience in measuring the current worth of these variables. *Monetary* (sometimes called *nominal*) economic variables and activities are those that involve only money as a measure of value without accounting for its command over real goods and services. Economists recognize that real and nominal economic activities influence one another, but typically real and monetary phenomena are analyzed separately and then compared.

Chapter 6 presented the evolution of the international financial markets and the influences of the international financial markets on the debt crisis. The monetary factors are important determinants of the world debt crisis, and, in fact, were the factors that resulted in LDCs not being able to continue to service their debts. However, real economic activity and the production and exchange of goods and services are important in setting the stage for the financial shocks that created the world debt crisis. Without real economic phenomena providing incentives for acquiring debt and extending credit, there could not have been a world debt crisis.

The brief financial history presented in Chapter 6 describes the Bretton Woods agreements and the various events that made the U.S. dollar decline in value so as to provide for a mutual attraction between industrialized countries' bankers and LDCs' government borrowers. However, this is but one episode in the credit markets involving LDCs. There is a long history of LDCs struggling to create sociopolitical stability and to foster economic growth that resulted in the LDCs becoming indebted. Even though the instability in the U.S. dollar's value relative to LDCs' currencies was one of the important contributors to the current round of reschedulings, it was not the sole cause of the debt crisis. Lest the reader believe that an international debt crisis can only be experienced because of monetary phenomena or an OPEC embargo, the history of indebted LDCs must be presented to demonstrate the previous causes of debt servicing problems, many of which arose from the markets for goods and services or from factor markets.

In truth, any economic problem of the magnitude and complexity of the world debt crisis has forces emanating from both the financial and real sectors that contribute to the observed difficulties. Economic events can often take years to produce observed financial crises. Throughout economic history, causality can be traced back for years from the actual event. In the most recent debt crisis, without the real economic changes in the world between 1950 and 1971 there could not have been the changes in exchange rates and balance-of-payment accounts that resulted in the increase in the value of the dollar in the 1980s that broke the debtors' financial backs and resulted in the significant rescheduling of debt that was witnessed during the 1980s.

HISTORY OF THE DEBT CRISIS

The history of the LDC debt crisis arises from the interdependence of the world's nations. The historical events that led to the debt crisis operated through global financial markets. Financial markets do not function in a vacuum. The economic environments in which both the developed and less developed nations of the world functioned influenced the directions of the world's financial markets and gave rise to the world debt crisis. Many of the factors that contributed to countries becoming developed or less developed also played significant roles in the indebtedness of a group of LDCs and their subsequent problems in servicing their debts.

Economic history, for the most part, is an examination of the rise and fall of economic activities, much the same as political or military history. Economic history is no less complex than other subjects of historical inquiry. A brief economic history will be offered to set the stage for understanding the developments in the global financial markets that gave rise to the world debt crisis.

Chapter 4 outlines the role of the guiding philosophies that resulted in several regions of the world experiencing problems in economic development. This section offers a brief review of the factors and events that help explain the economic and financial motivations of LDCs to acquire debt and of the developed countries to make loans to these countries.

LDC debts to industrialized countries are not new. Since the middle of the nineteenth century, LDCs have borrowed from industrialized countries for various purposes. Before turning to an explanation of the latest round of loans, a brief review of the pre-1944 history of LDC indebtedness will provide a useful background.

Pre-1944 Experience

The nineteenth-century economic involvement of industrialized countries with LDCs was of two specific natures. These two forms of involvement were industrialized countries colonializing less developed regions, hence direct economic and political domination; and interaction between independent nations. In the case of interaction between independent nations, the economic relations were typically trade and industrialized countries making loans to LDCs.

Colonies of European powers experienced siginificant direct investment from the industrialized countries. When an LDC became colonized, it was generally because the European colonial power had an incentive to do so. Many former colonies had an abundance of natural resources needed to keep the European factories running. Others had little more than a strategic location on trade routes or in militarily sensitive areas. In either event, the European power used direct investment in their colonies to assure that the bridges and railroads they needed were available.

There were also several independent nations in the developing regions, particularly in the latter half of the century. The economic relations of industrialized powers with LDCs were predominately loans or trade to obtain natural resources. This is not to say that the independent nations did not experience direct investment; they did, but not to the same extent as colonies.

From 1870 until the beginning of World War I, the world financial markets were dominated by British banks. As the Industrial Revolution in Europe entered its matured stages, foreign investment became increasingly important to Europeans to obtain agricultural commodities and the raw materials necessary for Europe's industrial base. The latter portion of the nineteenth century and the early twentieth century saw a marked increase in British investment in LDCs. The British engaged in direct investment in LDCs and the building of plants and equipment, financed through stocks and bonds and not loans to LDCs. One of the major reasons for this observed behavior, was that much of British investment was in their own colonies. For example, the amount of investment by the British in ten South American countries far exceeded U.S. investments in those countries from 1913 through 1929. See Table 7.1 for the specific comparisons of British and American investments in those Latin countries for the period.

During the colonial period, the British invested heavily in railroads and public utilities in LDCs. This investment was not motivated by a British desire to facilitate economic growth in their colonies, but to provide the infrastructure necessary to further the Crown's own objectives. These objectives focused primarily on political and military dominance of a particular region and the exploitation of the natural resources found in their colonies. This is not to say that the British did not have ideological reasons for their behavior. In fact, many historians attribute motives to the British that were, at best, close to altruistic (at worst, completely arrogant). The British, in some measure, believed that their

Table 7.1
Stock of Capital Invested in South America by the United States and United Kingdom, 1913–1929 (Millions of Dollars)

Country	U.S. investments		U.K. investments	
	1913	1929	1913	1929
Argentina	40	611	1861	2140
Bolivia	10	133	2	12
Brazil	50	476	1162	1414
Chile	15	396	332	390
Colombia	2	260	34	38
Ecuador	10	25	14	23
Paraguay	3	15	16	18
Peru	35	151	133	141
Uruguay	5	64	240	217
Venezuela	3	162	41	92
Total	173	2293	3835	4485

Source: M. Winkler, *Investments of U.S. Capital in Latin America* (Boston: World Peace Foundation, 1929).

system of governance and their economic values were superior to those found in the less developed regions and that they had a national responsibility to modernize their colonies. Whether these motives were sufficient to modify their quest for economic dominance of local resources is a matter of record.

The British also made loans to China, Egypt, and Turkey during this period. These loans were not tied to the creation of infrastructure to further British commercial interests. Rather, these loans were made to sovereign states for political purposes. The British perceived that there was competition for spheres of influence between themselves, the French, Germans, and Americans. Influence also meant trade and access to raw materials and military alliances that both the British government and their industries needed. Therefore, creditworthiness was not the primary concern of English government officials. The primary concern was consolidating influence in markets and governments that controlled resources and manpower. Even so, the British found that their direct investments overseas were more profitable than domestic investments and that they did not experience significant defaults on loans they had made to further their own political agenda.

In the first decade of the twentieth century, there were two major financial panics. These financial panics caused ripple effects through the world's currency markets and clearly demonstrated the need for some coordinated policies to assure a stable financial system. There were early attempts to create international organizations to deal with international financial problems. However, these attempts to create world organizations to deal with these matters failed and were ended abruptly by the outbreak of World War I. Europe suffered through four years of a brutal conflict that resulted in a new world order after the end of World War I. The late entry of the United States into World War I, together with substantial European investment in North America in anticipation of the outbreak of hostilities, left the United States as the dominant economic power between the two world wars. In fact, between the two world wars the United States replaced the United Kingdom as the world's largest creditor country.

It is also important to note that between the two world wars Europe had significant economic difficulties whose origins were in World War I. The Treaty of Versailles imposed burdensome reparations on the Germans that added significantly to the economic difficulties of that country following the war. Many European countries also experienced substantial destruction of their productive capacity during World War I. For example, Belgium, Germany, and France witnessed substantial fighting in areas in which industry had been located. This, however, is not to minimize the drastic impact that the millions of causalities had on all the belligerent nations' work forces. It was not solely the fact that the United States remained out of the war and developed substantial industrial strength. It was also the destruction of portions of Europe that helped to raise the United States to a leadership position.

During the 1920s and 1930s, neither the United States nor the European powers demonstrated much concern for the economic development of LDCs. There were loans extended to the independent nations of Latin America and Asia, but they were rather small (in number and size) compared to the loans extended to LDCs in the 1970s and 1980s. These loans were for various purposes. Several were for the construction of specific transportation networks (e.g., railroads) that were necessary for exploitation of natural resources. Unfortunately, many of the loans extended to the Latin American countries in the 1920s and 1930s resulted in default (albeit temporary default in most cases). The Latin American LDCs believed that default would not have any significant economic consequences. However, this experiment quickly produced unexpected results. In some cases, American and European creditors *persuaded* debtors to be more prompt with their payments using rather direct means. For example, British creditors sent gunboats to intimidate the debtor and encourage repayment, but such drastic encouragement was not unique to the British creditors.[1] The 1902 persuasion used by the British on their Venezuelan friends was somewhat less drastic than the Americans taking over the finances of Haiti (sound familiar?),

Cuba, Panama, and other Central American countries.[2] Most debtor countries were not difficult to persuade to repay their debts. Argentina and Brazil quickly found themselves in the position of needing additional credit. The governments of these two countries learned that default precluded them from obtaining further credit, and they decided to fulfill their debt obligations to prevent future credit problems.

It was not until after World War II that the LDCs became active participants in world financial markets. The modernization of industry that arose because of World War II was witnessed by most of the former colonies. These former colonies wished to increase their standards of living. Because these countries were now "independent," thus able to finance their own investment projects, they wished to seek capital through the international financial markets. There was also significant growth of consumer markets in many countries that had natural resources, particularly oil. These countries also wished to attract direct private foreign investment, which required these LDCs to invest in their infrastructure.

Further, as soon as World War II ended, the former allies—Russia and the Western allies—embarked on the Cold War. The rise of Communism in Asia and Eastern Europe caused Western nations to focus more on economic solutions to political problems than had been evident earlier in the century. Therefore, it is the economic and financial history of the post–World War II period that is most important to the understanding of the current debt crisis. This is not to say that the Russians did not seek economic influence among constituent nations; rather the Russians did not have resources nor access to organized international financial markets to have any influence whatever on the development of the world debt crisis.

Post–World War II Economic History

The interdependence that results from trade, both internationally and within countries, has the potential both for significant economic growth and for harm. The age-old suspicion that trade with other societies can threaten domestic economic and political interests has complicated economic progress. In fact, national interests—both political and economic—are often operable constraints on economic growth. However, it is the national interests of the developed countries together with the worldwide dispersion of endowments of natural resources that resulted in many nations becoming less developed.

The chance of geographic location is what caused the mercantile powers to colonize, explore, and exploit many of the countries that would be labeled "less developed" during the twentieth century. There were several factors that combined with mercantilism that restricted the development of many LDCs, which, in turn, gave rise to the LDCs' indebtedness. Primary among these factors were population growth, technological improvements, and changes in political variables.

For many LDCs, the Malthusian analysis of the pressure of population on agriculturally productive land certainly applies. Malthus argued that population grew at a geometric rate but that the production of agricultural commodities grew only at an arithmetic rate. The end result is that there would come a time that there would be too many people to feed, resulting in famine. The famines in East Africa over the recent decades has served to dramatically underscore the Reverend Malthus's warnings. Most low-income countries, even today, are dependent upon subsistence farming to support their populations. Capital formation under such circumstances is difficult if not impossible. The same constraints exist in many middle-income countries but are less severe. Domestic capital formation depends upon private domestic savings. If the majority of the country's population struggle to put food on the table and clothes on their backs, there will be virtually no domestic savings. Without domestic savings, there will not be excess resources that can be loaned to entrepreneurs to purchase capital equipment for the production of goods and services beyond those things absolutely necessary for human survival.

Production of commodities using modern capital-intensive, mass-production methods gives the industrialized nations significant cost advantages in many, if not most, markets. Advanced technology, as employed in the industrialized nations, typically requires large capital expenditures. As advanced technology began to be employed, profit margins in the industrialized countries increased, thereby enhancing capital formation, in turn, permitting further technological improvements. These large capital expenditures are generally beyond the financial abilities of even most middle-income countries. This has normally resulted, especially in Africa, in raw materials being exported to industrialized countries rather than in developing processing and fabricating industries in Africa.

The Politics of Economic Development

Geopolitics has also played a significant role. The Russians and Americans in post–World War II years entered into a competition for spheres of influence, much the same as the British and other European powers had during the post–World War I period. Even though it may have been well intentioned, the policies of providing finished products, military equipment, and food to LDCs that each of the superpowers wished to influence retarded rather than furthered economic development.

Rather than developing industries, which may take years, both the Russians and the United States embarked on strategies to have immediate and direct political influence. These strategies typically involved technical assistance in developing some industries, but relied heavily on provided arms, food, and other finished commodities. In the extreme, these policies breed some degree of dependence upon the industrialized world for manufactured goods and agricultural commodities, rather than the independence that economic development brings.

Had the well-being of the LDCs been the objective rather than economic dependence, hence political loyalty, the Russians and Americans would have transferred technology and supported capital formation rather than erecting missile sites and providing arms. However, both the Americans and the Russians were pursuing their own political aims and not the objectives of economic growth for LDCs.

Mercantilist Exploitation and Capitalism

Mercantilism gave way to a capitalist view of the functioning of markets. Production, division of labor, and specialization based on comparative and absolute advantage became the driving force for the modern economic powers. An economy based on the production of goods requires raw materials. Without domestic endowments of iron, oil, and other minerals necessary for manufacturing industries, an economy must rely on external sources of those natural resources. For example, countries such as England and Japan had few of the natural resources that are necessary ingredients to drive an industrial economy. To assure that their manufactories were properly supplied with the necessary raw materials, many of the world's developed countries needed to secure reliable sources of the natural resources. Colonization, military aggression, and political and economic dominance over realms containing these resources was often the solution—a solution available only to those countries with sufficient resources to build and support a modern military and naval capacity and administrative network to govern the spheres of influence or external realms.

Without capital formation from the profits of modern industrial economies, LDCs were placed at a significant comparative disadvantage, particularly in manufacturing. Lacking the capital to explore and utilize their own natural resources, most LDCs permitted enterprises from the developed countries to enter their jurisdictions to seek and exploit reserves of natural resources. After all, exportation of natural resources provided for some meager income, as was the case of most of the members of OPEC prior to the wave of nationalization that returned the oil wells to the countries in which they were drilled. Often, the treaties and contracts that permitted the industrial powers to explore and exploit were very one sided.[3] The natural wealth of the LDCs was often taken with little in return. The perception within many LDCs of these early commercial arrangements was that the colonialism of previous decades was replaced by economic domination.

The rise of nationalism in many regions of the world resulted in a change in the way business was conducted in many LDCs.[4] The solution adopted by several nations was to nationalize their natural resources or to seek alternatives to agreements with foreign investors that worked against their national interests. Ultimately, many LDCs realized the advantages that their endowments of natural resources provided them, especially in the Middle East. For example, the OPEC nations not only realized their natural advantage but also realized that through cooperative production planning they could exert monopoly influences over the price of oil. Unfortunately, for most African nations there was no significant change in who profited from the exploitation of natural resources.

Capital is necessary to exploit natural resources, build infrastructures, and create political stability to foster economic growth. Without economic growth, the LDCs could not break the perceived economic dependence on industrialized nations. Without economic independence, political independence is not a viable alternative. To achieve economic growth, most LDCs have a significant demand for capital and most do not have sufficient domestic sources of capital to support their needs. Therefore, their demand for capital, both public and private, could only be satisfied through global financial markets.

BUSINESS IMPLICATIONS

People learn from history. In many, if not most, of the developing regions of the world, there is suspicion of industrialized countries' governments and private businesses. Most of the economic history of the twentieth century gives little reason for trust in the goodwill and fairness of developed countries. This is not to say that there is widespread hostility to anyone or anything from the industrialized countries. In fact, just the opposite is true in most of the developing world. However, the history of the debt crisis should help the European or American businessperson understand that there are reasons why they may be viewed with a certain suspicion before they are accepted on their own merits.

The history of the debt crisis also shows that some of the retarded economic development results first from colonial dependence and later from dependence from aid programs from the competing nations of the Cold War. Most people in LDCs have the same desire for economic prosperity and independence that is observed in the Western industrialized countries. If the stereotype of lazy, unskilled, and indifferent workers in LDCs persists (and it should have been dispelled by now), it must be remembered that the United States and Russia actively sought to create dependence during the Cold War for political purposes. In fact, the populations of most LDCs face a lifestyle that is far more physically demanding, harsh, and uncertain than many people in Western industrialized nations can imagine. In many LDCs, what the work force lacks in skills is made up for with willingness to work and physical strength.

SUMMARY AND CONCLUSION

In the nineteenth century many of the world's LDCs were colonies of European powers. During this period, prior to independence, colonial LDCs experienced substantial direct investment in their economies by the nations that had colonized them. The independent LDCs also experienced some direct investment but for the most part had to rely on credit to make up for any deficiencies they may suffer in domestic credit markets.

During the pre–World War I period, the British financial institutions dominated the international financial markets. After World War I, the United States supplanted the British as the dominant financial force in the world's credit markets. However, the British and other European countries maintained important creditor positions in the international financial markets. This created a more competitive international financial market until after World War II, when agreements between the world's industrialized powers concerning the conduct of the international financial markets were made.

The debt crisis was brought to fruition by exchange rate and balance-of-payment changes. However, there is a substantial history of LDCs acquiring loans and then having problems servicing their debts. In fact, at the beginning of the twentieth century some Latin American countries defaulted on their loans and found themselves unable to obtain credit from industrialized countries. This provided a strong motivation for the defaulting countries to repay their obligations so as to assure future access to international financial markets.

There are business implications from the history of the debt crisis. There is a certain amount of suspicion that lingers in LDCs because of their former colonial status and the dependence creating policies implemented by the participants in the Cold War. Many of the stereotypes of the 1960s and 1970s of the labor forces in LDCs are more the products of the policies designed to achieve influence in the developing world than any factual characterization of the people who live and work in LDCs.

NOTES

1. Peter H. Lindert, "Response to Debt Crisis: What is Different about the 1980s?" in *The International Debt Crisis in Historical Perspective,* ed. Barry Eichengreen and Peter H. Lindert (Cambridge, Mass.: MIT Press, 1989), 236–238.

2. Ibid.

3. John H. Makin, *The Global Debt Crisis: America's Growing Involvement* (New York: Basic Books, 1984).

4. Nationalism rose in various regions for different reasons. Latin America came to view their Spanish overlords as oppressors and removed them in the nineteenth century. Africa, Asia, and the Middle East all have their own specific histories, ranging from the financial drain of World War II—making it impossible for some colonial powers to maintain their dominance—to purely economic reasons in some Middle Eastern countries.

Chapter 8

How the LDCs Used the Loans

Vinegar in hand is better than halvah to come.
>   —Persian Proverb

In business decision making concerning trade or the location of operations, it is important to know why an LDC acquired debt and how effectively the LDC accomplished the goals for which it borrowed money. As is discussed in detail in Chapter 11, the amount of the debt is important; but perhaps of greater importance is what the LDC has acquired with the borrowed money. In general, it is a positive sign to observe LDCs taking loans to purchase things that increase in the viability of the economy. However, if indebtedness has been used to finance current consumption, frivolous infrastructure, and possibly military equipment, this may be a warning of underlying difficulties for business operations in or trade with that LDC.

Historically, LDCs have borrowed from industrialized nations for several reasons. The financing of military establishments and transportation networks are among the most common reasons for LDCs borrowing in the pre–twentieth-century period. These reasons were still the major reasons for LDC indebtedness into the twentieth century. Many LDCs continue to borrow to finance military expenditures and to create highways, canals, and rail systems. However, technological progress and more complex social relations have resulted in LDCs borrowing for a broader range of activities.

The purpose of this chapter is to answer the question, *For what were LDCs borrowing money?* This chapter examines the major uses to which LDCs put their loans and what the implications of those purposes are for economic development, hence the business environment within the indebted LDC.

DEBT AND RISK

Most debt risk models rely on aggregate measures of debt and ratios of debt to various other financial and economic aggregates.[1] The Swiss Bank Corporation has formulated a method to monitor the risk of doing business in a particular country.[2] Among the variables used to monitor the potential risk of doing business in an LDC are the total external debt, international reserves, and external debt service. The Swiss Bank Corporation also recommends that the ratios of external debt and external debt service to exports be calculated. There are critical levels for these two ratios recommended by the Swiss Bank Corporation as guides to determine whether the overall debt of a country is cause for concern.

In the case of the ratio of external debt to exports, the Swiss Bank Corporation identified 150% as the critical value. If external debt is equal to 1.5 times of the country's total exports, there may be cause for concern. The Swiss Bank Corporation also identifies 0.25 as the critical value for the external debt service to export ratio. If debt service exceeds more that 25% of total exports, there may be serious financial risks in trade or operations involving that LDC.[3]

These critical values provide an interesting benchmark for business decision making. If the country exceeds these values, it means that there may be difficulty in the country obtaining sufficient foreign exchange to service their debts. A country borrows hard currency and is expected to repay its debts in hard currency. However, these critical values should be regarded as little more than a signal that more homework is necessary. The movement of these ratios over time is important. For example, if a country is well below these critical values but has an accelerating ratio of debt or debt service to exports, it may exceed the critical values within a short period. On the other hand, if the country already exceeds the critical values but has a history of reductions in the ratios, this may prove to be a positive signal concerning their debt position.

Unfortunately, there is no simple basis upon which to make an informed judgment. One must know something about the reasons the debt was acquired. A country that exceeds the critical values of these ratios may still be a good risk if the loans were for purposes that will increase economic output, hence exports over a period of a few years.

Aggregate measures can be misleading and opportunities missed if the nature of the indebtedness is not fully examined.

Many of the relevant debt ratios, the number and amount of debt rescheduling, and military expenditures as of percentage of GNP for each of the LDCs is presented in Appendix A. As can be readily seen from the data presented there, many LDCs have indebtedness that is a multiple of their GNPs. Many of these countries are severely indebted and have current low incomes, particularly in Africa. As can also be seen from these data, there are many relatively developed Pacific Rim countries that have significant foreign debt. In short, there is substantial variation in the amount of debt between the world's LDCs. There is also substantial variation in the reasons these countries acquired debt that are not evident from the aggregate data presented in Appendix A.

FOR WHAT WERE THE LDCS BORROWING MONEY?

The history of LDC indebtedness is in two distinct parts: the supply of loanable funds and the demand for credit. The first part involves the availability of credit (supply) and the operation of global financial markets that are examined in Chapter 7. Without the excess financial resources in the industrialized countries, there would be no capacity to make loans to LDCs. The development of orderly world financial markets resulted in the ability of LDCs to acquire debt, but it does not illustrate the specific national motivations for acquiring the debt. Each country or group of countries in a region acquired debt for specific reasons (demand for credit), and there is substantial variation in the causes of indebtedness.

If the indebtedness of an LDC was acquired for the purposes of capital formation, then the productivity and, hence, viability of that nation's economy should be improved. In other words, if loans were taken to foster economic development, then the creditworthiness of the LDC may not be jeopardized. If, on the other hand, debt was acquired for purposes other than to foster economic growth the creditworthiness of the underlying economy may actually be jeopardized. If the loans were used to finance consumption rather than investment, nothing was being done to enhance the economic development of that LDC. In such case, the creditworthiness of the LDC would have to be gauged using current economic output as the basis of determining the LDC's ability to service and repay the loan. If the loans were to finance military operations to eliminate political instability or to thwart external aggression, the debt may have a positive effect on the current political–economic environment, which, in turn, could be expected to have subsequent positive effects. Chapter 9 analyzes the rescheduling experiences of LDCs and presents evidence that there are significant differences in the determinants of debt rescheduling among the regions of the world. There also appear to be substantial differences in the reasons for borrowing across LDCs.

Table 8.1 presents evidence concerning for what LDCs spent the borrowed money in calendar year 1992. The manner in which the data are gathered does not permit easy reporting of the data in useful categories. This is primarily a result of politics between international organizations and the LDCs; however, some information is better than none.

It is interesting to note the similarities in most of the categories of expenditures between high- and low-income countries. Low-income countries use a slightly higher percentage of their borrowed funds for the military, on economic services, and for other uses. On the other hand, the middle-income countries spend a larger percentage of their borrowed resources on education, health care, and housing and social welfare. These data suggest that education and housing and social services become higher priorities as countries advance in the stages of economic and social development.

Table 8.1
Sectoral Allocation of Disbursements of Long-Term Debt (Percentages for 1992)

Category	Middle Income Countries	Low Income Countries
Defense	21.4	23.1
Education	12.3	10.6
Economic services[a]	20.1	22.5
Health care	6.5	5.2
Housing and social welfare	10.8	5.3
Other[b]	29.0	33.3

Sources: World Bank, World Development Report, 1994 (New York: Oxford University Press, 1994); World Bank, World Debt Tables, 1991–92 (Washington, D.C.: International Bank of Reconstruction and Development, 1991).
[a]Economic services comprise expenditures associated with both the regulation and the support and development of the economy.
[b]The "other" category includes general public services and interest payments on foreign debts.

Even though the World Bank does not gather the expenditure data to conform to the basic categories of expenditures, there are four causes for LDCs acquiring sovereign debt: (1) increased military strength, (2) improved infrastructure, (3) financing current consumption, and (4) because of government guarantees of loans to private entities within their jurisdictions.[4] Each of these causes of LDC sovereign debt will be discussed in turn in the following paragraphs.

Military Expenditures

Both sovereign and private economic well-being are dependent upon political and social stability. Investment is difficult to attract to areas of the world where civil war rages or where external military threats endanger markets, physical assets, or employees.[5] It is difficult to justify locating operations in a region or specific country where there is substantial risk that the assets of that firm may be caught between warring parties. If the firm is to rely on markets for intermediate goods or services or for its final products, then political and social stability are also of obvious importance.

Banking interests also have a direct concern with social and political stability in LDCs. If a government cannot survive, it cannot honor or service its debts. If violent revolution overthrows a government or the nation is conquered by another, the matter of debt of the original regime often becomes a moot point. The lender simply cannot collect from someone or something that no longer exists. In some cases, the successor government has honored the debts of the predecessor; but there is substantial risk that this will not occur.

Part of the United States's and other developed countries' economic interests in LDCs is the result of banking relations with these countries. Further, it is in the creditor countries' interests to avoid repayment difficulties associated with the political instability that could drain the debtors' resources to fight a civil war or otherwise constrain the ability of the debtor country to develop its economy (or even maintain current levels of output) and hence repay its loans.

In Latin America, especially Central America, there is a long tradition of civil unrest and military dictatorships. Argentina and Chile have also had notable military dictatorships during the twentieth century. The obvious cases of external conflict and civil disorder often require the international financing of military operations. However, there are other reasons for borrowing to finance the military. Because of the central role the military often plays, even in democratic political systems, in LDCs the governments of those countries must keep the military satisfied. Often, keeping the military happy means increased expenditures on modern equipment and salaries to assure continued military support of the government. However, in these cases there is cause for concern about the stability of the democratic institutions that may be found in those countries. If a democratic government is dependent upon the goodwill of the military, there are obvious risks for future political and social stability within that country.

There are also regions of the world in which aggressive powers are found. This is particularly true in the Middle East, Africa, and Southeast Asia. External threats can cause a country to use relatively large proportions of its GNP to defend itself from aggression. On the other hand, aggressors will also spend a substantial portion of their GNP on the military. In these cases, there is an inherent risk in doing business with either type of country. A case in point is Iraq. It is now clear that many U.S. and European countries did substantial business with Iraq, including arms. Doing business with a nation capable of such conduct not only risks the interests located in that country but may risk interests in other nearby countries (e.g., Kuwait). Intentions, particularly aggressive intentions, are often difficult to identify. However, the risks associated with doing business in such a region make it imperative that as much information be gathered as possible. Both the U.S. State Department and the Central Intelligence Agency (CIA) gather and make available substantial information concerning their perceptions of the future intentions of various nations and any treaties, alliances, or cooperative arrangements that country may have with others.

National Infrastructure

The rebuilding of the European nations and Japan under the Marshall Plan illustrates the motivation for the creation of infrastructure in LDCs. It is clear to the most casual observer that sanitation and disease control are prerequisites to human survival. Without an adequate sewer and waste disposal system, control of infectious diseases, and sources of clean water, human survival is difficult and economic progress almost impossible. A large number of LDCs, however, lack even the bare minimum facilities to support a healthy living or working environment.

The physical infrastructure necessary to support economic activity generally requires relatively large capital investments. Without a developed private sector, it is normally left to the public sector to create the infrastructure necessary for economic development. Even in most developed countries with extensive private sectors, most of the major infrastructure investments are, at least in part, public-sector activities. Telecommunications systems, ports, highways, airports, electrical power, and even railways are important physical assets necessary to support economic activity. For example, in the oil-exporting countries of the Middle East, telecommunications, highways, pipelines, and ports were necessary to successful exploration and discovery of oil. Once the oil is found and the reserves exploited, infrastructure was necessary to transport and market the oil. The more varied and complex the economic system, the more that is typically required of an infrastructure.

More labor-intensive infrastructures are also required for economic development. Education, police and fire protection, health care, and administration of these services require trained personnel. Without public safety systems, the lack of security is a significant deterrent to economic development. For example, almost any businessperson who has done business in Bogota, Colombia, has stories concerning the lack of police protection and the rather high levels of theft in the city. On the other hand, Singapore has a very effective public safety system. The case of one American teenager convicted of vandalism and sentenced to caning gained national media attention in 1994.

Even though the labor-intensive portions of the infrastructure may not require large initial outlays of capital themselves, the educational system necessary to educate the labor force and to train skilled labor may be relatively costly. Further, both capital and labor infrastructures require maintenance and improvements if sustained economic development is to be achieved.

To date, there has been little systematic analysis of infrastructure in LDCs. Most risk-assessment models have relied upon qualitative assessments of infrastructure and have not generally attempted to quantify infrastructure in a readily usable fashion. Appendix B presents an index of infrastructure found within LDCs. The index is entitled the HEETT (Health, Education, Electricity, Telephones, and Transportation) index. The description of data used to calculate this index is presented in Appendix B. The infrastructure index equally weights health care, education, transportation facilities, electrical generating capacity, and telecommunications facilities and compares these elements of infrastructure with the bottom four industrialized countries in each category of service. A 4 in this index system means that the LDC has equaled the bottom four industrialized countries in each category. This index provides only a quick and simple guide to whether a country's infrastructure is capable of supporting economic activity. In general, countries that have an index of 2 or less have infrastructures that are one-half the lowest four industrialized countries for each element of infrastructure. Therefore, 2 is a critical value. If a country has an index number of 2 or less, then substantial investigation may be required to assure that the elementary portions of infrastructure are present to support even the most basic of economic activities.

From the data contained in Appendix B, it is clear that there are several middle-income countries that have infrastructures that are at least comparable to the minimums found in industrialized countries. For example, the republics of the former Soviet Union have index numbers of 4, as do Israel, Chile, and Poland. Afghanistan (0.63) and Bangladesh (0.47) have the lowest index numbers, both well below 1, indicating that there is very little infrastructure in these countries.

Financing Consumption

There have been direct attempts to improve the standard of living of LDCs' populations. Aid to LDCs from developed nations often results from disasters such as famine. This aid from developed nations is generally motivated to save lives. However, because of political considerations, LDC governments have occasionally believed it prudent to directly subsidize the consumption of goods and services of the general population. Often, this was the result of reliance upon anticipated income from oil, as in the case of Mexico; but occasionally it has resulted from a desire to mitigate poverty and eliminate civil unrest, as in the case of El Salvador.[6] There is also a substantial history of industrialized countries providing direct aid for political purposes.

Financing current private-sector consumption without actions designed to facilitate economic growth can be a serious limitation on an LDC's future creditworthiness. However, many LDCs also engaged in government consumption expenditures, meeting payrolls, and day-to-day operations have also been funded by acquiring external debt. In fact, the U.S. government has an established history of budget deficits that were created because of the government's living beyond its means. To the extent that an economy is growing and is capable of at least servicing its debt, borrowing to fund current consumption poses no serious short-term financial difficulties. However, in the case of LDCs, the burden of a mounting budget deficit that must be financed by borrowing does pose a serious threat to creditworthiness of those countries. This is especially true when the LDC does not have a substantial private-sector economy or significant natural resources to generate resources to predictably service the budget deficits.

In some cases, funding current consumption expenditures from external debt is a function of some natural disaster or other catastrophe. The Mexico City earthquake resulted in some small external debt for current consumption purposes. However, very limited and short-run current consumption funded through external debt may not be a significant problem for economic development. Beyond very small, short-run debt acquired to fund current consumption, such behaviors are generally a signal that there is something seriously wrong in that particular country.

Publicly Guaranteed Private Loans

Debt originating from the private sector of LDCs is a small proportion of all LDC debt; however, much of this private debt is publicly guaranteed. It is common for banks to require that the government provide guarantees of repayment as a condition to loan money to private enterprises within the jurisdiction of an LDC.[7] If the private entity defaults, then the debt will become a sovereign obligation, leaving the LDC's government to collect from the private debtor.

To facilitate the development of the economy's private sector, many LDCs have been willing to provide public guarantees of private external debt. The risk to the government assumed by such public loan guarantees is motivated by a desire to see a private enterprise system evolve that can be used as a tax base to support the government's future activities.

The use of external debt for such purposes may be a signal that the country has embarked upon a strategy of economic development that is dependent upon the private sector. Most of the Pacific Rim countries that experienced rapid economic growth during the 1980s relied upon such strategies. There are dangers in this category, however. Without substantially developed political and social institutions, there is often significant corruption in the governments of some LDCs. Government guarantees may be used as a method for government officials (or private businesspersons) to increase their own personal wealth at the expense of the government (hence, the people) they serve. It is generally worthwhile to investigate to determine whether private loan guarantees are being used for legitimate purposes.

It is also interesting to note that some LDCs have a history of publicly guaranteeing loans, only later to find out that the private firm had no intention to repay its commitments. This is relatively rare and isolated but demonstrates something about the business culture in those few countries that have such problems. For example, in Mexico guaranteed loans were once used to invest in the United States. This resulted in the Mexican people bearing the burden of capital flight out of Mexico into the United States.[8] In fact, "Argentines, Mexicans, and Venezuelans holds dollar deposits and other assets abroad worth nearly as much as their countries' debt. Capital flight is arguably an important cause of the debt crisis, and its reversal is its most promising solution."[9]

Private capital formation in many LDCs may also provide the foreign investor with significant opportunities. The case of many Japanese firms locating operations in the United States is one with which most Americans are familiar. State and local governments have provided substantial financial incentives for foreign investors to locate in their locality. Many LDCs perceive themselves to be in competition with other LDCs to attract foreign investment. Many of these LDCs have policies that provide incentives for foreign investment, and these may be funded through government guaranteed loans.

Variations and Mix of Debt Sources

What makes the indebtedness of LDCs of such great interest to economists over the past decade is that there is a massive amount of LDC sovereign debt. However, the reasons for the governments of those countries to acquire debt are almost as unique as the 116 LDCs themselves. The stage of political, social, and economic development does much to determine the priorities set for the allocation of resources within the society of each LDC. Further, the historical development and endowments of resources enjoyed by each LDC also determine the availability of credit and the priorities established for the rationing of limited amount of credit by each society. It is, therefore, with great caution that any generalizations can be made concerning LDC indebtedness and creditworthiness.

The record shows that there are also substantial variations in the indebtedness and creditworthiness among the LDCs. Several LDCs have rarely, if ever, defaulted on their debt obligations or have been forced to reschedule. There are other LDCs who must frequently reschedule their debt to prevent default. Recent research shows that the purposes for which the loans were taken were important determinants of the creditworthiness of LDCs, particularly in sub-Sahara Africa and Latin America.[10] If these causes of debt can influence rescheduling behaviors of governments, these same factors may be important determinants of the efficacy of the business environments within those countries.

In practice, there is no specific mix of cause for debt that is optimal for sustained economic growth. The particular circumstances, stage of development, and development strategy adopted by the LDC will do much to determine the mix of types of debt. What is important is to examine the indebtedness of each country to determine whether the mix of expenditures funded by debt make sense with respect to the strategies for economic development of the specific country.

SUMMARY AND CONCLUSION

Reliance on aggregate measures of indebtedness can provide warning signals concerning the future business environment within specific LDCs. If standard financial analyses suggest there may be problems, further investigation may uncover opportunities or good reasons to avoid doing business in that country. The requisite examination of data means that the causes for loans should be fully examined to determine whether the loans fit a sensible economic plan for development that is consistent with the business's objectives in trading with or locating operations in that specific LDC.

The four general motivations for LDCs to take sovereign loans are (1) funding military expenditures, (2) creating national infrastructures, (3) subsidizing current consumption, and (4) providing public guarantees of private-sector loans. Few generalizations can be offered about the LDCs' debt portfolios, other than the unique character of each region and each country within that region affects the motivations for taking sovereign loans.

NOTES

1. Donald Ball and Wendell McCulloch, *International Business: Introduction and Essentials,* 4th ed. (Homewood, Ill.: BPI/Irwin, 1990), 321–325.

2. Swiss Bank Corporation, *Economic and Financial Prospects, Supplement,* various issues.

3. Ibid.

4. Seamus O'Cleireacain, *Third World Debt and International Public Policy* (New York: Praeger, 1990).

5. Ibid.

6. Ibid.

7. John Makin, *The Global Debt Crisis: America's Growing Involvement* (New York: Basic Books, 1984). In particular, see Chapter 2, "Treaties with Tyrants."

8. World Bank, *World Development Report, 1985* (New York: Oxford University Press, 1986), 64.

9. Eliana Cardoso and Ann Helwege, *Latin America's Economy: Diversity, Trends, and Conflicts* (Cambridge, Mass.: MIT Press, 1992), 121.

10. Mashaalah Rahnama-Moghadam, "Determinants of the Creditworthiness of LDCs: Global or Regional Debt Crisis?" working paper, 1994.

Chapter 9

Determinants of Debt Rescheduling for LDCs

> Any government, like any family, can for a year spend a little more
> than it earns. But you and I know that a continuance of that habit
> means the poorhouse.
> —Franklin D. Roosevelt, reported in David C. Colander,
> *Economics* (Homewood, Ill.: Richard D. Irwin, 1994), 381

Most public and private decision makers are aware that the economic
and sociopolitical environments in LDCs differ from those in industrialized nations. Cultural, legal, and governmental differences are also
well-recognized. What is too often left unrecognized is that the sovereign debt in LDCs creates far different problems in their economies
than the national debts of developed countries.

The history of LDC debt and the characteristics of LDCs have been
examined in the previous chapters. As discussed earlier in this book,
LDCs rarely default on their sovereign debts. However, when sovereign
debt becomes a constraining burden on the government of an LDC, the
LDC's government typically seeks to reschedule those debts. The rescheduling of debt is a clear signal concerning limitations in the LDCs'
economies and difficulties of their governments in providing public services, including those required to support the economic development of
the LDCs' private sectors.

Before strategies can be developed to guide business activities in indebted LDCs, one must understand something of the nature of the debt

problem in these countries. This chapter and Chapter 10 are concerned, not with how LDCs became indebted, but with the nature of the current LDC debt crisis. If the causes of LDCs' inabilities to service their debt obligations can be identified and examined, then it is possible to make use of this information in developing a strategic plan to enable a business to take advantage of any opportunities that may be available in these countries without shouldering any unnecessary risk that may be lurking in the economy of the LDC in which business is contemplated.

The indebtedness of LDCs is continuing to increase at a rapid rate. In Chapter 2, it is reported that the total indebtedness of LDCs was in excess of $1.4 trillion, with over $600 billion being rescheduled since 1980. This amount of rescheduling is a clear demonstration that many LDCs are incapable of servicing their debts, which is a clear warning to businesses operating (or contemplating operating) in those countries. What is of interest for present purposes is to determine why LDCs are having trouble servicing their debts.

The purpose of this chapter is to examine LDCs in aggregate to determine if there is some common explanation for their inability to service their debts. This chapter is divided into two sections. The first section of this chapter offers an explanation of the rescheduling process. The second section of the chapter is concerned with what factors have been identified in causing debt rescheduling for LDCs.

DEBT SERVICING PROBLEMS

The LDC debt crisis is a function of LDCs not able to service their debt. Not being able to service your debt as a company or even an individual operating in the United States generally means making financial arrangements more favorable to the debtor. In the extreme, it may mean bankruptcy. Often, a heavily indebted consumer or business will seek to refinance their debts at a more favorable interest rate, permitting the principal to be paid back over a longer period of time and possibly gaining forgiveness for a portion of the principal. This is generally accomplished through negotiations. Should negotiations fail and the debt be more than can be serviced (the extreme), then both businesses and consumers can seek protection for their assets through bankruptcy. Bankruptcy can mean either the reorganization of assets or the liquidation of assets to pay creditors. However, this book is examining nations, not companies or persons. The U.S. bankruptcy laws are not available to foreign sovereign countries that have developed inabilities to service their debts. Sovereign countries typically face situations in which commercial banks in developed countries are their creditors. In all but a very few cases, the reasons that an LDC's government went to a commercial bank in a developed country to obtain loan was the lack of domestic savings to fund sovereign loans within their own economies. Therefore, the creditworthiness of an LDC with the foreign banking community will determine the LDC's government's ability to obtain credit in the future. This is a powerful incentive for LDCs not to simply default on their loans. It is also the reason why LDCs do not prefer to enter a plea for rescheduling lightly.

Defaults are relatively rare. In the 1920s, Argentina, Bolivia, Chile, Colombia, and Peru decided to default on their international loans.[1] The 1920s were pre–Bretton Woods agreement days, but the error of these debtor nations soon became evident. An outright default means repudiation of the debt obligation, and the creditor is left with a worthless loan contract. However, a failure to service a loan in a timely fashion is also a clear warning to any other bank or nation contemplating making loans to that LDC. Even without the World Bank or the IMF, the banking community rapidly became aware of the defaults and no credit was extended to these Latin American countries. The result of Colombia's default was that potential creditors would not consider loans to Colombia. Within a few months of its default, the Colombian government had to obtain funds that it could not raise domestically. Because of its default, Colombia found potential creditors unwilling to consider extending credit. Colombia was left with no recourse but to make good on its obligations within thirty-six months of its first and only default. The four other debtor countries soon followed suit.

After the U.S. pullout of the Bretton Woods agreements in 1971 and the first rounds of loans to LDCs, the international commercial banking community formed a loose syndicate. The purpose of this syndication was to be able to share risks of loans and to be able to exert some monopoly power in the world's financial market, mostly for self-defense in dealing with sovereign nations. In large part, this quest for market power by the commercial banks was because there are no international bankruptcy laws. Market power was sought to provide a viable alternative mechanism to protect creditor rights in the absence of viable bankruptcy laws applicable to sovereign nations. During this period the IMF began to impose standards that should be met if an LDC was to be recommended as creditworthy. The IMF standards were concerned primarily with the viability of the country's economy and the purposes for which the loan was to be put. The IMF also monitored the country's debt management and historical creditworthiness. If the IMF declared a loan to be a bad risk, then the banking syndicate was very unlikely to make that loan. This process simply formalized what the five Latin American countries discovered in the 1920s.

However, the record of the IMF after 1982 was one of near complete failure in obtaining any cooperation from debtor LDCs in adhering to IMF standards. The IMF was reduced to a "grandmotherly role" of providing advice to debtor and creditors.[2] Teeth were put into credit policies by the industrialized nations combining into the Group of Seven (G-7 nations). These seven industrialized countries—the United States, Germany, Japan, Italy, the United Kingdom, France, and Canada—were the financial powers on the creditor side of the market. The economic and financial power of the G-7 nations could be exercised through the IMF to serve as disciplinarian for the world's debtors.[3]

Even with these precautions, the 1980s witnessed some minor default activity. The first formal default, after Bretton Woods, occurred in 1987 when North Korea defaulted. North Korea was a relatively insignificant debtor, but this default put international creditors and the IMF on alert. When North Korea defaulted, the IMF warned several countries that were in arrears in their debt service that future credit difficulties could arise if there was not a renewed effort to make good on their debt obligations. With the Group of Seven now seen as the force behind the IMF, there was little difficulty in getting these nations to be more timely in honoring their obligations.

Rescheduling

When a debtor LDC finds its debt servicing obligations to its ability to pay rather than default, the LDC petitions to reschedule its debt payments. Rescheduling means that the interest rate, length of loan, or principal payments will be renegotiated. Renegotiations are generally accomplished through direct agreements between the creditors and the debtors. However, there sometimes arises an impasse in the renegotiations. When this occurs, there is a mechanism for settlement.

The industrialized nations created informal processes to settle impasses concerning debt rescheduling; these were the Paris Club and the London Club. The mechanism for settlement of renegotiations impasses is an informal mediative system that is based on a simple set of rules for restoring debtors' abilities to service their debt. The membership of the Paris Club is comprised of all creditor countries who wish to join. The Paris Club limits its intervention to those cases involving sovereign debtors and sovereign creditors. Similar accords exist for commercial creditors, and this is called the London Club. Both clubs generally provide a grace period for reconsolidation of loans and requirements for meeting IMF standards and will serve as a forum to renegotiate mutually acceptable terms for loan contracts.[4]

Rescheduling is facilitated by the informal mechanisms of the London Club and the Paris Club. The incentives to reschedule for debtors is the maintenance of their ability to obtain credit. With both the IMF and the G-7 nations acting in cooperation, default would certainly result in denied access to international financial markets for any LDC choosing that path. By facilitating rescheduling, the creditor nations' interests in not losing their principal or interest payments are also served. Both the London and Paris clubs have been extremely successful in mediating rescheduling impasses. In fact, since the creation of these informal arrangements, neither the London Club nor Paris Club has failed to successfully mediate a dispute between creditors and debtors.[5] In general, the success of these informal arrangements depends on both debtors and creditors having an interest in mutually acceptable rescheduling arrangements.[6]

Assistance Programs for Highly Indebted Countries

LDCs have also been classified by the World Bank by the amount of the debt they have acquired. The two classifications of indebted countries are (1) severely indebted countries and (2) moderately indebted countries. Both low- and middle-income LDCs are found in both categories. However, during the late 1970s and early 1980s a group of severely indebted low-income countries were experiencing unusually difficult problems in servicing their sovereign loans. It was feared by many creditor countries, commercial banks, and international organizations that the large number of requests for rescheduling from these countries may result in one or more of these low-income countries defaulting on their sovereign loans.

Policies were needed to assist the severely indebted low-income countries with their debt problems. It was also clear that the policies should come from the G-7 nations that were the creditors. In October 1985, U.S. Treasury Secretary James Baker proposed a plan to mitigate the causes of the debt rescheduling problems that these severely indebted LDCs were experiencing at the time. This plan (commonly called the Baker initiative) consisted of three parts:

First and foremost, the adoption by principal debtor countries of comprehensive macroeconomic and structural policies supported by the international financial institutions, to promote growth and balance of payments adjustment, and to reduce inflation.

Second, a continued central role for the IMF, in conjunction with increased and more effective structural adjustment lending by the multinational development banks. . . .

Third, increased lending by private banks in support of comprehensive economic adjustment programs.[7]

The purpose of the Baker initiative was to develop the economies of the severely indebted LDCs so that the underlying economic causes of their debt servicing difficulties could be alleviated. Economic growth in the LDCs was seen by the G-7 nations as the key to preventing future financial crises in the international financial markets. Therefore, Mr. Baker proposed that $20 billion in commercial bank lending in the period of 1986 to 1988 and another $9 billion in loans from multinational development banks should be made for economic development purposes to the affected LDCs. The Baker targets were never reached, with only about $4 billion in commercial bank loans and something less than $3 billion in loans from the international development banks that was paid.[8] Little economic growth was observed in the severely indebted low-income countries since the Baker initiative. Therefore, the results were not generally successful in aiding the debtor LDCs in creating the economic base sufficient to service their debts.

The failure of the banks to adequately support the Baker initiative left many heavily indebted countries in danger of accelerating reschedulings and possible defaults. In March 1989, it was apparent that something had to be done for the fifteen most heavily indebted countries. The new U.S. Treasury Secretary, Nicholas Brady, proposed that there be a three-year program of voluntary debt and servicing obligation reductions. The Brady program called for a three-year waiver for existing debt-reduction waiver clauses so as to permit debt reduction and reductions in servicing costs financed by government sources to the most heavily indebted countries. This plan has been implemented, and there has been some success. The Brady Plan has assisted some of the most heavily indebted nations from having to continuously seek debt rescheduling.[9]

RESEARCH CONCERNING RESCHEDULING DETERMINANTS

Over the past two decades, there has been considerable scholarly effort expended in attempting to explain why debt rescheduling occurs. There have been numerous studies published since the early 1970s. These studies have included empirical examinations of aggregated data and case studies of individual countries during specific time periods. As should be expected, there have been mixed results reported in the literature. However, there are a few useful generalizations that have emerged from these scholarly studies that can potentially be of practical value in operating businesses in indebted LDCs.

Researchers have made serious attempts to approach this highly polemic problem using different methodologies. For instance, early studies concentrated on identifying the economic variables that could be used as indicators of debt servicing capacity of borrower countries.[10] These studies focused on the macroeconomics of the underlying economies into which the sovereign loans were made. Later, several authors applied statistical methods to the analysis of the debt repayment behavior of the debtor nations.[11] These studies used standard corporate financial ratio analysis, together with economic models, to predict the behavior of debtor nations. However, more recent studies, which utilized post-1971 data, have been limited primarily to descriptive analyses. The results of these studies have been mixed; however, these studies confirm that macroeconomic characteristics of the LDCs are important determinants of whether they will be capable of servicing their sovereign debts.

Palmer and Gordon analyzed the similarities and differences in the financial characteristics of two groups of countries using a descriptive approach.[12] Specifically, they computed and compared medians of several financial ratios for rescheduling and nonrescheduling countries from four years prior to debt relief until the time of debt rescheduling. Palmer and Gordon's study has shed some light on some specific financial patterns prior to the LDCs' being compelled to reschedule. It did not demonstrate how to make a judgment on the likelihood of an imminent payment interruption for a given country at a given point of time. What this study did confirm is that financial ratios for the indebted LDCs are correlated with their debt rescheduling behaviors. Any explanation of debt rescheduling in LDCs must account for many of the same types of financial ratios important to the analysis of the financial viability of private enterprises.

There has been one attempt to create a practical guide to the financial viability of LDCs. Fuad A. Abdullah developed a leading indicator of debt servicing vulnerability by compiling a weighted index combining several financial ratios.[13] These ratios are indicators of international liquidity position, internal debt growth, the domestic inflation rate, export position, and political stability of a country. The index is called the Payments Interruption Likelihood Index (PILI). Given the calculated value of PILI, countries can be categorized with respect to the likelihood of debt payment interruptions. As attractive as this approach may be, it is not without its problems.

In fact, there are two difficulties with the PILI. First, weights assigned to different financial ratios are based on subjective judgment. Second, the value of the index, which serves to place countries in different risk categories, may change over time as a result of changes in measurement methods and data inconsistencies. In other words, as a time series the index lacks stability because the size of "yardstick" may not be constant over time. This indexing system is a logical and useful approach, and if the measurement difficulties can be resolved, this system may provide information in economical manner for decision makers.

Political variables have been shown to be an important determinant of debt rescheduling in several cases. Shapiro criticized pre-1985 studies of the LDC debt crisis for failing to account for the probable effects of the political environment on debt rescheduling.[14] Brewer and Rivoli incorporated political phenomena into their study of national creditworthiness by quantifying and including different types of instability within the country (i.e., armed revolts or ongoing wars). They contend that "our results suggest that political variables are at least as important as economic variables in explaining perceived creditworthiness."[15]

There have also been numerous case studies of specific countries. These case studies have used a variety of methods and data sources in an attempt to explain the debt rescheduling experiences of specific countries.[16] The experiences of several Latin American, Middle Eastern, and Pacific Rim countries have been examined, finding that there are sometimes factors unique to that specific country. These results suggest that studies of all LDCs may provide misleading evidence for specific countries when competing results are in evidence in the literature.

There have also been several studies of specific regions of the world. Typically, these studies have focused on regions as defined by the World Bank. These studies have not used consistent methods and have often reported conflicting results, particularly across regions. However, these studies fill the intermediate area between case studies and broad aggregate studies focused on all debtor LDCs.[17] As Rahnama-Moghadam, Samavati, and Haber have noted:

> The models suggest that the analysis of debt can best be accomplished by segmenting the world into groups of countries (here, a geographical region) that exhibit similar geographic, structural and institutional characteristics. According to this interpretation, then, there may be no world debt crisis, but rather a series of regional debt crises with different determinants.[18]

In fact, the evidence demonstrates that there are regional differences in predicting LDC debt rescheduling. Chapter 10 focuses on a detailed analysis of debt rescheduling by region.

Last, there have been empirical studies that have attempted to identify the institutional, economic, and financial determinants of debt rescheduling on an aggregate level (for all LDCs). To better understand the relationship between the probability of debt rescheduling and the financial profile of debtor countries, Rahnama-Moghadam and Samavati examined the behavior of ten financial ratios for forty-four debtor countries.[19] The financial ratios that were used as explanatory variables in this study were the ratios suggested in other studies and considered the relevant factors for debt servicing capacity by the IMF and the World Bank. This study drew the following conclusions: First, the debt/service ratio that is touted as one of the most common rules of thumb for creditworthiness evaluation is not an important factor. In all the models that were estimated using cross-section data, pooled data, and forecasted data, this ratio was significant but with an implausible sign. Second, five economic ratios were tested: international reserves to imports of goods and services, international reserve to debt outstanding and disbursed, debt outstanding and disbursed to exports of goods and services, debt outstanding and disbursed to GNP, and interest payments to exports of goods and services. These economic ratios can be used credibly to judge the debt quality of debtor nations. Third, from among those five ratios, the ratio of interest payments to exports of goods and services (interest/service ratio) is most enlightening. This ratio was found to be significant and of correct sign in all of the models including, the forecasted data model.

In other words, there are some LDC characteristics that consistently predict debt rescheduling across all countries. The macroeconomic and financial indicators concerning international reserves, international trade, amount of debt, and interest payments appear to be stable across time and countries as reliable predictors of debt rescheduling.

BUSINESS IMPLICATIONS

It is clear that the LDC debt problem has not been solved. It should also be equally clear that the LDC debt problem is not going to disappear in the near future. However, there are policies in place that provide for organized rescheduling of LDC debt without resorting to default. The Paris Club and the London Club have been successful in bringing order out of potential chaos. In general, these efforts have significantly improved the business climate in LDCs.

There are two classifications of indebtedness: severely indebted and moderately indebted LDCs. The recent policies coming from the G-7 nations provide some useful insights. The severely indebted low-income countries have experienced significant difficulties in servicing their debts. The Baker initiative clearly identified the problem with debt rescheduling as an inability to create and sustain economic growth in some LDCs. The initiative failed because it attempted to solve the growth problems through more loans and grants. Financial resources are only a portion of the problem because they must occur with capital, labor, political stability, and infrastructure if production is to occur. As the Great Depression demonstrated, without consumer income, production means very little if there is no domestic demand for that production.

Not only have the severely indebted low-income countries witnessed financial instability, but they are also prone to political instability. These countries may be bad risks because of the political instability that is often present in these countries. What is also interesting is that these countries have had problems sustaining economic growth. Some lack the infrastructure necessary to create and sustain growth. The result is that standard manufacturing, wholesale, or retail trade maybe risky in these countries. What may be profitable is transportation, communications, and other enterprises associated with infrastructure. Particularly, contracts with governments to build infrastructure may have some potential.

The academic literature provides some guidance to business decision making. The literature has focused on economic, financial, and political variables in attempting to explain debt rescheduling. Further, the studies published to date can be classified into groups by the scope of the study. Studies have focused on individual countries, all of the world's LDCs, and regions of the world. It is clear that there are unique characteristics of some countries that predict rescheduling. The limitation with country-specific studies is simply that there are 116 LDCs that report to the World Bank's Debtor Reporting System (DRS). The study of 116 LDCs has produced competing results, suggesting that this level of aggregation hides problems experienced by individual countries or regions. It is true, however, that there are variables that behave in an orderly fashion across all LDCs. Where consistency across all LDCs is not observed, the regional studies have provided some explanation for the competing results and suggest that these may be the most useful to both public and private decision makers. In examining Appendix A and Chapters 2 and 3, it is clear that there are reasons why regional information is likely the most useful. Most low-income countries are in Africa; most of the Latin American countries are middle-income countries. In addition, differences in climate, culture, and even location may predict similarities in economic development and financial limitations. Chapter 10 examines LDC debt rescheduling predictors by region of the world in more detail.

SUMMARY AND CONCLUSION

There were relatively few defaults on sovereign loans in the history of the twentieth century. Early defaults by several Latin American countries were follies that were quickly corrected when those nations discovered the implications for their future creditworthiness. In the post–World War II era, only North Korea has defaulted on a sovereign loan. When debt servicing problems arise, it is to the advantage of both the creditor and the debtor to reschedule the loan.

In recent years, particularly since North Korea's default, the IMF and the Group of Seven have increasingly become the disciplinarians for debtor LDCs. Debtor LDCs can reschedule their loans through the informal provisions of the Paris Club, in the case of sovereign lenders and sovereign debtors, or through the London Club, in the case of commercial lenders and sovereign debtors. There have also been proposals made to help mitigate some of the problems experienced by debtor LDCs in servicing their debts; these are the Baker initiative and the Brady Plan. The Baker initiative failed to attract sufficient loans to create the economic development that was thought to be necessary, but no conclusions can yet be reached on the success of the Brady Plan.

To date, there have been several scholarly studies published concerning the determinants of LDC debt rescheduling. These studies range from aggregate studies of all LDCs to case studies of specific countries. There have been descriptive studies and more statistically sophisticated empirical studies. The variables thought to influence debt rescheduling are varied but have been narrowed to institutional, economic, and financial variables that have recently been refined sufficiently to be relatively accurate in predicting LDC debt rescheduling.

There are substantial implications for business from both the recent policy initiatives and the academic research concerning the determinants of debt rescheduling. Severely indebted low-income countries obviously require infrastructure and have had difficulty maintaining both sustained growth and political stability. The results of attempts to explain debt rescheduling using the economic, financial, and political variables reported in the academic literature suggest that there are significant similarities between countries by regions of the world. Studies examining all indebted LDCs provide evidence that may be misleading. Because of the large number of LDCs (116 DRS countries), it appears that the most fruitful approach to examining the causes of the world debt crisis is by region. That is the purpose of Chapter 10.

NOTES

1. Barry Eichengreen and Peter Lindert, eds., *The International Debt Crisis in Historical Perspective* (Cambridge, Mass.: MIT Press, 1991), 71–74.

2. Morris Miller, *Debt and the Environment: Converging Crises* (New York: United Nations Publications, 1991), 209–212.

3. Ibid.

4. World Bank, *World Debt Tables, 1992–93* (Washington, D.C.: International Bank of Reconstruction and Development, 1992), 58, 73.

5. Mashaalah Rahnama-Moghadam, Hedayeh Samavati, and David A. Dilts, "Partisan Mediation in International Financial Markets: The Cases of the Club of Paris and the Club of London," *Journal of Dispute Resolution* (in press).

6. See ibid. for further explanation for why the parties' relative market power results in natural solutions when mediation is employed, regardless of whether the mediator is a neutral or a party to the dispute.

7. Peter B. Kenen, "Organizing Debt Relief: The Need for a New Institution," *Journal of Economic Perspectives* 4 (1; Winter 1990): 8.

8. World Bank, *World Debt Tables, 1992–93*, p. 87.

9. Kenen, "Organizing Debt Relief," pp. 8–9.

10. R. F. Mikesell, ed., *U.S. Private and Government Investment Abroad* (Eugene: University of Oregon Press, 1962); and Henry J. Bitterman, *The Refunding of International Debt* (Durham, N.C.: Duke University Press, 1973).

11. William R. Cline, *International Debt: Systematic Risk and Policy Response* (Cambridge, Mass.: MIT Press, 1984); and Nicholas Sargen, "Use of Economic Indicators and Country Risk Appraisal," *Economic Review of the Federal Reserve Bank of San Francisco* (Fall 1977): 19–35.

12. Michael Palmer and Kenneth Gordon, "External Indebtedness and Debt Servicing Problems of Developing Countries: A Financial Profile of Debt Rescheduling and Non-Rescheduling Countries prior to Debt Relief," *Columbia Journal of World Business* 20 (Spring 1985): 37–45.

13. F. A. Abdullah, "Development of an Advance Warning Indicator of External Debt Servicing Vulnerability," *Journal of International Business Studies* 16 (Fall 1985): 135–141.

14. Alan C. Shapiro, "Risk in International Banking," *Journal of Financial and Quantitative Analysis* 17 (5; 1985): 727–739.

15. Thomas L. Brewer and Pietra Rivoli, "Politics and Perceived Country Creditworthiness in International Banking," *Journal of Money, Credit and Banking* 22 (3; August 1990): 357–369.

16. Jeffrey D. Sachs, ed., *Developing Country Debt and the World Economy* (Chicago: University of Chicago Press, 1989).

17. Mashaalah Rahnama-Moghadam, Hedayeh Samavati, and Lawrence J. Haber, "The Determinants of Debt Rescheduling: The Case of Latin America," *Southern Economic Journal* 58 (2; October 1991): 510–517; Joshua Greene, "The External Debt Problem of Sub-Saharan Africa," *IMF Staff Papers* 36 (4; December 1989): 836–874.

18. Rahnama-Moghadam, Samavati, and Haber, "Determinants of Debt Rescheduling."

19. Mashaalah Rahnama-Moghadam and Hedayeh Samavati, "Predicting Debt Rescheduling by Less-Developed Countries: A Probit Model Approach," *The Quarterly Review of Economics and Business* 31 (1; Spring 1991): 3–14.

Chapter 10

Regional Determinants of Debt Rescheduling

I don't believe in princerple,
But, oh, I du in interest.
—James Russell Lowell, *The Biglow Papers: First Series* (1848)

As was discussed in Chapter 9, LDC debt rescheduling has been the subject of substantial scholarly research, much of which has been consistent with the examination of corporate indebtedness. The empirical studies of the debt crisis have relied primarily upon financial ratios to predict LDC debt rescheduling. The preponderance of the published research has focused on the case of a single country or on pooled data for all LDCs. There have been a few studies that focused on some specific region of the world; however, relatively few regional studies have been reported.[1]

The close geographic proximity and observed similarities in economic and political characteristics of LDCs in specific areas of the world suggest that examination of data segmented by region may provide more reliable results than studies of the entire population of LDCs. Case studies limited to single nations have offered some insights into the debt crisis but do not lend themselves well to drawing general economic inferences or business planning beyond that single country.

A recent study of debt rescheduling in Latin America and the Caribbean has found evidence that debt rescheduling by LDCs may have different determinants across regions of the world. This suggests that there may be a series of regional debt crisis rather than a generalized world debt crisis.[2]

Unfortunately, there has been no systematic attempt to differentiate between regions of the world in examining the statistical associations of financial (or other) predictors with the incidence of debt rescheduling to date. The aggregation of rescheduling data for all of the world's LDCs may fail to uncover important regional differences in the predictors of debt reschedulings. If regional differences exist, it should be obvious that empirical evidence obtained from data for all 116 LDCs may provide misleading results.

The purpose of this chapter is to present an empirical analysis of LDC debt rescheduling so that conclusions can be drawn as to whether there is evidence that LDCs reschedule for different reasons across regions. Much of the information presented in this chapter relies upon a previously completed research project.[3]

RESCHEDULING DATA BY REGION

There are six World Bank geographic classifications into which debtor LDCs have been categorized. These regions are (1) Africa, South of the Sahara, (2) East Asia and the Pacific, (3) Latin America and the Caribbean, (4) North Africa and the Middle East, (5) South Asia, and (6) Europe and the Mediterranean. Table 10.1 presents descriptive statistics for the reschedulings of the debtor nations in each of the World Bank's six regions for the period 1980 to 1989.

From examination of Table 10.1, it is clear that there was only one debt rescheduling in South Asia and six in East Asia and the Pacific over the ten-year period. No meaningful inference can be made about the determinants of creditworthiness in these regions because there were few incidents of debt rescheduling.

In Europe and the Mediterranean, there were twenty-nine reschedulings. The majority of the reschedulings for this region came from Poland and Romania for which no systematic data for any of the predictor variables are available for the period (*World Debt Tables, 1991–92*). In this region, with the exception of Poland's debt, the reschedulings were for relatively minimal amounts. Turkey and Yugoslavia were responsible for virtually all of the remaining European debt reschedulings. Only limited systematic data are available for Yugoslavia's predictor variables. The relatively infrequent rescheduling of debt by a total of four countries in the Europe and the Mediterranean region results in insufficient variation in the data to meaningfully apply statistical models.

There were only sixteen reschedulings in the North Africa and Middle East region. Morocco accounted for over one-half of the region's resched-

Table 10.1
Amount and Number of Debt Reschedulings by Developing Countries from 1980 to 1989 (Billions of U.S. Dollars)

	Amount Rescheduled	Number of Reschedulings
All Debtor LDCs	556.3	386
Latin America and Caribbean	396	150
Africa, South of the Sahara	60	184
East Asia and the Pacific	18	6
North Africa and the Middle East	16	16
South Asia	0.3	1
Europe and the Mediterranean	66	29

Source: World Bank, *World Debt Tables,* various issues.

uling, and these were also of relatively small amounts (*World Debt Tables, 1991–92*). Again, the lack of variation makes inference from statistical models applied to this data problematic.

The evidence shows that two of the regions had virtually no debt rescheduling and two more had only modest rescheduling. Virtually all LDC debt rescheduling comes from only two regions. This evidence indicates that the LDC debt crisis is not a global phenomenon but is limited, for the most part, to only two regions.

The next question to be answered is whether the determinants of debt rescheduling are the same and behave similarly across the remaining two regions—Africa, South of the Sahara and Latin America and the Caribbean. This question was addressed in the paper by Rahnama-Moghadam, and the relevant results from this study will be examined here.[4]

EMPIRICAL EVIDENCE

Rather than replicate the study of regional determinants of debt rescheduling here, only the portions relevant for present purposes of this study are reported here. A probit model was used to estimate coefficients for this study, and the technical details of the method are deleted here for continuity.[5]

Financial Predictor Variables

The data used in this study are from the *World Debt Tables* (various issues). These tables are published by the World Bank, which gathers and publishes financial and economic information concerning its member countries. The financial ratios used as financial predictor variables in this study were constructed from the data published in *World Debt Tables*. Each of these ratios are defined as follows:

X_1 = RES/DOD is the ratio of total international reserves to debt outstanding and disbursed.

X_2 = TDS/GNP is the ratio of total debt service to gross national product.

X_3 = TDS/XGS is the ratio of total debt service to exports of goods and services (debt/service ratio).

The effects of the financial characteristics of LDCs on debt reschedulings are tested using financial ratios that are standard measures of the systematic risk of sovereign loans. RES/DOD is a measure of liquid assets available for short-term debt servicing by the LDC. This variable is hypothesized to have a negative relation with the probability of debt rescheduling. Both TDS/GNP and TDS/XGS are leverage measures and are expected to be positively related to the likelihood of debt rescheduling. Each of these ratios have been commonly used in studies of sovereign indebtedness and found to be significant determinants of the probability that a country will reschedule.

Since 1982, creditors have demanded that variable interest rate loans be accepted by LDCs to afford the creditors protection from the inherent risks of inflation and increases in world interest rates. The economic predictor variable, X_4 = VIR/DOD, public loans with variable interest rates as percentage of total debt outstanding and disbursed, was calculated using the data published in the *World Debt Tables*. The variable interest rates for loans to LDCs have been indexed to the London Interbank Offer Rate (LIBOR) with a premium to reflect the perceived historical creditworthiness of the specific debtor country. The ratio VIR/DOD is expected to be positively associated with the probability of rescheduling. LDCs will have a higher probability of default when interest rates increase, the larger the proportion of loans with variable interest rates, as in the case of the decade of the 1980s.

Political Predictor Variables

As was discussed in Chapter 9, economic and financial variables are not the only factors that affect LDC debt rescheduling. It has been shown in previous studies that the political environment is also an important influence on LDC debt rescheduling. Variables that contain information concerning the political dimensions important to the determination of debt rescheduling must be included to have a fully specified model. The relative size of the public sector and a measure of political instability are used as the political predictor variables.

To measure the relative size of the LDC's public sector, the variable X_5 = CGE/GNP, the ratio of total central government expenditures to gross national product, was constructed. LDCs with rather limited private economic development or excess reliance on the public sector will exhibit CGE/GNP ratios that are higher than countries with a more developed private sector and less reliance on the public sector. Thus, it is expected that CGE/GNP will be positively correlated with the likelihood of rescheduling.

It is possible that political instability may limit a willingness for foreign investment in a particular country. It is hypothesized that political instability is positively associated with rescheduling. Political instability is measured using X_6 = ME/CGE, the ratio of total military expenditures to total central government expenditures. Military expenditures are an objective and direct measure of a country's preparations to deal with perceived or actual political instability (either from internal or external sources). To date, political instability has been measured using proxy variables such as dummies for warfare or armed revolt. These proxies do not provide information concerning the government's perceived need for protection against political instability and may fail to reflect the actual economic impact of political instability. Military expenditures as a percentage of government expenditures directly measures the government's preparations for and cost of reaction to instability. This ratio is hypothesized to be positively associated with the probability of debt rescheduling. The central government expenditures and military expenditures data are from *World Military Expenditures and Arms Transfers* (various issues), published by the U.S. Arms Control and Disarmament Agency.

Method

The technical aspects of the statistical methods employed in the original study will be minimized in the following discussion. A probit model is used to test the correlations of the financial and political predictor variables with debt rescheduling of debtor LDCs.[6] A probit model transforms a dichotomous dependent variable into a probability. The response (dependent) variable is categorical. Because the question is whether rescheduling will occur rather than the magnitude of any observed rescheduling, the dependent variable (debt rescheduling) is a discrete random variable that assumes one of two possible values: 0 if a country does not reschedule during a given year and 1 if it does. The independent variables may be either continuous or discrete, but they are assumed to be nonstochastic. In other words, the probit model is a correlative method that permits coefficients with essentially the same interpretative value as a regression model to be calculated and presented. The greatest difference is that the probit model uses something similar to a dummy variable as the dependent variable. The proper inferences from this model are, therefore, not related to how much of the debt will be rescheduled but whether debt rescheduling will be observed.

The probit model used to test the correlation between the predictor variables and debt rescheduling for the two LDC regions may be summarized as follows:

$$Y_{it} = a_o + \sum_{j=1}^{m} a_j X_{jit} + \varepsilon_{it}$$

where

$$Y_{it} = \begin{cases} 1, \text{ when country } i \text{ has rescheduled its debt payments in year } t \\ 0, \text{ when country } i \text{ has not rescheduled its debt payments in year } t \end{cases}$$

X_{jit} = the jth financial ratio or the jth political variable of country i in year t

Thus, the qualitative response model determines the probability that a country i with given attributes $X_{1i}, X_{2i}, \ldots, X_{mi}$ will reschedule its debt, against the alternative response that it will not. Coefficients a_1, $a_2, \ldots, a_m$ may be interpreted as the partial derivatives of the probability of rescheduling with respect to the independent variables, X_{1i}, $X_{2i}, \ldots, X_{mi}$.

The estimated probit equation and relevant test statistics are included in Figure 10.1 and Tables 10.1 to 10.3. Further, because there were countries that did not report the relevant data for many of the variables included in this study, twenty-two countries were deleted from this study. The deletion of these twenty-two countries should not pose significant difficulties because they were virtually all Eastern Bloc countries or very small countries, such as the Solomon Islands. A listing of the countries included in the study is also found in Figure 10.1.

DISCUSSION OF RESULTS

Again, the reader is referred to Figure 10.1 and Tables 10.1 to 10.3 to find the relevant empirical results of the Rahnama-Moghadam study. However, the following discussion assumes that the reader is not famil-

Figure 10.1
LDCs Included in Study

Africa, South of the Sahara

Benin, Botswana, Burkina Faso, Burundi, Cameroon, Central African Republic, Chad, Congo, Ivory Coast, Ethiopia, Gabon, Gambia, Ghana, Guinea, Guinea-Bissau, Kenya, Lesotho, Liberia, Madagascar, Malawi, Mali, Mauritania, Mauritius, Mozambique, Niger, Nigeria, Rwanda, Senegal, Seychelles, Sierra Leone, Somalia, Sudan, Swaziland, Tanzania, Togo, Uganda, Zaire, Zambia, Zimbabwe

Latin America and the Caribbean

Argentina, Bolivia, Brazil, Chile, Colombia, Costa Rica, Dominican Republic, Ecuador, El Salvador, Guatemala, Guyana, Haiti, Honduras, Jamaica, Mexico, Nicaragua, Panama, Paraguay, Peru, Uruguay, Venezuela

iar with probit models. If the reader is familiar with the statistical methods, the technical aspects of the methods can be gleaned from the following section by referring to Figure 10.1 and Tables 10.1 to 10.3.

Financial Characteristics

Table 10.2 presents the expected signs for each of the financial variables. All are positive except for the sign of the reserves/debt outstanding ratio (RES/DOD), which is expected to be negative. This means that for the variables with an expected positive sign, we anticipate a direct relation between that variable and LDC debt rescheduling. That is, as the value of the ratio increases, we would expect the probability of the LDC to reschedule increases. Conversely, if the ratio declines in value, we would expect the probability of rescheduling to decline. For the variable with an expected negative sign, we anticipate an inverse relation between the value of the ratio and the probability of debt rescheduling (in other words, lower [higher] values of the ratio predict there will [will not] be debt rescheduling). For all variables in the Latin America and the Caribbean equation, the expected sign was obtained, except for the ratio of total debt service to exports (TDS/XGS). The coefficient for this variable is not a significant determinant of debt rescheduling. In other words, there is not evidence that TDS/XGS is related to LDC debt rescheduling. Oddly enough, this ratio is one that the Swiss Bank Corporation uses to determine whether an LDC is a risky loan customer or a bad risk for the location of operations (see Chapter 8).

However, in Africa, South of the Sahara, only one financial variable was found to be a significant determinant of debt rescheduling. The

Table 10.2
Goodness of Fit Measures Comparing Regions

	Latin America & the Caribbean	Africa, South of the Sahara
Chi-Square	64.12	51.35
Maddala R^2	0.27	0.13
Hit Ratio	0.71	0.71

reserves/total debt ratio (RES/DOD) variable had a significant coefficient, with a negative sign as expected.

The evidence presented here demonstrates that there are substantive differences in the determinants of debt rescheduling between regions. The results reported here demonstrate that there is only one financial ratio that is a significant predictor of debtor LDC creditworthiness regardless of region. The ratio of reserves to total debt outstanding and disbursed (RES/DOD) has a negative coefficient in both equations. Liquidity in the form of international reserves cannot compensate for poor economic performance for prolonged periods. However, in the event of short-term problems, the lack of liquid assets can result in an inability to service debt. In other words, reserves serve as a buffer between downturns in economic performance and debt rescheduling. In LDCs without a significant buffer (reserves), short-term economic downturns result in an increased probability of debt rescheduling.

In Latin America and the Caribbean, as the ratio of total debt service to gross national product (TDS/GNP) increases (decreases), the probability of debt rescheduling also increases (decreases). In the Africa, South of the Sahara equation, the ratio TDS/GNP is insignificant. The average annual total debt service in the Latin America and the Caribbean countries is 6.35 percent of GNP over the decade of the 1980s. Total debt service in the Africa, South of the Sahara countries averages only 4.35 percent of GNP for the same period (*World Debt Tables, 1991–92*). In other words, the burden of debt in Latin America and the Caribbean is large enough to influence debt rescheduling, but the burden has not yet reached that magnitude in Africa, South of the Sahara.

The ratio of total debt service to exports (TDS/XGS, debt/service ratio) is insignificant in both the Latin America and Caribbean and Africa, South of the Sahara equations. The debt/service ratio has been

Table 10.3
Estimated Probit Models of Debt Rescheduling

	Expected Sign	Latin America & the Caribbean	Africa, South of the Sahara
Constant		-1.54 (-3.66)*	-0.94 (-3.32)*
RES/DOD	-	-0.02 (-3.34)*	-0.03 (-4.25)*
TDS/GNP	+	0.07 (1.94)	0.01 (0.17)
TDS/XGS	+	0.00 (0.13)	0.01 (1.03)
VIR/DOD	+	0.02 (3.09)*	0.01 (1.14)
GCE/GNP	+	0.02 (2.54)*	0.01 (1.23)
ME/CGE	+	0.02 (1.15)	0.02 (1.68)

*Significant at 0.01

found to be a significant determinant of LDC creditworthiness in virtually every study published to date for aggregated data.[7] However, it has been argued that the debt service ratio "is not a very good indicator of a country's ability . . . to pay its debts. The debt service ratio is merely an indicator of the proportion of foreign exchange earnings free to purchase imports."[8] In other words, if a country is reliant upon foreign exchange to repay debts, this ratio would be expected to be a significant determinant of an LDC's creditworthiness. Contrary to the results for all debtor LDCs, the evidence suggests that neither the Latin American nor the African nations' debt rescheduling is sensitive to the debt/service ratio. Thus, even the widely used debt/service ratio provides inconsistent evidence as to the creditworthiness of debtor LDCs depending on whether specific regions are examined or the data are pooled.

This evidence suggests that standard and widely used measures of country risk may be unreliable. For example, the Swiss Bank Corporation uses the TDS/XGS ratio as one of its measures of country risk. The evidence presented here suggests that this ratio is not a significant determinant of debt rescheduling. Further, the evidence presented here suggests that the TDS/XGS average values in both the African and Latin countries are approximately one-fourth of the suggested critical value of this variable under the Swiss Bank Corporation rating system (see Chapter 8 for further discussion).

The ratio of variable interest rate loans to all loans (VIR/DOD) is significant and positive for Latin America and the Caribbean but is not significant in Africa, South of the Sahara. The average for this ratio in Latin America and the Caribbean from 1980 to 1989 was 41.29 percent (*World Debt Tables, 1991–92*). The Africa, South of the Sahara region had only 10.43 percent of all sovereign loans negotiated with a variable interest rate (*World Debt Tables, 1991–92*). These types of loans are negotiated so as to permit the creditor to transfer the interest rate risk of a loan to the debtor. Therefore, creditors are not locked into low interest rates should the world interest rates (LIBOR) increase. If interest rates increase, as was the case during the 1980s, debtors with variable interest rate loans will experience an increase in their debt maintenance payments, which increases the probability of rescheduling.

Perhaps the reason so few of these loans are observed in African countries is that many of the region's LDCs are low-income countries, and over a dozen of these countries are severely indebted. The transfer of the interest rate risk to these countries may simply be replaced with systematic risk for creditors. For the most part, the Latin region's LDCs are middle-income countries, and because of their greater level of economic development, it may be prudent to transfer interest rate risk to them because of their increased ability to pay for such risk.

Political Characteristics

Previous studies of debt rescheduling in LDCs have demonstrated that economic and financial variables alone are not adequate to explain all of the variations in debt rescheduling. Economic development experts have long recognized that the social and political institutions of an LDC can present as many problems for economic development as can economic and financial variables. The results presented here suggest that these variables are important but are not consistent across regions of the world.

The ratio of central government expenditure to gross national product (CGE/GNP) is significant and of the correct sign for Latin America and the Caribbean but not for Africa, South of the Sahara. As central government expenditures grow relative to GNP, the probability of debt rescheduling increases for Latin America and the Caribbean. During the 1980s, central government expenditures as a percentage of GNP grew by 16 percent in Latin America and the Caribbean but by only three percent in Africa, South of the Sahara (*World Military Expenditures and Arms Transfers, 1990*). Latin America and the Caribbean countries have experienced difficulty in sustaining economic growth based on private-sector activities, which results in rather large public sectors when the private sector falters. The governments in this region have typically responded by financing the subsidization of commodities, investment in public enterprises, and the building of infrastructure through sovereign loans (*World Development Report, 1985*, pp. 62–63). This variable is insignificant in the African region, suggesting that the relative size of the public sector is of little consequence in determining whether debts will be rescheduled. This is probably a result of the fact that most African countries are low-income countries with little private market activity.

The ratio of military expenditures to central government expenditures (ME/CGE) is significant and of the correct sign for the Africa, South of the Sahara, region but insignificant for Latin America and the Caribbean. During the 1980s in Africa, South of the Sahara, annual average military expenditures were 15.56 percent of central government expenditures; but for Latin America and the Caribbean, military expenditures were only 5.34 percent of government expenditures (*World Military Expenditures and Arms Transfers, 1990*, pp. 48–49). In other words, the relative proportions of military expenditures in the two regions probably reflect the higher amount of political instability in Africa, South of the Sahara.

As can be readily seen, there are significant differences in the determinants of debt rescheduling between the two regions of the world in which debt rescheduling occurs. These differences have significant implications for trade and operations within these regions. The political instability in Africa is not duplicated in Latin America. The low-income status of African countries causes fixed rate loans in that region, while banks impose variable interest rate loans on the middle-income countries in the Latin American area. The remaining financial variables are of significance in Latin America, but only reserves to total debt were significant in Africa. This suggests that the African countries have far greater development problems than do the Latin countries.

SUMMARY AND CONCLUSION

East Asia and the Pacific, South Asia, Europe and Mediterranean, and North Africa and the Middle East have not experienced significant debt rescheduling. The statistical results for Latin America and the Caribbean and for Africa, South of the Sahara, demonstrate that the determinants of debt rescheduling vary significantly between the two regions. The evidence strongly suggests that inference concerning debt rescheduling determinants of a specific region cannot be reliably drawn from studies of data pooled across all debtor LDCs or from data examined from other regions.

RES/DOD was significant and negative in both estimated equations. This evidence is consistent with the results of virtually all previous studies, confirming that an LDC's international reserves are important to its ability to meet its debt obligations and has substantial policy implications. Debtors that wish to maintain the creditors' perceptions of their creditworthiness must manage their assets so as to maintain adequate international reserves to meet short-term debt obligations. Creditors may also focus on international reserves as a proportion of debt outstanding as a generally applicable measure of LDC creditworthiness.

The remaining financial characteristics lack consistency in their predictive value for debt rescheduling. These results suggest that creditors cannot formulate a uniform set of credit policies applicable to all LDCs. Creditors must examine the determinants of debt default and rescheduling by region and possibly country by country to determine what policies are appropriate.

The results support the hypothesis that the political environment is an important determinant of debt rescheduling. In Africa, South of the Sahara, ME/CGE was significant and of the correct sign but CGE/GNP was insignificant. In the case of Latin America and the Caribbean, military expenditures were insignificant; but the size of the public sector relative to the total economy was a significant determinant of debt rescheduling. Political instability limits African debtors' ability to meet their debt obligations, but in Latin America and the Caribbean political instability does not appear to be an operable constraint. The growth of the public sector appears to be the operable political constraint in meeting debt obligations in Latin America and the Caribbean. Policies designed to bring political stability to the African LDCs appear to be necessary to protect creditors' interests in the region.

Great caution must be exercised in relying on the standard country risk-assessment measures. As this study demonstrates there are serious questions about at least one of the measures' applicability concerning creditworthiness.

NOTES

1. See Chapter 9 for a brief review of this literature.

2. Mashaalah Rahnama-Moghadam, Hedayeh Samavati, and Lawrence J. Haber, "The Determinants of Debt Rescheduling: The Case of Latin America," *Southern Economic Journal* 58 (2; October 1991): 516.

3. Mashaalah Rahnama-Moghadam, "Debt Rescheduling in Less Developed Countries: World or Regional Crisis?" unpublished paper, 1994.

4. Ibid.

5. Copies of the Rahnama-Moghadam study are available from the authors upon request.

6. The reader without a background in statistics may wish to skip this section and begin with the discussion of results. Little is lost to the reader by doing so. If the reader has limited knowledge of the probit model, see Takeshi Amemiya, "Qualitative Response Models: A Survey," *Journal of Economic Literature* 19 (December 1981): 1483–1536.

7. Mashaalah Rahnama-Moghadam and Hedayeh Samavati, "Predicting Debt Rescheduling by Less-Developed Countries: A Probit Model Approach," *The Quarterly Review of Economics and Business* 31 (1; Spring 1991) 3–14.

8. Charles Frank and William Cline, "Measurement of Debt Servicing Capacity: An Application of Discriminant Analysis," *Journal of International Economics* 1 (March 1971): 327–344.

Part IV

DOING BUSINESS IN INDEBTED LDCS

Live together like brothers and do business like strangers.
—Arabic Proverb

Chapter 11

Introduction to Business in Indebted Less Developed Countries

> If you allow men to use you for your own purposes, they will use you for theirs.
>
> —Aesop, *The Horse, Hunter and Stag from Fables*
> (sixth century B.C.)

The increasing global competitiveness of the modern economic environment presents many challenges for entrepreneurs, governments, scholars, and workers who have grown accustomed to local or national operations. Local and national operations rarely involve having to adjust to significant differences in sociopolitical, legal, or economic institutions. In fact, the globalization of the economy also provides many opportunities along with the challenges. The manner in which business adapts to its environmental changes will determine the future success of that enterprise.

International trade complicates the conduct of most businesses. Instead of one set of government regulations and social and institutional expectations, an enterprise may need to adapt to and master several when it enters global markets. The numerous barriers to trade, treaties, and tariff structures also complicate the conduct of business. In developed nations with stable governments, economies and institutions enjoy certain predictable patterns of conduct that facilitate business. However, LDCs—as the name implies—are developing and evolving which reduces the predictability of the conduct of business, government, and society. This lack of predictability makes business more risky.

The first ten chapters of this book have focused on the analysis of indebted LDCs and the foundations of trade with and operations in indebted LDCs. Many LDCs have little or no sovereign debt. The result of being debt free is that a large number of constraints associated with burdensome sovereign debt in LDCs are not present. Lower levels of economic development present significant constraints on business without the further complications created by large sovereign debts.

The strengths and weaknesses of developed countries' economic systems have been extensively examined.[1] Cultural constraints, legal systems, and political–economic environments are generally country specific. Most of the cultural, legal, and political–economic differences in doing business in LDCs have been examined in general terms elsewhere. The unique problems of doing business in indebted LDCs have not been fully examined. The general purpose of this chapter and Chapters 12 and 13 is to introduce the unique challenges and opportunities of doing business in indebted LDCs.

The specific purpose of this chapter is to examine the characteristics of indebted LDCs and their implications that are important to the decision to do business in such jurisdictions. This chapter is divided into three separate sections. The first will examine sociopolitical stability, the second focuses on infrastructure characteristics, and the final section is concerned with optimal rates of economic growth in LDCs.

The political and social stability of LDCs has probably been the greatest constraint on business throughout history. These issues have been examined at various points throughout this book but are of sufficient importance that a consolidated presentation of the impact of this issue on business decision making is necessary before examining business strategies and management in Chapters 12 and 13.

Infrastructure includes both public and private goods and services to facilitate business and consumption activities. Businesses in developed countries have grown accustomed to having at least adequate infrastructure to support their activities. LDCs, on the other hand, may lack elements of infrastructure that were taken for granted in the developed countries, thereby causing inconvenience or even serious difficulties for the enterprise. Again, these issues have been briefly examined throughout this book but are of such importance so as to be consolidated and examined here.

Economic growth occurs in varying ways and varying rates in different countries. Academic economists have identified numerous growth paths and the causes of these differences. Because strategic issues become critically important to success in doing business in LDCs, a rudimentary understanding of growth paths will aid the reader in understanding appropriate business strategies in LDCs and the constraints facing international trade with LDC trading partners.

SOCIOPOLITICAL STABILITY

The social and political order in any nation is the result of the historical evolution of that society. There are numerous observed paths toward social and political development within states. Because there is no single development path, the social and political variations on stability and development may appear to be a muddle. However, there is some order to development on the social and political plains. Former colonial status, the setting of geographic boundaries, values systems (including individual, political, social, and religious), and the interaction of these variables will all do much to determine the path of social and political development of any nation.

LDCs not only are often economically less developed but also suffer from a lack of social and political structures. The rise of a large number of LDCs out of colonialism after World War II left several of these countries with established government bureaucracies and social traditions. However, others were not so fortunate. The political boundaries of some nations were established without much consideration of the implications of including or excluding certain territories for the future of that nation. To date, many of these countries have border disputes and, in some cases, no firmly identified borders, as in the case of Sudan.[2] Countries like Kenya are geographically diverse, but contain dozens of tribes, several of whom have little in common save a history of animosity. The civil war in Rwanda between two tribes serves to illustrate this point rather dramatically. India, of all the world's former colony LDCs, has about the most established and stable democratic government. The years of former British rule established traditions that extend throughout the Indian government and have been refined and adapted to suit the specific needs of that nation. But even India, with its British bureaucratic traditions, experienced substantial civil unrest, particularly in the 1940s and 1950s and culminating in the Bangladesh–Pakistan War in 1971. Other countries have few, if any, stable political traditions, such as many of the Central American countries. The lack of such traditions has resulted in substantial civil unrest and, in many countries, one civil war or governmental change right after another.

It is not necessary for political and social stability to exist simultaneously. For example, the tribal difficulties in Kenya have not always resulted in political instability. At the other extreme, Mexico has a stable government, but the social unrest caused by the one-party rule in that country has been well reported in the popular press. However, it is more common for social instability to create political instability. In other words, the underlying causes for future political instability may lie under the surface for years before it is translated into problems for the current government (e.g., the changes that occurred in South Africa).

The Iranian example is a case in point. Iran had a democratic government when, in 1953, it was suddenly changed through external intervention by developed countries. The Shah of Iran was installed as the monarch. The Shah's policies of modernization and his pro-Western political views were resisted initially by few Iranians. However, as Western value systems supplanted many Islamic traditions, more devote Shiite Muslims became increasingly disenchanted with the Shah's regime. Further problems were added by some of the repressive tactics used to maintain the Shah's power that were generally applicable to Iranians regardless of religious views. Many Iranians who were comfortable with modernization and the pro-Western change in values became disenchanted with the direction the country was taking and began to resist. The social instability created by one segment of society with Western values clashing with the traditional Muslim values and both clashing with an increasingly repressive regime finally resulted in revolution and the dominate social group establishing an Islamic Republic. This brief history simplifies what happened in Iran, but it illustrates the dependence between political and social environments. Social phenomenon influences political actions, and the lines of causation work both ways. The result in Iran was the loss of American business opportunities in a relatively large market (the biggest U.S. market in the Middle East before the fall of the Shah).

However, change is also not necessarily bad. Every four years or so, the United States experiences a change in government. The change in government in the United States has caused significant political instability only on one occasion—in the beginning of the second half of the nineteenth century. India has experienced several social and political upheavals over the course of its independent nationhood, but the strength of its institutional arrangements have prevented outright political instability. Strong constitutional standards and widely held respect for the tenets of the constitution will often provide political stability, even in the face of extreme social unrest (i.e., 1968 to 1969 in the United States).

In the absence of the widely held belief in constitutional democracy, several solutions are possible. Social strife that breeds political unrest or simple political instability tends to result in totalitarian forms of government. If a totalitarian form of government supplants democratic principles, it is still not clear that political or social instability will result. Franco's Spain and Tito's Yugoslavia existed for several decades without substantial political or social difficulties (however, the Basques would not be expected to agree with this assessment). Unfortunately, after a dictator dies, there are often very unfortunate consequences. Yugoslavia is a case in point. If economic progress improves the well-being of the general population without the excesses too often observed with totalitarian regimes, there may not be an incentive for resistance to the political or social order that results in instability.

Table 11.1 presents data concerning international disputes and civil wars across developed and developing countries. As can be readily observed from the table, the industrialized countries experience proportionately fewer current civil wars and international disputes than do either category of LDC. Eighty-four percent of low-income countries experience an international dispute, which is 1 percent higher than middle-income countries with international disputes. It therefore appears that the stage of development is negatively correlated with the incidence of international disputes. It is also clear that this correlation does not extend to civil wars in LDCs.

Implications

Political or social instability at its extreme results in revolution. Such violent events typically result in the loss of life and property. Without stable government institutions, there is no check on violent activity, and the security necessary for businesses to flourish is absent. Social unrest need not result in violent revolution if there are strong traditions of constitutional democracy or nonrepressive totalitarian regimes (the latter being exceedingly rare and given to repression).

The political and economic interests of developed countries are often perceived to be influenced by the internal social and political conditions within an LDC. Frequently, the governments of developed countries err in their handling of their perceived interests, and the consequences of

Table 11.1
International Disputes and Civil Wars

	Number of Countries		Countries in
	Civil Wars	International Disputes	Category
Industrialized Countries	0	11	19
Middle-Income Countries	8	64	77
Low-Income Countries	7	43	51

Source: Central Intelligence Agency, *The World Factbook* (Washington, D.C.: U.S. Government Printing Office, 1993).

those errors are often the loss of access to markets within the country experiencing the instability. For example, the corruption of the previous Cuban regime caused a great deal of social unrest that was translated into a violent revolution. The United States and other developed countries had perceived business and political interests, and they supported those interests by supporting the Batista regime. When Batista fled Cuba on January 1, 1959, U.S.–Cuban relations deteriorated because of the Cubans' perceptions of U.S. support for Batista. The end results were that the Castro regime seized $1 billion of U.S. assets in Cuba and the U.S. government imposed a trade embargo on Cuba on October 17, 1960. In addition, three months after the economic sanctions were imposed, the United States withdrew diplomatic recognition of Cuba. The history of Cuba provides very valuable lessons concerning the conduct of business and foreign policy.

Economic growth requires stability. Without several years of sociopolitical stability, it is difficult to develop institutions necessary to continue economic growth. Security for life and property, laws protecting personal and property rights, a judiciary to interpret and apply the laws, and peaceful methods to provide for legal change are prerequisites to economic development. East Africa has numerous examples of countries without established institutions that make even the distribution of food in times of famine nearly impossible without outside intervention.

Without established government and social institutions, it is nearly impossible to acquire and maintain the infrastructure upon which business is founded. It is not uncommon in low-income countries to see partially completed railroads, ports, and roads. With constantly changing governments and social unrest in an LDC, the simple completion of a port or highway may be impossible.

Sovereign debt may be a key to recognizing the potential for unrest. The causes for LDCs acquiring debt have been examined earlier in this book. One of the most significant reasons for LDCs acquiring debt is to fund military expenditures. Military expenditures in LDCs may be for simple self-defense, but large expenditures become burdensome. Relatively large military expenditures suggest that the LDC may perceive that it has aggressive neighbors or reasons to fear violent internal uprisings. It is prudent for any business considering trade or the location of operations to an LDC to determine what the motivations were for any LDC's government to borrow to establish a large military establishment.

Many standard country rating services include sociopolitical risks within the region and specific country. For example, beginning in 1986, the Euromoney Country Risk Ratings weighted political risk as 20 percent of their total index.[3] These types of indices have continued to recognize the importance of the political and social institutions to economic risk. The CIA also provides approximately one paragraph for each country concerning international disputes in its annual *Factbook*. Further, the U.S. State Department typically has general information concerning the internal stability within a country and external disputes. The State Department also issues advisories and warnings concerning business and travel in countries that are currently experiencing difficulties that present immediate dangers.

In gathering information concerning the sociopolitical environment for trade or business in any country, there is almost always conflicting evidence. One is always well advised to seek information from several independent sources. This can even include direct interviews with persons currently in the country or who have recently visited the country. It is generally unwise to rely solely on government or banking industry sources alone. Many of these sources have certain biases or rely on survey methods to gather information.

INFRASTRUCTURE CHARACTERISTICS

The stage of economic development will often first be reflected in the infrastructure characteristics of an LDC. The development of infrastructure will normally be accomplished in stages. The first elements to appear will be the things necessary to human survival: sources of safe water, sewer and sewage treatment systems, distribution systems sufficient for allocating the necessities of life, and basic public safety. With basic public safety comes courts, legal systems, and correctional institutions. With the formalization of codes of conduct into law comes a need for centralized government to enact laws and administer security provisions and their corollary courts and correctional facilities. A society of subsistence farmers can survive nicely with little more infrastructure than what has already been described. However, this basic society is not going to experience much economic growth. To support more complex economic systems, including mining, manufacturing, and financial services, there will be more complex infrastructure requirements. Telecommunications, larger electrical-generating capacity, more complete educational systems, better transportation networks, and other modern conveniences will be required to operate more complex operations.

To attract private foreign investment, LDCs will need to have competitive infrastructures. To exploit natural resources requires ports, highways, and often railroads. To develop and maintain a domestic work force requires more sophisticated social services, including health care, education, and government administration. If foreign work forces or businesses are to be attracted, even more of the modern amenities of life are required. Unless there is a locational or natural resource advantage, an LDC will find itself in a position where it is in competition with other LDCs for trade and foreign investments. Because of the need for foreign investment in development strategies, many LDCs focus a substantial amount of their resources on the development of infrastructure.

However, infrastructure must be developed consistent with the needs and the values of the society in which the infrastructure is expected to function. Kuwait's superhighways are simply luxury items that serve no practical purpose with its relatively small population of automobiles; they simply are the trappings of industrial development. With Kuwait's oil income, such trappings of economic development impose no significant difficulties for Kuwait; however, LDCs with far greater limitations on their resources must be careful in distinguishing between the trappings of development and things that will foster development. Such behaviors by LDC governments may be a warning to businesses that the potential for mismanagement is present within that government.

Educational and health care systems are necessary elements to create a competitive work force and maintain it. Taiwan and Korea invested heavily in educational and health care delivery systems at one particular stage in their development to permit them to achieve higher levels of economic well-being. Both Taiwan and Korea began their economic development by attracting industries for which their large pools of unskilled labor could effectively compete. As the standards of living rose and available resources increased, education provided the stepping-stone to the next level of development. Industries requiring more skilled workers and more sophisticated supporting activities require educational assets.

As an economy develops and diversifies, there will be further requirements imposed on the necessities of economic development.[4] Heavy industry and raw materials extraction requires highways, railroads, and ports. Oil and gas extraction have their own special pipeline requirements and often refinery capacity is necessary. Tourist industries require hotels, beaches, and the development of attractions. For example, without the beaches and the Aztec and Mayan ruins, it is doubtful that the Yucatan area in Mexico could be developed into a tourist area. However, Mexico invested in the restoration of many of its archaeological sites, provided telecommunications and transportation networks, and assisted in the development of electrical power for the region. It now enjoys a brisk tourist trade.

Infrastructure is also an important determinant of the overall standard of living of the residents of an LDC. Airports that are important to business also provide an opportunity for the general population to travel. Safe water to attract industry also provides a better standard of living for the LDCs' residents. The development of a nation's infrastructure normally not only contributes to the facilitation of business development but also assists in bringing a higher standard of living, hence more social and political stability to the country.

Implications

The development of an infrastructure to support economic growth is also an evolutionary process. If a society expects and wishes nothing more than subsistence farming, the infrastructure requirements are rather minimal. However, if economic development is to produce more, then there are greater requirements placed on the infrastructure systems. Desirability of direct investment or the location of economic activities in LDCs is dependent upon the existence and the maintenance of the required elements of the infrastructure.

Specialized elements of the infrastructure may be necessary to support specific industries such as aluminum ore mining or oil extraction. In the development of non–resource-based industries, the infrastructure typically advances in stages, reflecting and facilitating the total economic development of the economy.

If an LDC's debt has been acquired to invest in infrastructure, this is a clear signal that the country's government is sensitive to attracting foreign investment and trading partners. Much of the sovereign debt acquired by Asian countries, particularly prior to the mid-1970s, was for the purpose of acquiring infrastructure. The development of the infrastructure spurred rather spectacular rates of economic growth in many of these countries. On the other hand, Mexico's substantial debt problems arose because their national debt was to subsidize current consumption with very little being invested in infrastructure.

It is clear that expenditures on infrastructure are signals that an LDC is pursuing a strategy of economic development. The appropriateness of those expenditures is another question. The development of basic infrastructure to support and attract realistic business opportunities is a very positive signal. Expenditures for modern airports is a case in point. A modern airport may be necessary to support a tourist or service trade and may be a wise investment. On the other hand, a fancy, modern airport in a country struggling with subsistence agriculture makes virtually no sense. Careful attention to current economic conditions, location, resources, and the types of trade and foreign investment may give the potential business clues as to the probability of continued economic growth within a particular LDC.

Large amounts of debt are not necessarily a negative signal concerning business conditions in an LDC if that debt improves the LDC's ability to participate in the global economy (and thereby service its debt). If the debt is beyond the LDC's means to service and is not an efficient allocation of resources, there is reason to be cautious in economic relations with that LDC.

Appendix B presents an index of infrastructure development within LDCs. There has been a paucity of systematic information concerning specific elements of a country's infrastructure. The index presented in

Appendix B is constructed from published data sources, including *World Development Report* and *World Debt Tables*. These data were then checked against the data published by the CIA in its annual *Factbook*. Like any index, the HEETT index is intended only as a basic guide to the overall performance of the LDC in creating infrastructure. One is well advised to seek detailed information on any elements of infrastructure necessary for any business contemplated in an LDC, particularly if that LDC is indebted.

OPTIMAL RATES OF ECONOMIC GROWTH

This section is concerned with putting the previous two sections together in a coherent fashion. Economic growth is a function of the current level of economic performance and the manner in which the sociopolitical environment and the infrastructure fit together with the current abilities of the economy to produce. There is rarely only one path that can be selected. Generally, there are allocative decisions that must be made at both the public and private levels. These are the decisions that will provide opportunities for some businesses and eliminate opportunities for others.

Unlike the United States, most LDCs have some elements of centralized planning for their economic systems. The government not only influences economic activities in these countries but also controls certain segments of the economy through regulation or, in some cases, public ownership. In most respects, the United States is atypical of even most industrialized countries in that there is relatively little government planning or regulation. This fact alone creates certain difficulties, particularly to the relatively unexperienced in global economic matters.

The selection of an appropriate path for economic development is often the most difficult policy decision for an LDC or for the international organizations supporting development. The growth path will, in turn, substantively affect businesses' decisions concerned with investing in an LDC. Since the 1920s, economists have wrestled with the idea of what conditions must be met to experience an optimal growth rate.[5] The cause of this academic concern is that economic growth, particularly in LDCs, is a critical determinant of the economic welfare of that society. The optimal rate of growth is a function of the productivity of labor and capital and is constrained by the available technology and the sociopolitical environment in which the economy operates.

The Golden Rule of Accumulation is one standard by which growth paths may be judged. There is an optimal growth path, which permits the maximum consumption for a given level of continued growth. That growth path conforms to what Edmund Phelps called the Golden Rule of Accumulation which is obtained by permitting the highest consumption per worker to be no more than the exogenous rate of growth of the labor force. In other words, each generation should save an amount equal to what it would have had the previous generation saved for it, hence the "Golden Rule" of economic growth.[6] The underlying assumption is that growth can only occur if there is savings from which capital is accumulated. By accumulating capital, an economy can provide for itself and future generations the ability to produce, and the ability to produce determines the standard of living.

Without the accumulation of capital it is unlikely that any significant economic growth will be observed in an economy. Capital accumulation can be facilitated in several ways. The simplest and easiest to understand is through domestic savings. What people save is deposited in the banking system; and the banks, in turn, loan the money to people who want to buy a machine or a manufactory or an apartment house (all of which is capital accumulation). Without domestic savings, an economy must attract foreign investment or borrow from external sources.

If the world is experiencing a transformation into a global economy, the saving–investment recycling view is still valid. In a global economy, it makes little difference if the Japanese save during this generation and the Costa Ricans invest and in the following generation the Costa Ricans save and the Nigerians invest. World economic growth occurs as long as the recycling of savings creates productive investments. A problem can arise if savings by one group results in consumption by another, with no net growth in productive capacity.

There are contrary views. There are a group of economists that do not view economic growth as being desirable by definition.[7] There are costs of economic growth. Pollution, which can be internalized as an external diseconomy; changes in lifestyle (two wage earners in a family); and the depletion of our endowment of natural resources are but a few of the arguments against unrestrained economic growth. One needs only to view the Rio Grande (Rio Bravo side) valley to see the potentials for harm from pollution in an LDC resulting from unregulated environmental abuse.

Implications

The models of economic growth suggest that capital accumulation is the driving force behind economic growth. Savings is how banks finance investment in capital and without savings banks (or an LDC's government) must seek external sources of funds. The lack of domestic savings in LDCs has caused reliance on foreign lending to accumulate capital in most LDCs. Whether intended, the need for capital in LDCs will create greater global interdependence, at least in capital markets.

Economic growth requires the development of infrastructure and an appropriate sociopolitical environment. It is the economic growth models that explain how these characteristics come together to support and facilitate economic progress. However, there are economists that are suspicious that unregulated economic growth may contribute more to economic misery than to well-being. Pollution, changes in lifestyles, and the depletion of nonrenewable resources are all causes for concern. Without appropriate planning or regulation of economic activity, there is a great potential for harm arising from the development of LDCs.

Business decisions must take into consideration the potential negative results of economic growth, particularly in countries that have little or no sophistication in regulatory matters. The potential for shifting policies and extreme responses to observed difficulties are relatively important considerations in deciding to invest in LDCs. This is particularly true when the LDC is indebted and may not have the ability to assist in environmental cleanups or the will to appropriately manage the extraction of natural resources. LDCs are not developed countries, and one must be careful not to apply lessons concerning regulation in developed countries to LDCs.

Again, indebtedness becomes an important issue in the selection of growth paths. If an LDC has debt and a history of rescheduling, it becomes subject to international control or influence of economic decision making. The rescheduling process is subject to negotiations and the settlement processes embodied in the Paris Club and the London Club. To obtain favorable terms for rescheduling, an LDC must generally agree to conditions concerning its ability to service its debt. The IMF often makes recommendations concerning the allocation of resources within the LDC, and the G-7 nations will frequently impose their own limitations. The result is that once rescheduling occurs, there are significant limitations imposed on the freedom of an LDC to select its own growth path. These limitations may actually enhance the economic viability of the LDC; however, it must be remembered that the G-7 nations and the IMF have their own concerns and may limit foreign trade and investment in those nations. It is always prudent to examine the external limitations placed on indebted LDCs because of their debt service or rescheduling activities.

Growth paths are an interesting academic tool for explaining observed economic activity. However, an understanding of the directions that an LDC is headed makes it far easier to determine whether trade with or operations in that LDC will be profitable. It is, therefore, imperative for success that as much information concerning the LDC's strategies for and limitation upon growth be accumulated and analyzed.

SUMMARY AND CONCLUSION

The conduct of business in LDCs has significant limitations that are not often observed in developed countries. Social and political stability is often taken for granted in the developed nations of the world. Most elements of the economic infrastructure are also taken as a given by most people in the developed nations of the world. In LDCs, nothing can be taken for granted. There is wide variation in the stage of development among LDCs. The stages of development apply not only to the production and market systems but also to the social, political, and infrastructure systems within an LDC.

The stages of development in each of the arenas discussed in this chapter have substantial implications for doing business in a particular LDC. Because each LDC has its own unique characteristics and enjoys differing stages of development, great care must be exercised in deciding to do business in LDCs. Further, because LDCs are on various growth paths, what can be expected of LDCs in the future may differ significantly from what is presently observed.

The indebtedness and creditworthiness of an LDC will also have much to do with the directions the growth path will take in that LDC. If an LDC has credit problems, these may provide future limitations that are not presently observed. An LDC with relatively little infrastructure but with no history of debt rescheduling may have the financial potential for growth and economic development that may be absent in countries with histories of default or rescheduling. What is needed is a framework for strategic planning that accounts for the implications of operating in an LDC and for the indebtedness that country may be experiencing. That is the purpose of Chapters 12 to 14.

NOTES

1. For example see, David Ricks, Marilyn Fu, and Jeffery Arpan, *International Business Blunders* (Columbus, Ohio: Grid Press, 1974); Stefan Robock, Kenneth Simmonds, and Jack Zwick, *International Business and Multinational Enterprises* (Homewood, Ill.: Irwin, 1977).

2. See Central Intelligence Agency, *The World Factbook* (Washington, D.C.: U.S. Government Printing Office, 1993).

3. *Euromoney* (September 1986), pp. 364–365.

4. H. G. Jones, *An Introduction to Modern Theories of Economic Growth* (New York: McGraw Hill, 1976).

5. See Irving Fisher, *The Theory of Interest* (New York: Macmillan, 1930); F. P. Ramsey, "A Mathematical Theory of Saving," *Economic Journal* (1928): 543–559.

6. Edmund S. Phelps, *Golden Rules of Economic Growth* (New York: Norton, 1966).

7. For example, see E. J. Mishan, *The Costs of Economic Growth* (London: Staples Press, 1967).

Chapter 12

Strategic Planning and Business Activity in Indebted LDCs

> Merchants have no country. The mere spot they stand on does not constitute so strong an attachment as that from which they draw their gains.
>
> —Thomas Jefferson,
> Letter to Horatio G. Spafford, March 17, 1814

Business strategies are similar to the blueprints for a building. A building can be constructed without a blueprint, but the resulting structure may leave much to be desired. The purpose of a business plan is to create a blueprint for the activities of an enterprise that will, hopefully, lead to a profitable venture. Without a business plan, the firm risks the same poor results that would be expected of the contractor who attempted to construct a building without a blueprint.

In the case of LDCs, and especially those with sovereign debt, effective business planning may become of critical importance. The more complicated the environment in which a business contemplates operating, the greater the number of contingencies that may arise and, in turn, the more important are appropriate strategies to the firm's successful operation. LDCs and their government's ability to influence the business environment provide specific problems for the strategic planning process that must be fully understood for an enterprise to be successful.

American businesses have been criticized for failing to take a strategic view of their enterprises.[1] Many foreign competitors of American businesses have consistently based their business activities on effective strategic plans. In global markets, reactive management styles are often disasters. The coordination of activities across national boundaries, dealing with numerous different governments, and the cultural diversities among countries cannot be accomplished effectively without significant planning and contingencies.

The purpose of this chapter is to introduce the concept of strategic planning and its role in doing business abroad. This chapter is divided into two sections. The first section is a brief examination of strategic planning. The second section is concerned with the application of the strategic planning concepts in determining whether to attempt a particular project. Chapter 13 will develop specific models of planning for doing business in indebted LDCs.

STRATEGIC PLANNING

Strategic planning is the blueprint for implementing the firm's mission statement. Planning horizons and types of plans differ by the type of activity they are designed to support. The strategic plan is based on the company's mission and begins a four-step process for determining the activities necessary to accomplish the company's mission. In other words, there must be a mission before there can be a strategic plan. The implementation of the strategic plan is the tactical or operational activities of the firm.

There are numerous types of business plans and missions. A brief examination of planning horizons and types of plans will be offered before discussing mission statements. Once the strategic planning process has been developed, a brief discussion of operational activities will be offered.

Planning Horizons and Types of Plans

Planning horizons are concerned with the time frames in which certain activities of the firm are to be accomplished. Planning horizons can be established in several ways. Time frames are often a function of the activity in which the firm is engaged. For example, the length of a growing season may require that a farmer use a two-year planning horizon for crop planning. The first-year crop and its location may affect what is planted in the same field the next year in a crop-rotation system. Planning horizons can also be determined by external or internal organizational constraints. The chief executive officer of a firm may impose a particular planning horizon on operational aspects of the firm because of policies set by the board of directors. Competitive position in the marketplace, external regulatory authorities, or customer demands may also impose planning horizons on the firm.

In general, plans that respond to the various time frames can be classified into three broad categories. *Short-range* plans generally focus on time frames of one year or less and often deal with specific one-time activities. *Medium-range* plans are for periods of more than one year and generally two or more years. Medium-range plans are often associated with building or major capital acquisition projects. *Long-range* plans are for periods of five or more years and involve a variety of activities focused on growth, retrenchment, or other such activities that require relatively prolonged efforts. It is not uncommon to find each planning time frame included in a firm's strategic plan.

Plans can also be categorized as either *single-use* or *standing-use* plans. *Single-use* plans are blueprints designed to meet the firm's needs in a unique, typically nonrecurring situation. For example, a flood or other natural disaster may require an unanticipated reaction from the organization. The plan to correct the problems caused by a natural disaster is called a single-use plan. *Standing-use* plans are ongoing guides to action for recurrent needs. Marketing plans or the global plan for an organization are examples of standing-use plans. Standing-use plans are typically associated with the creation of policies, procedures, and rules as guides to the actions necessary for their implementation. Single-use plans are often short range, some extending into the medium-range category. Standing-use plans are normally long-range plans, with some requiring shorter time frames associated with medium-range planning.

Mission Statements

Mission statements are brief statements of what the business is and what it does; they must be succinct and to the point. Mission statements are also an indication of the character of the enterprise. Lengthy mission statements have a tendency to cloud the purposes of the firm and may portray to the reader an organizational culture that lacks focus. If the firm cannot represent itself in a crisp and clean statement consisting of a sentence or two (certainly no more than four sentences), considerable thought should be given to what is the firm's mission. There is probably nothing in business that is more difficult to do than to write a mission statement, but there are also probably few things as important to an organization gaining clear focus on what activities are necessary to its success.

Each operational segment of the firm should also be able to communicate its mission in a short and concise mission statement. The mission statement at the various organizational levels should convey to the reader what it is that organizational unit is and what it does. Typically, the subunits of an organization are supporting elements of the overall organization, and as such, the subunit's mission statement must reflect subservience to the organization's mission statement.

The firm's strategic plan is the support document for the mission statement. In other words, the purpose of the strategic plan is to identify the activities and the assets to be used to accomplish the mission. An organizational mission statement requires an organizational strategic plan. These organizational wide strategic plans are called *global plans*. If sub-units exist, they must have mission statements and supporting strategic plans; these subunit plans are called *operational* or *tactical plans*.[2]

The Strategic Plan. The strategic plan takes shape through a four-step process. The first step in the process is the creation of the mission statement that the plan is to support. Once the mission has been set, then there are four activities that must be undertaken.[3] The first two steps in the process are often undertaken simultaneously. The first step is to identify environmental opportunities and threats and to identify organizational strengths and weaknesses. This step is also called *SWOT (strengths, weaknesses, opportunities, threats) analysis*. Once the assessments of the business environment and the organization are completed, attention can be turned to the second step of the process. The second step is the establishment of the organization's goals and objectives.

With global operations or international trade, SWOT analysis becomes critically important. As has been repeatedly mentioned throughout this book, many of the threats that exist in indebted LDCs are things with which the initiated may not have experienced before. Before an effective planning process can be undertaken, the threats and opportunities that exist with the specific areas in which business is contemplated must be identified. Identification of the threats and opportunities that may be present in an environment with which one is not familiar is every bit as difficult as conceiving the initial mission statement. It does not significantly differ from walking into a darkened room that you have never been in before. Information and its accurate analysis are the key to success at this stage of the game.

In the third step, strategies can be formulated to accomplish the organization's goals and objectives. Once the strategies are identified, they must be implemented in the final step. Implementation also includes assessment of performance, accountability, and monitoring progress toward the firm's goals. The strategic plan is not a one-time activity. Strategic management also involves periodic assessment of the effectiveness of the strategies in accomplishing the firm's goals and objectives. Therefore, the strategic planning process is an ongoing activity through which the strategic plan is being consistently assessed and revised so as to effectively support the firm's mission and to facilitate changes brought about by either internal or external considerations.[4]

Each of the stages of strategic planning will be reviewed, in turn, in the following paragraphs of this section.

SWOT Analysis. SWOT analysis contains two component activities. There is an internal assessment to determine what strengths and weaknesses the firm possesses. There is also an external assessment to identify opportunities and threats from outside the organization. The standards which translate SWOT into strategies are that a firm should select the strategies that maximize the use of their strengths and minimize reliance on weaknesses to take advantage of environmental opportunities while avoiding threats.

The purpose of SWOT analysis is provide a realistic appraisal of the firm and the environment in which it operates. SWOT provides a basis for the formulation of realistic goals and objectives and strategies for their implementation. Without a SWOT analysis the firm's planning process is fatally flawed. Planning is an information-based activity and, without information planning, quickly degenerates into a political exercise in selling individual biases and preconceptions. Further complicating matters is that if SWOT is not essentially conducted, there is no basis upon which to assess progress toward the accomplishment of goals and objectives; and the accountability upon which managerial control is based also quickly degenerates.

There are significant benefits to SWOT. By the identification of the strengths and weaknesses of the organization, strategies can be designed to efficiently allocate the organization's resources, hence increasing overall organizational effectiveness. SWOT can identify profitable opportunities and high-risk ventures that enhance the firm's effectiveness. Preventive measures can be designed to avoid major environmental threats that may save large amounts of resources that might otherwise be required to correct damage from those environmental threats.

The identification of organizational strengths provides valuable information concerning what competencies exist within the firm upon which to base strategies. The same activities also result in information that permits avoidance of reliance on weaknesses that may not be capable of fulfilling strategic roles within the organization. The effectiveness with which strengths and weaknesses are assessed will, in large measure, determine the effectiveness of the organization's strategies.

There are several environments in which a firm functions. These environments are the economic environment, the sociopolitical environment, and the technological environment. Each of these environments has important components and implications for the strategic planning process.

The economic environment consists of both factor and product markets considerations. The availability of supporting market structures, intermediate goods, labor, and the price levels within these areas will determine the costs of production for the firm. The product market; its relative competitiveness, whether it is expanding or contracting; and its continued viability will determine the ability of the firm to generate revenues from that market.

Indebted LDCs have their own peculiarities. The first two-thirds of this book focus on the issues that must be accounted for in the SWOT analysis necessary to business in indebted LDCs. Most industrialized countries and few debt-free LDCs have the range of opportunities and threats that are present in the indebted LDCs.

The sociopolitical environment consists of both government activities and private value systems. Government regulation, political stability, and public goods can all influence the viability of an enterprise. The values commonly held by the population will affect not only the firm's ability to compete in the market but also its public image. For example, a firm that sells liquor may be viewed with suspicion in a traditionally Islamic society and go virtually unnoticed in Latin America.

The technological environment is concerned with the availability of both physical and human capital. Without skilled labor or electricity, most manufacturing firms would find production to be a difficult, if not impossible, situation. The technological environment also includes the ability of the population to be served by a market. For example, an on-line computer information service may find low-income countries with few, if any, personal computers a hard market to service.

Goals and Objectives. Goals and objectives can be classified into two broad categories: *organizational objectives* and *operating objectives.* Organizational objectives are broad statements of official goals. These typically focus on the basic purpose for the organization's existence. Within the organizational objectives, *domains* of the firm's operations will typically be identified. The firm's domains are generally identified by the markets the company intends to serve or the products it produces.

More specific objectives must also be identified. The critical outcomes expected by the organization are called *operating objectives.* The following list presents the most important operational objectives as categories(in no particular order of priority):[5]

1. Profitability
2. Cost efficiency
3. Market standing

4. Quality

5. Innovation

6. Human resources

7. Capital and physical resources

8. Financial resources

9. Social responsibility

Depending upon the nature of the business in which the firm is engaged and its current performance, the priorities assigned to each of these objectives may vary. For example, private firms may value profitability; however, it is unlikely to be an objective for a public agency. The operating objectives serve to guide day-to-day operations and form the base upon which policies, rules, and regulations are founded. The desired results for each activity (the goal) under each operating objective must be identified. Further, a statement of a measurable goal to be attained is desirable to permit monitoring of progress in each area.

Organizational Strategies

Once the SWOT analysis is completed and the goals and objectives identified, the next step is the formulation of strategies to accomplish the firm's objectives. The major elements of strategy formulation include two factors in addition to those in the SWOT analysis. Both of these additional factors are macro-organizational considerations. An organization must analyze its organizational values and corporate culture to determine what strategies are most compatible with those values and cultures. An organization must also formulate strategies that are consistent with its overall mission. Strategies that stray too far from either the current culture and value systems will cause dissidence within the organization. Such dissidence is generally the result of a perceived departure from established norms for the organization and, in extreme cases, tends to be dysfunctional. The strategies selected must conform to the firm's mission. If there is inconsistency, the value of the strategic planning process is mitigated.

Strategies are the anticipated activities, by identified units within the organization, that are designed to support and accomplish specific goals. Strategies involve identifying the activities that are appropriate for attaining established goals and the assets required to best accomplish those activities (hence strengths and weaknesses assessments). Assets in this sense are the productive resources necessary to operations. When activities and assets are identified, the next question to be answered is how those assets are to be used in what activities so as to accomplish the identified goal. Strategies also require identifying the standards by which progress toward the accomplishment of goals can be gauged. These elements together are called a strategy.

There are four levels in which strategies are observed: (1) functional, (2) business, (3) corporate, and (4) institutional. The functional strategies serve to direct the day-to-day operations of functional areas within the organization. Business strategies are concerned with overall conduct of business in a particular market. Corporate strategies are more inclusive and generally identify the businesses that the organization should pursue. Institutional strategies are concerned with the structure and nature of the organization as an entity. These strategy levels reflect the relative focus of the specific level of the organization. In turn, the levels also identify where strategic planning occurs within organizations and the subject matter appropriate to that organizational level's planning.

There are four basic types of grand strategies: (1) growth, (2) stability, (3) retrenchment, and (4) mixed.[6] Growth strategies are activities designed to foster the development of the organization and increase its size. Stability strategies include efforts designed to maintain the present level of performance or size. Retrenchment strategies are concerned with activities necessary to downsizing, liquidation of assets, or divesting the company of divisions or assets. Mixed strategies include activities that are appropriate for more than one of the pure strategies identified previously. For example, a corporation may be involved in retrenchment strategies in one division while employing growth strategies in another. The corporate strategy would be categorized as a mixed strategy in such cases.

Strategies are simply guides to activity. However, strategies at each level are interrelated and each level must support the levels both above and below it. The types of strategies employed at each level may also differ but must be designed at each level to support the mission of the organization. In other words, there are both elements of feedback and feedforward to establish appropriate strategies at each organizational level that will support the global organizational strategy.

Implementation

Strategy implementation is a matter of managerial effectiveness. No strategic plan is any better than the management that is asked to assure that the plan is accomplished. The prerequisite to effective strategic implementation is managerial commitment to effective strategic planning and management. Effective implementation requires that management at each level understands the role that their level plays within the overall organization, understands the value of the plan, and is willing to assume full responsibility for the implementation of parts of the plan that fall under that level's responsibility.

Top management's responsibility is to assure that the highest level of planning is properly managed but also to initiate the planning process and to assure that lower organizational levels are performing their planning functions effectively. In fact, the concept of teamwork applies more readily to strategic planning than most management activities. The interdependence among planning levels and the individual responsibility for planning at each level requires a cooperative–team approach to assure that the management of the strategic aspects of the firm properly bring the strategic plan to bear on the relevant goals of the firm.

In other words, the basic elements of management apply to strategic management. Organizing, leading, and controlling is how appropriate planning is implemented in organizations. Failure in any aspect of the management function can spell failure in the implementation of the strategic plan. However, strategies alone will not assure success of the organization. Intervening external variables, failures at one or more levels, and deficiencies in one or more aspects of the management function may cause the best laid plans to fail.

Operational Considerations

The strategic planning process is not an artificial construct. In every walk of life, the old adage that prior planning prevents poor performance has attained the status of principle. The operationalization of strategic planning has been found many times to have been the difference between success and failure in business activities.[7] Without strategic planning and the appropriate managerial activities to implement the plan, organizing of activities can be accomplished only in a limited and piecemeal fashion. Individual managers must learn to think on a strategic plane, not as a cog in a wheel. In many important respects, strategic management is as much a state of mind as a set of activities.[8]

The strategic planning and management processes are also those activities that are used to systematically decide whether a business or a project should be undertaken. The identification of markets to serve and the viability of serving identified markets is a strategic management question requiring the application of the procedures and processes identified in this chapter. Chapter 13 focuses on the application of the concepts presented here on business decisions concerning markets in indebted LDCs.

STRATEGIC PHILOSOPHY

Because LDCs typically lack at least elements of infrastructure and many of the supporting economic institutions, many things cannot be accomplished with the convenience and speed common to industrialized countries. Most businesses that successfully operate in the world's indebted LDCs have adopted a deliberate and patient approach to their businesses. Institutions move more slowly in LDCs and often have more bureaucratic hurdles (and sometimes more corruption) that try most people's patience, particularly if they have grown accustomed to the way things are typically done in industrialized countries. This patient, yet deliberate, approach can be accurately characterized as a strategic philosophy.

Plans, contingencies, and a willingness to adapt to a constantly changing sociopolitical and economic environment requires skillful strategic management. The attitude that something needed to be done yesterday and an unwillingness to learn the culture of the various environments will be self-defeating. The adoption of the strategic philosophy will open doors and gain goodwill among officials and business people in an LDC. With economic growth comes opportunities that simply are not present in developed economies. A business presence in a developing economy can provide significant opportunities that had not been considered in the original planning activities but only if one intends a long-term business commitment and is patient. In other words, businesses operating in LDCs, in general, and in indebted LDCs, in particular, must have a long view of their operations in those markets.

SUMMARY AND CONCLUSION

Mission statements are the formal pronouncement of what an organization is and what it does. The strategic planning and implementation processes are supporting activities for the firm's mission statement. It is the firm's mission that provides the *glue* that keeps everyone headed in the same direction throughout the organization, particularly during the planning phase of operations.

The strategic planning process consists of four steps. The planning process requires a SWOT analysis, establishing goals and objectives, designing strategies to accomplish the firm's objectives and implementing the strategies. SWOT analysis is the gathering and analyzing of information concerning the strengths and weaknesses of the organization and the opportunities and threats posed by the firm's environment. Goals and objectives may be categorized into several schematics. The goals and objectives of each organization and its subunits are influenced by the nature of the business and internal institutional considerations. Strategies are designs of activities that are necessary to operationalize the firm's goals and objectives. Implementation of strategies are managerial activities necessary to assure the activities contained within the strategy are effectively brought to bear to accomplish the firm's goals and objectives. The strategic planning and management occurs at each level of an organization, and each level supports the total enterprise.

The concepts that comprise strategic planning and management are applicable to deciding what businesses should be undertaken. The systematic approach to strategic planning and management presented here are the same activities that are necessary to determine whether activities in indebted LDCs are opportunities or unwarranted risks. The application of these concepts to indebted LDCs is the topic to be examined in Chapter 13.

NOTES

1. "The New Breed of Strategic Planner," *Business Week*, 17 September 1984, 62–64.

2. Laura Nash, "Mission Statements—Mirrors and Windows," *Harvard Business Review* (March/April 1988): 155–156.

3. John A. Pearce and Richard B. Robertson, *Strategic Management: Strategy Formulation and Implementation*, 2nd ed. (Homewood, Ill.: Irwin, 1985).

4. James B. Quinn, "Strategic Change: Logical Incrementalism," *Sloan Management Review* 20 (Fall 1978): 7–21.

5. Peter Drucker, *Management: Tasks, Responsibilities, Practices* (New York: Harper & Row, 1973).

6. William Glueck, *Business Policy: Strategy Formulation and Management Action*, 2nd ed. (New York: McGraw Hill, 1976).

7. See, for example, J. Scott Armstrong, "The Value of Formal Planning for Strategic Decisions," *Strategic Management Journal* 3 (1982): 197–211; Christopher Orphen, "The Effects of Long-Range Planning on Small Business Performance," *Journal of Small Business Management* 23 (1985): 16–23.

8. Larry E. Griener, "Senior Executives as Strategic Actors," *New Management* 1 (1983): 11–15.

Chapter 13

Indebted LDCs: To Do or Not to Do Business

> Oh Dear Lord, you made many, many poor people. I realize, of course, it is no shame to be poor, but it's no great honor either.
> —Tevye, *Fiddler on the Roof*

The decision to invest in any enterprise involves risk. Understanding the nature of the risk in an investment frequently helps to determine whether a profit or a loss will be realized. Investing in LDCs over the years has been a risky proposition. The experience of sovereign countries and commercial banks making loans to the governments of LDCs has conclusively demonstrated that economic activity in the developing world can be very risky. On the other hand, the majority of the world's population lives in LDCs. Several LDCs are also rich in natural resources, culture, and historical sites. Therefore, the market potential of LDCs is substantial and cannot be ignored.

The commercial banking system has created mechanisms for their own protection because of the perceived high risk of loans to indebted LDCs. Among the mechanisms the banks created were the London Club, syndicate banking practices, and frequently high-risk premiums. These practices all demonstrate the banks' trepidation in conducting business with these countries. Sovereign countries have not been without their own collection of defensive efforts: The Paris Club, the Brady Plan, the Baker initiative, and the Group of Seven are all reactions to the business environments in the indebted LDCs.

The purpose of this chapter is to utilize the concepts of strategic planning and management to provide a framework in which managers can assess the various characteristics of indebted LDCs to determine whether projects in those nations pose greater environmental threats or greater economic opportunities. The first section of this chapter is the development of a decision tree model than can be used by almost any manager to assess the relative risk of doing business in an indebted LDC. The second section of this chapter is a discussion of the application of the decision model to doing business abroad.

THE DECISION PROCESSES

Models are abstractions from reality that are useful in analyzing and understanding phenomena. A good model is one that is descriptive of reality and, therefore, aids in decision making rather than hindering the decision maker by leading to false conclusions. Simple models, other things being equal, are the best models. The simpler the model, the less data, mathematical, or statistical sophistication required, and the easier it is to understand and to communicate to others.

The simplest of all decision-making models is a description of the flow of activities through which a decision is made. The five steps in decision making are as follows:

1. Identifying and defining the problem.
2. Identifying alternative solutions.
3. Evaluating alternatives.
4. Implementing the preferred alternative solution.
5. Evaluating the results and adjusting if necessary.

The simple five-step decision model is a simple flow of activities from identifying and defining the problem to identifying and evaluating alternative solutions, choosing an alternative, implementation, and the evaluation of the results and adjusting the solution if necessary. The general nature of the model makes it applicable to almost any problem; however, the lack of specificity (which gives it its general applicability) may reduce its utility in specific applications.

Probably the two most difficult parts of problem solving involve the identification of the problem and alternative solutions. Identification of a problem requires recognition that something is a problem. Unfortunately, there is no good substitute for the perceptive abilities necessary to recognize and identify a problem. Perception is the key to understanding that there is a problem. The systematic analysis of information and experience with similar activities can often aid in the recognition of a problem.

Creativity is the key to creating alternative solutions. Again, systematic analysis of available information can greatly assist a person's ability to determine what are viable solutions to the recognized problem. Often, it is worthwhile to examine solutions others have used or recommended with similar problems. The analysis should also provide a more complete understanding of the nature of the problem, which, in turn, can serve to improve creativity in identifying alternative solutions.[1]

Deterministic and Stochastic Decision Making

The amount of information and its reliability are important influences on the quality of decisions. The definition of problems and selection of possible alternative solutions depend on how much information is available upon which to make decisions. Decision making is categorized by the amount of information available. The two situations are (1) decision making with perfect information and (2) decision making under uncertainty (less-than-perfect information).

Decision-making systems that involve perfect information are called deterministic systems. If there is perfect information, then there is certainty concerning the relevant aspects of the problem. With certainty, the best alternative solution will also be known. Unfortunately, perfect information—hence deterministic—systems rarely exist outside of textbooks. Most real-world decision making is stochastic (i.e., depends on probabilities because of the lack of perfect information) and not deterministic.

Stochastic decision making relies on assigning probabilities to events and results that are uncertain. In most cases, there is far-less-than-perfect information available. Further, in most cases the results of alternative solutions are not known with certainty. If a problem is identified, there may be several alternative solutions, each with a probability of having a desired result and a probability of having an undesired result. The assignment of the probabilities of results depends on the available information. In the real world, probabilities are assigned as a matter of an educated best guess and are not known with any certainty. The selection of an alternative solution then depends on a decision maker's degree of risk aversion.

For example, a lottery contestant wins a chance to appear on a weekly television show in which $1,000,000 is the top prize. The contestant may select one of four boxes. In one box is $1,000,000, in another is $500,000, in another is $100,000, and in the last box is nothing. The game rules permit the contestant to keep the contents of only the last box selected, but the contestant can select boxes until the empty box is discovered. If the contestant selects the empty box he wins nothing, regardless of previous selections, and the game ends. If for the first selection the contestant selects the box containing $500,000, what will the contestant do? If the contestant is risk averse, he keeps the $500,000 and leaves. Why? Because there are three selections left: One makes him better off (the box containing $1,000,000), but there are two that make him worse off (the box containing $100,000 and the empty box). The one chance in three of being better off will not likely induce a risk-averse person into further play. For example, most contestants in Indiana's lottery game, similar to that in this example, stop if they win anything, even in cases where two of three remaining selections would make them better off. A risk-assuming person who selected the $500,000 box will play on because the chances of obtaining the $1,000,000 have been narrowed from one chance in four to one chance in three. Notice that the expected value of the second selection is $366,667 for either person ($1,100,000 divided by 3). The risk assuming is labeled so because the expected value of the second selection is less than the amount already won.

The stochastic nature and limitations on available information about most real-world decisions complicate matters. The element of human values, perceptions, and human error are important components in the process. Human judgment simply cannot be factored out of most real-world decisions, but it can be improved by more systematic approaches to decision making and more information upon which to base decisions. This is clearly the case in doing business in risky environments such as indebted LDCs.

LDCS, DEBT, AND RISK

Deciding whether to do business abroad requires the consideration of a wide array of variables. Climatic, cultural, geographic, institutional, and resource differences between the host country and the one from which the enterprise is expanding or relocating can make such a move seem so complex as to be hardly worth the effort. The generic difficulties of doing business abroad have been thoroughly examined and will not be rehashed here.[2] The standard financial considerations concerning the recovery period, changing currency values, transformation risks, and the time value of money will all effect the decision, but these matters are also applicable to business decisions in the developed countries. Only one technical portion of the business decision process will be examined here, and that is the effects of LDCs and their indebtedness on deciding to locate an enterprise in the Third World.

The risks associated with doing business in LDCs come from the sociopolitical environment, from the markets for resources and products, and from the availability of public goods and services. LDCs are in various stages of development, not only in their economies but also in virtually all of their institutions. The indebtedness of an LDC can be the result of underlying phenomena that pose a risk to the business environment, such as political instability. The debt can also pose a risk to the continued growth and viability of the LDC's markets.

As demonstrated earlier in this book, there are significant differences between regions of the world as to what predicts debt rescheduling. These differences suggest that the causes and burden of the debt vary substantially across LDCs. In other words, any decision to invest in enterprises in an indebted LDC requires specific information concerning the causes and the burden of the sovereign debt of that particular country. Generalizations concerning debt, particularly aggregated for larger cross-sections than specific regions, are clearly indefensible.

Investment Decisions

Investment decisions in LDCs can be modeled as a decision tree. A decision tree is a set of standards, normally posed as conditions and relevant alternatives facing the decision maker. Decision trees are simple flow charts that are used to describe the decision-making process to be employed. In the case of indebted LDCs, the decision tree model is relatively simple and straightforward. The business environment of LDCs creates additional factors for consideration; and if the LDC also has a significant sovereign debt, another set of potential relevant variables also enter the decision-making process. The environmental influences of the LDC's business environment and the debt must be taken into consideration before proceeding to the standard decision-making processes typically used in the firm.

Figure 13.1 presents a simple decision tree model that fits above the flows of the business decision-making processes that would be used if the location for the enterprise was not an indebted LDC. Notice that the decision tree simply imposes a SWOT analysis on top of the normal decision-making models. The first step in the decision tree—labeled (1) in the figure—is to identify the threats and opportunities resulting from the country's LDC status. The result is that the LDC's environment presents net threats or opportunities. The second step—labeled (2) in the figure—is to identify the economic consequences of the LDC's debt, if any, to determine if risk caused by the sovereign debt is likely to offset any gains from environmental opportunities. Once this portion of the analysis is completed, then standard business analyses—labeled (3) in the figure—may be relied upon to reach a conclusion concerning whether the LDC is an appropriate location for the proposed enterprise.

The decision tree simplifies the model to propositions and alternatives. Countries that have net threats and governments with difficulties servicing debt are unequivocally bad risks. If net nonfinancial threats exist and the country is servicing its sovereign debts, there may be hope for future improvement in the sociopolitical and economic en-

Figure 13.1
Decision Tree

(1)

Threat or opportunity
exclusive of sovereign debt

Enviroment is net
threat to success

Environment is net
opportunity for success

(2)

Debt service
problems

Sovereign debt
servicing problems

No debt service
problems

Bad risk

Mixed results

Good risk

(3)

Input into standard business decision models

vironments and more information is needed. In the other two cases, there are unambiguous decisions indicated.

The simple decision tree, however, does not reflect the complexity of most of the underlying questions that must be answered at each step in the process. The flows of decision making contained in Figure 13.1 are rather simple; however, the questions that must be asked at each step are not. To operationalize the decision tree model, the right questions must be asked and answered. The following sections present the typical lists of the types of questions for which answers must be forthcoming before any conclusions can be reached with confidence.[3]

Doing Business in Indebted LDCs

The relevant decision processes in the case of LDCs are to examine the characteristics of the LDC as suggested in the SWOT portion of the strategic management procedures of Chapter 12 (step 1 in Figure 13.1). Opportunities and threats from the environment within the LDC must be fully analyzed. The types of questions that must be resolved are

1. Is the political and social environment stable? If so, is it favorable for the proposed type of business (especially from your country or firm)?

2. Are the regulatory, statutory and judicial environments favorable?

3. Is there an absence of domestic industries who are competitors that may be given preferential treatment by the government or the indigenous population?

4. Are the quantity and quality of humans, capital, and other resources con-sistently available in the quantities and qualities required?

5. Are there adequate public services, such as sewage treatment, electricity, transportation, and telecommunications for the proposed business?

6. Is the tax environment stable and favorable to the proposed business?

7. Are adequate and reliable private-sector support industries in place?

8. Are there stable cost advantages to operations in the LDC?

9. Are the domestic market opportunities limited or nonexistent in the host country? Do stable trade arrangements that permit exportation of proposed products exist?

10. Are there economic trends in the host country that may result in future business advantages for the proposed enterprise?

11. Are competitors from other nations unlikely to be attracted to this coun-try that may cause competitive problems?

12. Is the government of the country debt free?

Before any of these questions can be answered, relevant information must be gathered and analyzed. The gathering of information is an expensive proposition, in both time and money; however, it must be remembered that any decision is no better than the reliability and va-lidity of information upon which that decision was based. Relevant evi-dence must be gathered, sources checked, and corroboration sought for each bit of information before any analysis is conducted. Once there is confidence that the data are valid and reliable, then appropriate analy-ses must be conducted to permit answers to be formulated to each of the preceding twelve questions.

If the information gathered concerning any of the preceding twelve questions suggests an answer of no, then a potential environmental threat exists. Further, investigation will normally be warranted and strategies developed to effectively deal with such potential threats. Where the answers are all yes, then there are potential environmental opportunities that also warrant further investigation and the formula-tion of strategies to take advantage of any opportunities that may exist.

This suggested approach is a rather straightforward application of the standard strategic planning and management models. These twelve questions represent the critical elements of the opportunity and threat portions of the SWOT analysis. Strengths and weaknesses of the en-terprise or proposed firm must be matched with the appropriate oppor-tunities and threats to determine whether goals and objectives and their supporting strategies can be formulated and implemented. If the SWOT analysis produces results that suggest realistic strategic plans are unlikely to attain desirable goals and objectives, the proposed en-terprise must be rethought to make the proposal potentially profitable.

If this cannot be done, then it is recommended that the proposal be refocused on other ventures or other countries or simply abandoned.

The model becomes more complicated where all of the questions except Question 12 yield satisfactory answers. If the country has significant sovereign debt, several more questions need to be asked:

13. Has the country had difficulties servicing its debt?
14. Has it rescheduled its debts? If so, recently? If recently, why?

If the answer to Question 13 is no, then the first checklist (Questions 1 through 12) are probably sufficient for present purposes. If, however, the answer to Question 13 is yes, then Question 14 must be answered. If the answer to the first part of Question 14 is yes but the answer to the second part is no, then the sovereign debt difficulties may have been resolved over time. This could be a positive indication. Debt servicing may have been a difficulty in the past, in lesser stages of development; but if the loans eventually created infrastructure and fostered economic growth, this is a positive signal concerning the country's future economic viability. If the answer to Question 14 is yes, the country has taken loans beyond its ability to service and has a history of debt servicing problems that resulted in rescheduling; then the reasons the loans were taken become important. If the country has used the loans to create infrastructure and foster economic growth, then the future growth potentials for domestic markets and political stability may be relatively strong. If, however, the loans were for military expenditures or to finance present or past consumption, these may be signs of social unrest that may likely produce political unrest at some point in the future.

In the case of the loans being used for public investments for infrastructure and to facilitate economic growth, this also may not be all good. If the government is involved in partnership arrangements or owns and operates specific industries, then there may be precedents for public ownership of what would normally be considered private enterprise in the United States. In these cases, the legal, political, and institutional traditions and structure of the country deserve careful and thorough examination to assure that there is little chance for the loss of the proposed enterprise. It is also possible in many regions of the world that the firm could be forced into unfavorable partnership arrangements should the proposed business succeed.

If Question 14 is answered in the affirmative (any part), then there is a readily available source of information concerning the reasons. Before a country can reschedule its debts, the IMF requires several types of information. There must be a full explanation of the reasons why the country cannot service its debts and what its plans are for servicing the rescheduled debt. This information should be requested from

IMF and fully examined if Question 14 is answered yes.

If the answer to Question 13 or Question 14 is yes and the loans were from international sources, then another question should be asked:

15. Are there viable domestic financial markets?

The fact that the government of an LDC had to seek international financing for sovereign debts suggests limited domestic financial markets in the host country. If the proposed enterprise is a capital-intensive operation, it may need to be financed from current revenues or may be left seeking financing through international capital markets. The international capital markets may or may not view the proposed business as being resident to the LDC, depending on the type of proposed business and corporate affiliations, if any.

There is also a forecasting function that is inherent in answering any of these questions. The current state of affairs is only one point in time in the dynamic process of economic development. The historical trends, together with current conditions, may give a reasonable basis upon which to forecast the future directions that the various institutions and economic activities within the country may take. However, forecasting—even with sophisticated models and accurate data—is an imperfect art form. All forecasts are nothing more than educated guesses and should be regarded as such.

Use of the Questions

The decision tree model examined in this chapter is the basis for deciding whether to do business in an indebted LDC. This model is adapted for the strategic planning and management models presented in Chapter 12. Rather than simply take a chance, a systematic approach to gathering evidence and decision making will provide for better decisions. Once the decision to operate in an indebted LDC is made, then there will be differences in the way that the enterprise must be operated. This brings the discussion presented in this book full circle. In Chapter 1, it is stated that there are several sources of information concerning operations overseas. The point is made that there are already adequate treatments of cultural, political, legal, and institutional differences between developed countries and LDCs available.

SUMMARY AND CONCLUSION

Managerial decision making can be modeled, but there is a trade-off between ease of application and sophistication. Whether this trade-off affects the utility of the model on net is subject to debate. Decision trees can be constructed to demonstrate investment decisions in indebted LDCs. However, it is the strategic planning and management models of Chapter 12 that provide the questions that must be asked if contemplating operations in an indebted LDC.

The SWOT analysis of the strategic planning model provides a systematic method to analyze the environment to determine whether opportunities and threats exist in a proposed business. The SWOT model feeds information into the creation of realistic goals and objectives and the formulation of strategies for the implementation of the business plan. Outside of the sovereign indebtedness status of the LDC's government, there are numerous questions that must be resolved before deciding whether the opportunities outweigh the threats. When the sovereign indebtedness of the country is added to the decision-making process, both current threats and opportunities change; but the effects of the creditworthiness of that country's government may also influence the future directions of the institutions and economy in that LDC.

NOTES

1. For further discussion, see George P. Huber, *Managerial Decision Making* (Glenview, Ill.: Scott, Foresman, 1975).

2. For example, see Michael Porter, *The Competitive Advantage of Nations* (New York: Free Press, 1990); Kenichi Ohmae, *The Borderless World* (New York: Harper Business Publications, 1989); Philip Harris and Robert T. Moran, *Managing Cultural Differences,* 2nd ed. (Houston: Gulf Publishing, 1987).

3. See R. C. Garg and R. Aggarwal, "Risk Analysis in Bank Lending to Developing Countries: A Survey of International Bankers," *Issues in International Business* 4 (1; Spring 1987): 17–24 for a checklist of questions for bankers considering making loans in less developed countries.

Chapter 14

The Imperative of Globalization

He who lives by fighting with an enemy has an interest in the preservation of the enemy's life.
—Nietzsche, *Human, All Too Human* (1878)

Economic globalization has received considerable attention in the past couple of decades. In the United States, consideration of NAFTA revitalized the debate. Before the ratification of NAFTA, organized labor actively resisted the treaty because of its perceived threat to American jobs. In the European Economic Community, the political unification treaty was roundly defeated. In other words, there continues to be considerable suspicion of possible adverse effects from globalization. The trend for the U.S. and European economies to become importing rather than exporting nations probably has contributed to the resistance to globalization.

For the past two decades, business schools have increased curricular emphasis on international business.[1] This increased emphasis is, at least in part, a result of the belief that international trade will become an increasingly important component of economic life. As discussed in Chapter 1, international trade continues to decline in relative importance in the United States economy. Even though business schools may be overly optimistic concerning international business contribution to the U.S. economy, the internationalization of business curricula is well advised.

The purpose of this chapter is to examine some of the more important controversies concerning economic globalization. With the rise of free trade areas in recent decades and political resistance to NAFTA in the United States, the positions of opponents to free trade should be examined. There are elements of those arguments against NAFTA that are worthy of serious consideration. Further, the need for economic progress in the developing regions of the world have been dramatically demonstrated with some of the difficulties experienced in East Africa during the early 1990s. These issues will also be examined. Last, some concluding comments concerning nationalism are also in order.

RESISTANCE TO FREE TRADE

French farmers rioted in 1992 and 1993 about agricultural imports and their adverse effects on farm commodity prices. Since the mid-1970s, American automobile workers have argued that restrictions had to be placed on Japanese imports. In fact, the United Automobile Workers (UAW) distributed bumper stickers during the recession in the latter part of the 1980s that said "Hungary—Eat Your Import." Less rational than American union workers and French farmers has been the racist attacks of groups of thugs in Germany. Attacks by bands of German neo-Fascists against immigrant labor in Germany, particularly Turks, have been increasing at an alarming rate through the 1990s. All these events are unfortunate symptoms of resistance to the globalization of national economies.

The resistance to free trade should come as no surprise. There are real economic reasons why we should expect to observe various groups of people to resist free trade. Some of these concerns are legitimate; some are not so legitimate. Everyone would recognize that racism and the creation of an industrial–military complex for purely aggressive purposes fall into the latter. However, there are several reasons, based on sound economic reasoning, for resistance to free trade. These reasons exist in both developed and developing countries and present difficulties for businesses wishing to enter markets abroad. Each of these reasons will be discussed in the following sections.

Economic Reasons to Resist Free Trade

The economic reasoning for resisting free trade can be generally classified into two categories: (1) national or societal reasons and (2) harmful effects on a specific group. In the case of harm to a specific group, the affected group will generally resist; however, it is not uncommon for national policy to be formulated to protect that group.

Among the most common reasons for protectionist policies are national security and infant industry. These arguments have been long advanced as reasons for protectionist policies.[2] These arguments are applicable to both industrialized countries and LDCs and are worth brief discussion here.

National security in the developed nations is frequently based on the protection of technology as it is on the protection of industrial capacity. Without industrial capacity, a nation becomes reliant on international markets for arms, hence their national defense capabilities become dependent on trading partners. This is common in LDCs; however, most developed countries have sufficient industrial capacity to defend themselves.

Computer, nuclear, optic, chemical, biological, and metallurgical technologies, among others, are generally very sensitive because of their direct military applications. In modern military endeavors, it is frequently technology that provides the margin necessary to prevail (e.g., the reports concerning the campaign against Iraq). Perhaps of greater importance are biological, chemical, and nuclear technologies. Almost everyone is familiar with the nonproliferation treaty and the controversy with North Korea in 1994.

To maintain a technological edge can provide as much national security as large standing militaries. Therefore, both the technology and the industrial capacity necessary for the production of military goods will be sensitive issues that will typically be heavily regulated by developed countries in international trade. LDCs rarely have a technological base that requires protection for military purposes; however, those countries that have heavy industry capable of producing arms generally will protect those industries from direct foreign competition. In fact, several LDCs will provide incentives to locate heavy industry to their jurisdiction, especially those that can be readily converted to military applications in unstable regions of the world.

Infant industry arguments are based on the country attempting to protect production of some essential good from competition from large foreign competitors that have a comparative advantage. Often, the industry that is being protected has a military implication; however, industries that produce the necessary items of daily life are often the most protected. The infant industry argument generally has closure, even though it is rarely observed. The argument is generally that the subject industry needs to be protected from foreign competition until such time as it attains an efficient scale that permits it to compete with imports. While this may sound logical, too often the protections are never lifted or are applied to industries that will never be anything but infants. France, Japan, the United States, and many other industrialized countries protect their agricultural markets from foreign competition simply because food is a necessity and farmers are politically active.

The comparative advantage argument has an implication that should not go unnoticed. Specialization and trade imply that countries will put more resources into certain activities and less or none into others. Under free trade arrangements, it is likely that certain industries will be displaced in some of the countries involved. When an industry is displaced, workers are unemployed, demands on the public sector increase, and political problems arise. The increased unemployment and job search associated with being displaced by foreign competition, even if fair and honest, generally cause political backlash that can have an effect on governments and even the market for goods of companies thought to be culpable. If the trade practice of the exporters are suspect, then even greater political and economic backlash can be reasonably expected.

Companies contemplating economic relations abroad must consider resistance from two sources. Governments may resist trade or locating of operations into their jurisdictions because of domestic political ramifications. Consumers, especially those who were displaced from their jobs because of the foreign competition, may be a potential source of problems. Many of these same problems may also be present in the country of origin for many businesses.

On the other hand, there are many companies that have taken domestic products, particularly consumer products, to foreign markets with rather phenomenal success. The case of Coca-Cola has few equals. U.S. residents have a well-known sweet tooth and have been the largest consumers of soft drinks in the world for decades. Most other regions of the world have different tastes, even in Europe. Further, the soft drink industry is very competitive in the United States. It is a risky enterprise to devote energies and resources to international marketing when facing a domestic market that accounts for the bulk of sales and is highly competitive. Coca-Cola took the risk (as did Pepsi) and has become extremely popular in many regions of the world. In these cases, there is no domestic displacement of workers, and there is expansion of employment opportunities in the countries where these companies located. These types of international economic relations are win-win situations.

LDCs as Markets

In Chapter 1, the fact that Mexico is the second largest consumer of American exports is brought to the reader's attention. Mexico has an annual per capita GDP of just over $3,000. One of the strongest arguments for the passage of NAFTA was to increase workers' incomes in Mexico that, in turn, could be spent on U.S. goods.

In low-income countries (see Chapters 2 and 3), the per capita GDP is so low that there are very limited markets for imported goods. As countries move into the middle-income classification with per capita incomes approaching $7,000 per year, those economies become viable markets for imported goods from industrialized countries. Again, the majority of the world's population live in LDCs, and the market potential is proportional to the income that can be generated in these countries.

The free trade treaties that have been ratified in many regions of the world have had positive effects for trade in that region. The EEC, the African Common Market, and the Latin Free Trade Agreements have all had positive influences on trade and with some varied positive influence on economic growth. As growth continues, especially in the middle-income countries of Latin America, there is cause for optimism concerning the development of consumer markets in those regions. Unfortunately, most of the African nations, south of the Sahara, are low-income and politically unstable countries that have far greater hurdles to leap before they become positioned to be consumer economies.

Other Incentives for Industrialized Countries

Especially during the 1950s and 1960s, the United States had ambitious programs to assist in the economic development of LDCs. Much of the motivation for this assistance was the Cold War; however, many of these aid programs continue directly through the United States Agency for Industrial Development (USAID) or indirectly through various U.N. agencies, that derive much of their financial support from the United States. The financial burden of these foreign-assistance programs is not trivial.

The potential markets for industrialized countries' goods is no minor implication of economic growth in LDCs. However, the increased stability that higher incomes bring to such regions will make the world a safer place in which to live, with positive implications for all.

In sum, the poverty in LDCs serves nobody's interests. Nobody is made better off by anyone being worse off. If viable growth paths can be implemented in each of the LDCs, the world can make economic progress in which all nations can share, LDC and industrialized alike. If the globalization of economic relations is to generate such idealistic results, it must start with the LDCs.

NATIONALISM

Nationalism has been an impediment to free trade and increased economic relations among countries. Attachment to home or love of country is a natural human emotion. Nationalism is often the root cause of the lack of acceptance of foreign products and labor. Many persons see globalization of the economy as inconsistent with nationalism, and at the extreme it may be. The EEC was unable to overcome this view in 1993 to 1994.

Economic interdependence does not require the diminishing of sovereignty nor home rule. Trade and multinational production has existed throughout recorded history alongside of political independence. In fact, the argument that globalization of economic activity is a threat to the existence of independent political states is inconsistent with the historical evidence. In LDCs where the argument is often used against foreign investment or trade, it is based on Cold War influences or suspicion of former colonial powers. In many cases, businesses will find that nationalism will be an impediment to developing business relations in certain regions of the world. It is a real consequence of the events of the past, but it can be overcome. The patient but diligent approach suggested earlier in the book is the key to winning over government officials, workers, and consumers.

SUMMARY AND CONCLUSION

Protectionism is a very real constraint on global economic relations. National security and infant industry have been among the more persuasive arguments for protectionist policies. However, trade based on comparative advantage has the real potential to harm certain classes of employees; and these individuals and their unions will naturally seek to protect their economic interests. The adverse effects of nationalism, made worse by the suspicion of industrialized countries' motives, are a real problem in business relations in many LDCs. However, the patient and diligent approach can do much to eliminate those barriers.

LDCs have the potential of becoming extensive markets for industrialized countries' goods. The majority of the world's population live in LDCs, and middle-income countries already have importing relations with industrialized countries that are significant. As low-income countries enter the mainstream and middle-income countries continue to progress, even greater markets for industrialized countries' goods should open.

NOTES

1. The American Association of Collegiate Schools of Business require accredited business programs at both the graduate and undergraduate levels to have substantial international components in their curricula.

2. Adam Smith, *An Inquiry into the Nature and Causes of the Wealth of Nations,* ed. Edwin Cannan (New York: G. P. Putnam & Sons, 1877), 103. Original work first published under the same title in 1776.

Appendix A

Debt Rescheduling Determinants of Less Developed Countries, Commercial Bank Claims on Developing Countries, and Net Foreign Direct Investment Flows to LDCs

Table A.1
The Debt Rescheduling Determinants of Less Developed Countries

Country Group	GNP per Capita in U.S. Dollars, 1992	Debt in Millions of U.S. Dollars, 1992	Debt to GNP Ratio (%), 1992	Debt to Exports of Goods and Services Ratio (%), 1992
Middle-Income Countries				
1. Albania	760	625.00	0.21	750.80
2. Algeria	1750	26349.00	0.60	204.30
3. Angola	950	9645.00	140.50	279.20
4. Argentina	3400	67569.00	30.10	453.50
5. Armenia	780	10.00	10.00	11.00
6. Azerbaijan	740	1300.00	23.00	1.60
7. Barbados	7000	620.00	36.70	78.30
8. Belarus	2930	181.00	40.00	90.00
9. Belize	1635	170.00	38.50	68.00

Table A.1 *(continued)*

Country Group	GNP per Capita in U.S. Dollars, 1992	Debt in Millions of U.S. Dollars, 1992	Debt to GNP Ratio (%), 1992	Debt to Exports of Goods and Services Ratio (%), 1992
10. Bolivia	670	4243.00	83.60	536.40
11. Botswana	2450	545.00	15.10	24.50
12. Brazil	2350	121110.00	31.30	310.70
13. Bulgaria	3800	12146.00	111.00	203.20
14. Cameroon	1040	6554.00	67.20	303.80
15. Cape Verde	800	160.00	45.20	210.00
16. Chile	2730	19360.00	49.30	149.30
17. Colombia	1330	17204.00	36.70	161.80
18. Congo	1030	4751.00	185.20	349.10
19. Costa Rica	1960	3965.00	63.20	149.70
20. Czech Republic	2450	9328.00	28.80	70.00
21. Djibouti	1030	189.00	39.50	67.00
22. Dominica	2100	93.00	51.20	83.00
23. Dominican Republic	1050	4639.00	62.00	185.00
24. Ecuador	1070	12280.00	102.10	339.00
25. El Salvador	1170	2131.00	33.40	130.40
26. Estonia	2760	51.20	1.10	30.00
27. Fiji	1900	337.00	22.20	36.00
28. Gabon	4450	3799.00	71.00	150.00
29. Georgia	850	84.80	20.00	90.00
30. Grenada	3000	109.00	53.00	111.00
31. Guatemala	980	2749.00	27.00	150.00
32. Hungary	2970	21900.00	65.00	157.00
33. Iran	2200	14166.00	12.80	67.50
34. Jamaica	1340	4304.00	153.60	154.40
35. Jordan	1120	7977.00	179.10	223.00
36. Kazakhstan	1680	24.90	5.00	25.00
37. Korea Republic	6790	42999.00	14.60	47.20
38. Kyrgyz Republic	820	0.00	0.00	0.00
39. Lebanon	1400	1812.00	30.20	93.40
40. Lithuania	1310	37.70	8.00	15.00
41. Malaysia	2790	19837.00	36.10	42.30
42. Malta	7600	603.30	24.20	26.60
43. Mauritius	2700	1048.00	35.00	54.60
44. Mexico	3470	113378.00	35.20	243.20
45. Moldova	1300	37.50	2.00	3.00
46. Mongolia	1000	375.00	29.60	96.00
47. Morocco	1030	21418.00	78.00	258.50
48. Oman	6480	2854.00	28.00	46.00
49. Panama	2420	6485.00	111.00	223.00
50. Papua New Guinea	950	3736.00	97.00	171.00
51. Paraguay	1380	1747.00	28.00	114.00
52. Peru	950	20297.00	95.40	453.00
53. Philippines	770	32589.00	61.00	185.00
54. Poland	1910	48521.00	54.00	301.00
55. Portugal	7450	32046.00	40.00	103.00
56. Romania	1130	3520.00	16.00	88.00
57. Russia	2510	78658.00	40.00	88.00
58. Senegal	780	3607.00	58.00	226.10
59. Seychelles	5200	181.00	48.00	68.00
60. Slovak Republic	1930	1900.00	6.00	53.00
61. Solomon Islands	600	90.90	39.00	109.00
62. St. Kitts and Nevis	3500	43.30	23.40	48.00

Table A.1 *(continued)*

Country Group	GNP per Capita in U.S. Dollars, 1992	Debt in Millions of U.S. Dollars, 1992	Debt to GNP Ratio (%), 1992	Debt to Exports of Goods and Services Ratio (%), 1992
63. St. Lucia	1650	96.40	21.20	29.20
64. St. Vincent/Grenadines	1500	62.60	29.00	54.00
65. Swaziland	800	240.00	25.00	33.30
66. Syria	2300	16513.00	104.00	301.00
67. Thailand	1840	39424.00	36.30	95.00
68. Tonga	900	43.10	31.10	81.00
69. Trinidad & Tobago	3940	2262.00	46.00	110.00
70. Tunisia	1720	8476.00	55.50	125.50
71. Turkey	1980	54772.00	51.00	193.00
72. Ukraine	1820	415.00	0.40	88.00
73. Uruguay	3340	5253.00	47.00	196.00
74. Uzbekistan	850	15.50	2.00	20.00
75. Vanuatu	900	40.40	21.00	31.00
76. Venezuela	2910	37193.00	62.50	220.00
77. Western Samoa	690	117.60	78.00	225.00
78. Former Yugoslavia	1600	16294.00	20.40	88.00

Low-Income Countries

Country Group	GNP per Capita in U.S. Dollars, 1992	Debt in Millions of U.S. Dollars, 1992	Debt to GNP Ratio (%), 1992	Debt to Exports of Goods and Services Ratio (%), 1992
1. Bangladesh	20	13189.00	55.70	397.30
2. Benin	410	1367.00	64.50	232.20
3. Bhutan	180	83.40	34.90	94.40
4. Burkina Faso	300	1055.00	35.90	191.20
5. Burundi	210	1023.00	94.40	1037.30
6. Central African Republic	410	901.00	68.40	523.30
7. Chad	220	729.00	56.10	318.30
8. China	470	69321.00	16.00	76.00
9. Comoros	540	173.00	66.20	328.70
10. Egypt	640	40431.00	116.80	246.60
11. Equatorial Guinea	380	246.00	165.50	391.00
12. Ethiopia	110	4354.00	65.60	562.00
13. Gambia	325	379.00	102.00	171.00
14. Ghana	450	4275.00	63.10	380.80
15. Guinea	510	2652.00	86.00	384.00
16. Guinea-Bissau	220	634.00	290.00	9753.00
17. Guyana	370	1879.00	769.00	675.00
18. Haiti	340	773.00	29.00	186.00
19. Honduras	580	3573.00	114.20	334.00
20. India	310	76983.00	32.30	297.00
21. Indonesia	670	84385.00	67.00	231.00
22. Kenya	310	6367.00	76.00	268.00
23. Laos	200	1922.00	165.50	1670.00
24. Lesotho	590	472.00	42.00	77.00
25. Liberia	400	1952.00	161.00	395.00
26. Madagascar	230	4385.00	154.00	951.50
27. Malawi	210	1699.99	96.00	392.00
28. Maldives	620	97.00	81.30	49.00
29. Mali	310	2595.00	93.20	452.00
30. Mauritania	530	2303.00	206.00	445.00
31. Mozambique	60	4928.00	584.00	1360.00
32. Myanmar	100	5326.00	14.10	682.00
33. Nepal	170	1797.00	62.20	314.00

Table A.1 *(continued)*

Country Group	GNP per Capita in U.S. Dollars, 1992	Debt in Millions of U.S. Dollars, 1992	Debt to GNP Ratio (%), 1992	Debt to Exports of Goods and Services Ratio (%), 1992
34. Nicaragua	340	11126.00	823.00	3466.00
35. Niger	280	1711.00	74.00	491.00
36. Nigeria	320	30998.00	111.00	251.00
37. Pakistan	420	24072.00	48.00	243.10
38. Rwanda	250	873.00	55.40	584.00
39. Sao Tome and Principe	315	190.00	510.20	1824.80
40. Sierra Leone	160	1265.00	202.50	550.00
41. Somalia	100	2447.00	284.00	2600.00
42. Sri Lanka	540	6401.00	66.50	168.00
43. Sudan	184	16085.00	221.00	3265.30
44. Tajikistan	490	9.70	25.00	125.00
45. Tanzania	110	6715.00	268.40	1210.00
46. Togo	390	1356.00	86.50	247.00
47. Uganda	170	2991.00	97.00	1518.00
48. Yemen	600	6516.00	86.20	286.00
49. Zaire	235	10912.00	111.00	442.00
50. Zambia	550	7041.00	386.00	576.60
51. Zimbabwe	545	4007.00	74.00	217.00

	Total Debt Services to Exports of Goods and Services (%) (Debt/Service Ratio), 1992	International Reserves to Imports of Goods and Services Ratio (Months), 1992	Number of Rescheduling of Debt from January 1980 to September 1993

Middle-Income Countries

1. Albania	80.00	3.00	0
2. Algeria	71.90	3.00	1
3. Angola	7.20	2.00	1
4. Argentina	34.90	6.00	10
5. Armenia	5.00	3.00	0
6. Azerbaijan	10.00	1.00	0
7. Barbados	16.80	1.20	0
8. Belarus	15.00	2.00	0
9. Belize	7.90	2.00	0
10. Bolivia	39.10	3.70	9
11. Botswana	3.40	17.60	0
12. Brazil	24.40	8.00	9
13. Bulgaria	6.90	5.00	2
14. Cameroon	16.20	0.10	2
15. Cape Verde	10.10	6.00	0
16. Chile	21.00	8.40	10
17. Colombia	35.30	8.60	3
18. Congo	11.40	0.10	2
19. Costa	20.70	3.90	8
20. Czech Republic	11.00	3.80	0
21. Djibouti	4.40	2.50	0
22. Dominica	5.00	1.50	0
23. Dominican Republic	13.50	2.00	5
24. Ecuador	27.10	3.30	7

Table A.1 *(continued)*

	Total Debt Services to Exports of Goods and Services (%) (Debt/Service Ratio), 1992	International Reserves to Imports of Goods and Services Ratio (Months), 1992	Number of Rescheduling of Debt from January 1980 to September 1993
47. Uganda	41.00	1.50	6
48. Yemen	9.10	1.10	0
49. Zaire	15.00	1.00	13
50. Zambia	29.30	1.40	6
51. Zimbabwe	32.00	1.80	0

	Amount of Debt Rescheduling from January 1980 to September 1993 (in Millions of U.S. Dollars)	Military Expenditure as a Percentage of GNP, 1989
Middle-Income Countries		
1. Albania	0	4.10
2. Algeria	100	5.10
3. Angola	365	24.00
4. Argentina	40813	3.40
5. Armenia	0	30.00
6. Azerbaijan	0	32.00
7. Barbados	0	0.60
8. Belarus	0	1.00
9. Belize	0	2.00
10. Bolivia	2364	4.30
11. Botswana	0	2.80
12. Brazil	108,739	1.30
13. Bulgaria	706	11.90
14. Cameroon	1227	1.30
15. Cape Verde	0	11.00
16. Chile	21755	3.40
17. Colombia	350	2.10
18. Congo	1610	6.50
19. Costa Rica	0	0.50
20. Czech Republic	0	6.80
21. Djibouti	0	2.00
22. Dominica	0	3.00
23. Dominican Republic	2382	0.80
24. Ecuador	8562	1.70
25. El Salvador	135	4.00
26. Estonia	0	5.00
27. Fiji	0	2.20
28. Gabon	1979	4.50
29. Georgia	0	12.00
30. Grenada	0	5.00
31. Guatemala	440	1.60
32. Hungary	0	6.30
33. Iran	0	7.00
34. Jamaica	2465	1.10
35. Jordan	2060	12.70
36. Kazakhstan	0	6.00
37. Korea Republic	0	4.30

Table A.1 *(continued)*

	Amount of Debt Rescheduling from January 1980 to September 1993 (in Millions of U.S. Dollars)	Military Expenditure as a Percentage of GNP, 1989
38. Kyrgz Republic	0	7.00
39. Lebanon	0	11.00
40. Lithuania	0	10.00
41. Malaysia	0	2.90
42. Malta	0	1.10
43. Mauritius	0	0.20
44. Mexico	131832	0.50
45. Moldova	0	3.00
46. Mongolia	0	10.00
47. Morocco	13550	5.50
48. Oman	0	20.30
49. Panama	780	3.40
50. Papua New Guinea	0	1.40
51. Paraguay	0	1.40
52. Peru	9827	5.20
53. Philippines	21069	2.20
54. Poland	80767	8.90
55. Portugal	0	3.30
56. Romania	4194	6.10
57. Russia	15000	15.00
58. Senegal	1125	2.00
59. Seychelles	0	2.00
60. Slovak Republic	0	10.00
61. Solomon Islands	0	2.00
62. St. Kitts and Nevis	0	1.00
63. St. Lucia	0	1.00
64. St. Vincent/Grenadines	0	1.20
65. Swaziland	0	1.70
66. Syria	0	11.60
67. Thailand	0	2.70
68. Tonga	0	3.30
69. Trinidad & Tobago	891	1.60
70. Tunisia	0	2.80
71. Turkey	4869	4.10
72. Ukraine	0	10.00
73. Uruguay	3787	2.10
74. Uzbekistan	0	12.00
75. Vanuatu	0	2.00
76. Venezuela	41477	1.00
77. Western Samoa	0	12.00
78. Former Yugoslavia	16358	3.60

Low-Income Countries

1. Bangladesh	0	1.60
2. Benin	362	2.00
3. Bhutan	0	1.00
4. Burkina Faso	101	2.10
5. Burundi	0	2.60
6. Central African Republic	107	1.70
7. Chad	33	4.30
8. China	0	3.70

Table A.1 *(continued)*

	Amount of Debt Rescheduling from January 1980 to September 1993 (in Millions of U.S. Dollars)	Military Expenditure as a Percentage of GNP, 1989
9. Comoros	0	2.00
10. Egypt	27535	5.00
11. Equatorial Guinea	26	3.00
12. Ethiopia	330	12.80
13. Gambia	38	0.70
14. Ghana	0	0.60
15. Guinea	606	1.20
16. Guinea-Bissau	64	2.40
17. Guyana	498	2.70
18. Haiti	0	1.90
19. Honduras	893	3.20
20. India	0	3.10
21. Indonesia	0	1.70
22. Kenya	0	2.70
23. Laos	0	11.00
24. Lesotho	0	2.20
25. Liberia	131	4.80
26. Madagascar	1908	1.50
27. Malawi	179	2.30
28. Maldives	0	3.00
29. Mali	183	2.00
30. Mauritania	399	4.30
31. Mozambique	2067	9.70
32. Myanmar	0	3.70
33. Nepal	0	1.20
34. Nicaragua	1571	18.00
35. Niger	577	1.30
36. Nigeria	24053	0.50
37. Pakistan	263	6.80
38. Rwanda	0	2.00
39. Sao Tome and Principe	0	1.60
40. Sierra Leone	470	0.70
41. Somalia	221	6.00
42. Sri Lanka	0	3.20
43. Sudan	3323	2.20
44. Tajikistan	0	5.00
45. Tanzania	1949	4.10
46. Togo	892	3.30
47. Uganda	565	1.60
48. Yemen	0	9.10
49. Zaire	5617	2.60
50. Zambia	2961	1.40
51. Zimbabwe	0	6.70

Sources: The data reported in Table A.1 were calculated by Mashaalah Rahnama-Moghadam. Each of these variables was calculated from data available from published sources. Per capita income is from CIA's *Factbook, 1994* (Washington, D.C.: U.S. Government Printing Office, 1994). Debt, debt to GNP ratio, debt to export ratio, total debt services to exports ratio, international reserve to imports ratio, the number of reschedulings of debt, and the amounts of debt rescheduled are from *World Debt Tables, 1993–94* (Washington, D.C.: World Bank, 1993). Military expenditure is from the CIA's *Military Expenditures and Arms Transfers* (Washington, D.C.: U.S. Government Printing Office, 1991).

Table A.2
Commercial Bank Claims on Developing Countries
(Millions of U.S. Dollars)

Country Group	1992	1993
All Developing Countries	691385	703490
Sub-Saharan Africa	34614	32078
East Asia and the Pacific	191665	205399
Europe and Central Asia	155353	158028
Latin America and the Caribbean	224903	225347
Middle East and North Africa	61187	59551
South Asia	23663	23087
Severely Indebted Middle-Income	254234	252509
Severely Indebted Low-Income	29987	29473
Moderately Indebted Low-Income	60686	60918
Moderately Indebted Middle-Income	136656	138925

Source: Financial Flows and the Developing Countries (Washington, D.C.: World Bank, August 1994).

Table A.3
Net Foreign Direct Investment Flows to LDCs
(Millions of U.S. Dollars)

Country Group	1990	1991	1992	1993
All Developing Countries	26339	36876	47267	56283
Sub-Saharan Africa	856	1774	1613	1765
East Asia and the Pacific	11038	14029	20487	25462
Europe and Central Asia	4711	7011	8529	8987
Latin America and the Caribbean	7668	12374	14506	17510
Middle East and North Africa	1595	1211	1564	1892
South Asia	469	475	566	667
Severely Indebted Middle-Income	5658	9814	13004	15745
Severely Indebted Low-Income	1764	1254	1655	1752
Moderately Indebted Low-Income	1502	1906	2255	2495
Moderately Indebted Middle-Income	4210	7650	7787	8677

Source: Financial Flows and the Developing Countries (Washington, D.C.: World Bank, August 1994).

Health, Education, Electricity, Telephones, and Transportation (HEETT) Index

The HEETT index is a measure of infrastructure calculated from published data sources. The narrative portion of this appendix is divided into three sections. The first section describes the data and their sources. The second section discusses the structure of the HEETT index (e.g., how it was constructed). The third section describes the inferences that may be appropriately drawn from the index, and what inferences cannot.

Table B.1 reports the raw numbers for each of the component areas, with only the transportation numbers being adjusted for population density. The total HEETT index was calculated and reported in the table.

DATA AND THEIR SOURCES

The data from which the HEETT index was constructed are from published sources. There are nine sub-indices that were constructed to describe each of the five areas contained in the HEETT index. Health has two sub-indices, education has two sub-indices, electricity has only kilowatt hours (kwh) per capita, telephones has only number of telephones per thousand persons, and transportation has three sub-indices. The data used to construct HEETT are for calendar year 1993. Each of these components of the HEETT index will be discussed in turn in the following sections.

Scaling across All Categories

An index is simply a scale. In this context, the absolute value of the index means nothing. It is the relative value either across countries or over time that has meaning. In each category, the index is constructed so that the maximum number in the scale (4) indicates that the particular country has infrastructure that is at least equal to the four worst industrialized countries.

To make the HEETT comparable to developed countries, the base for the index was constructed using the four developed countries with the least infrastructure in the particular category being examined. To eliminate scalar problems, the industrialized countries' average is used as the denominator if a larger number reflects more or better infrastructure. If a smaller number reflects more or better infrastructure, then the developed countries' average is used as the numerator. This process eliminates scaling problems that would make inference from the index impossible.

Health

The health portion of the HEETT index consists of two sub-indices. These are infant mortality per thousand live births and number of physicians per thousand persons. Both series of data are published by the World Bank in *World Development Report, 1994* (New York: Oxford University Press, 1994).

For the infant mortality rate, the four worst industrialized nations were Ireland, New Zealand, Australia, and Italy. The average infant mortality index for these four industrialized countries is 8.25. Because a higher infant mortality rate is associated with less infrastructure capability, the industrialized countries' average is used as the numerator in the infant mortality index and the observation for each country is used as the denominator.

For physicians per thousand persons the four worst industrialized countries were Ireland, New Zealand, Sweden, and Japan (1.6 per thousand persons). The average number of physicians per thousand persons is the denominator in the fraction for the physician per thousand persons index, with the individual country observation being the numerator.

Again, remember that the reason the worst four industrialized countries were used as the numerator in the infant mortality index and the denominator in the physicians per thousand index is to make the scale consistent. The higher the infant morality per thousand live births, the worse the health care system, ceteris paribus; and the more physicians per thousand persons, the better the health care system, ceteris paribus.

Education

Student/teacher ratios in primary schools and literacy rates are the two subcomponent indices for education. The standard measure of the effectiveness of educational systems in LDCs has been the student/teacher ratios in primary schools, most other measures of education are known to be highly correlated with this ratio.[1] However, even though there is a strong correlation between these two indices, literacy rates are descriptive of present labor force characteristics, while student/teacher ratios in primary schools are indicative of future qualitative aspects of the labor force in that country. Therefore, these two indices are complementary in the information they contain about education over time.

The literacy rate is from *The World Factbook* prepared by the CIA (Washington, D.C.: U.S. Government Printing Office, 1993). The four industrialized countries with the lowest literacy rates were Spain, Italy, United States, and Japan (97 percent). The industrialized countries' average was used as the denominator and the individual country's observation was used as the numerator in the literacy rate index.

The student/teacher ratios are from *World Development Report, 1994*. The four industrialized countries with the highest student/teacher ratios were Ireland, Japan, Spain, and the United Kingdom (22.25 students per teacher). The industrialized countries' average for student/teacher ratios was used as the numerator and the denominator was the individual country observation in the students per teacher index. Again, the data reported in the table for this variable are the raw numbers.

Electricity

The kilowatt hours of electricity per capita data are from the CIA's *Factbook* (1993). The lowest four industrialized countries in this category were Italy, Ireland, Netherlands, and Spain and their average was 4,095 kilowatt hours of electricity per person. The industrialized countries' average was used as the denominator and the country's observation was the numerator in this index. Remember that the data in the table for this variable are the raw numbers.

Telephones

The data concerning telephones per thousand persons are also from the CIA's *Factbook* (1993). The four industrialized countries with the fewest telephones per thousand persons were Spain, Ireland, Italy, and Belgium, with an average of 447.6 telephones per thousand people. In constructing this component of the index, the industrialized countries' average was used as the denominator, and the country's observation is the numerator in this fraction. Again, the raw numbers appear in the table.

Transportation

All the data for these three sub-indices are from the CIA's *Factbook* (1993). Each of the indices in this group are adjusted for population and land mass (population density). Population divided by land in square kilometers yields a number called population density. The population densities for each country in the world were indexed against the four industrialized countries with the lowest population densities. Each of the transportation components were also standardized using the total kilometers of railroads and highways and number of airports. The four industrialized countries with the lowest number of kilometers of highways divided by population density were Spain, United Kingdom, Italy, and Germany (average = 5.26 kilometers). The industrialized countries with lowest kilometers of railroads divided by population density were Spain, United Kingdom, Netherlands, and Japan (average 0.29 kilometers). The four industrialized countries with the lowest number of airports divided by population density were New Zealand, Netherlands, Belgium, and Switzerland (average 64 airports). The industrialized countries' average was used as the denominator and the individual country observation as the numerator in each of these ratios. Remember that the numbers reported in the table are raw numbers.

Index Structure

Again, the HEETT index is reported as an equally weighted average of the nine sub-indices calculated. Each of the sub-indices and the total HEETT index are reported in Table B.1. Therefore, the total HEETT index is a weighted index. The health component comprises two-ninths of the total, education is two-ninths, electricity is one-ninth, telephones is one-ninth, and transportation is one-third. The direct capital portion of infrastructure (electricity, transportation, and telephones), therefore, comprises five-ninths of the index; and the human resources portion is four-ninths of the index.

The HEETT index is constructed by calculating each of the sub-indices and then adding them. The sum of the sub-indices is then divided by nine. This process equally weights each of the sub-indices. If the averages for each of the industrialized countries are calculated for each subcomponent of the HEETT index, the value for these averages will be one.

The index number calculated is multiplied by four. Numbers greater than four are ignored. This scaling permits variations in the index to be more readily noticed and is similar to the process used in the Gorman Report for colleges and universities. A value of four for any LDC indicates that the infrastructure in that country, as measured here, is equal to the average of the four worst industrialized countries for each category.

Some Caveats in the Use of the HEETT Index

It must be remembered that this indexing system results in a quantitative measure of the development of the level of a country's infrastructure. Nothing concerning the quality of any particular component of the infrastructure is explicitly included in the measures. However, to the extent that infant mortality or literacy rates imply something about quality, there can be qualitative inference.

The weighting of the HEETT index of 40 percent human resources and 60 percent physical capital was dictated by the availability of data rather than the empirical evidence that capital/labor ratios of businesses operating in LDCs is about 1.5. However, the assumed capital/labor ratio for infrastructure of 1.5 does not appear to be out of line with the experience of most operations in LDCs.

The HEETT index is no more accurate than the underlying data from which it was constructed. The sources of data used here were the U.S. CIA and the World Bank. Neither organization has any particular ax to grind, and the data-gathering processes they used are available in their publications. It is left to the reader to decide how trustworthy these data sources are.

An LDC with a HEETT index of 4.0 has infrastructure that is quantitatively comparable to the worst infrastructure available in the developed countries.

As the index number moves toward 0, one may infer that there is quantitatively less physical or human capital available in those LDCs. For example, in the former Soviet Republics, 4.0 is commonly observed for this index. In fact, most of the human resources and capital characteristics found in the former Soviet Republics are comparable to those found in the industrialized countries with the least infrastructure. In countries such as Afghanistan and Bangladesh, the HEETT indices calculated are less than 1, indicating that there is very little physical capital and relatively poor stocks of human capital, consistent with the raw data reported here.

The authors intended the HEETT index to be only a rough quantitative guide to the availability of infrastructure. Low numbers in this index are a clear warning that there may be serious problems with normal infrastructure-related support systems. Clearly, numbers less than 2.0 are cause for concern. Numbers close to 4.0 indicate that there may not be quantitative difficulties with infrastructure, but quality may still pose constraints. Even with an index number of 4.0, the reader would be well advised to seek specific information concerning any element of infrastructure that is critical to the prospective business enterprise in that country.

NOTE

1. Daniel Cohen, "Low Investment and Large LDC Debt in the 1980s," *American Economic Review* 83 (3; June 1993): 437–449.

Table B.1
HEETT Index and Component Indices, 1993

Country Group	Scaled Railroads (km)	Scaled Highways (km)	Scaled Number of Airports	Telephone per 1000 People	Electricity per capita (kwh)
High-Income Countries					
1. Australia	2.27	46.90	52.17	488.00	8475
2. Austria	0.72	47.00	177.42	488.00	8475
3. Belgium	0.35	10.30	144.80	470.00	6790
4. Canada	5.30	31.84	117.35	648.20	17900
5. Denmark	0.50	12.80	655.50	871.00	6610
6. Finland	1.17	20.39	313.70	621.70	11050
7. France	0.60	26.90	222.20	681.00	7430
8. Germany	0.40	5.80	199.60	498.90	7160
9. Ireland	0.55	26.15	235.30	254.90	4120
10. Italy	0.34	5.14	74.40	441.20	4060
11. Japan	0.30	10.00	443.00	500.00	6700
12. Netherlands	0.18	7.09	63.60	616.50	4200
13. New Zealand	1.40	27.50	300.00	626.30	9250
14. Norway	0.90	18.50	214.60	722.00	25850
15. Spain	0.39	3.85	66.40	391.00	4000
16. Sweden	1.40	11.10	346.60	939.00	16560
17. Switzerland	0.60	8.90	287.00	843.00	8200
18. United Kingdom	0.31	6.26	275.50	520.90	5480
19. United States	1.00	30.00	814.70	500.00	12690
High-Income Less Developed Countries					
20. Hong Kong	0.00	0.20	14.18	540.00	4980
21. Israel	0.12	0.96	353.30	366.00	4600
22. Kuwait	0.00	2.30	63.60	59.00	8890
23. Singapore	0.02	0.90	12.60	393.00	6420
24. United Arab Emirates	0.00	0.70	231.20	145.30	6718
Middle-Income Countries					
25. Albania	0.16	5.00	100.00	45.00	1520
26. Algeria	0.15	3.30	5.00	30.16	630
27. Angola	0.33	7.73	188.75	4.22	84
28. Argentina	1.02	6.20	422.90	79.00	1559
29. Armenia	0.24	3.25	100.00	74.70	2585
30. Azerbaijan	0.30	4.84	216.70	85.00	2990
31. Bahamas	0.00	0.03	60.00	368.00	3599
32. Bahrain	0.00	0.35	214.30	173.00	8500
33. Barbados	0.00	6.15	3.35	348.60	2118
34. Belize	0.00	13.29	42.00	42.40	393
35. Bermuda	0.00	3.46	66.70	67.90	8370
36. Bolivia	0.49	5.10	850.70	19.13	250
37. Botswana	0.54	8.70	138.90	19.60	846
38. Brazil	0.19	9.00	262.60	65.00	1531
39. Brunei	0.05	3.90	153.80	119.00	3300
40. Bulgaria	0.50	4.18	1055.60	294.40	5070
41. Burma	0.09	0.62	43.70	1.20	65
42. Cameroon	0.08	5.09	67.82	2.04	190
43. Cape Verde	0.00	0.00	375.00	4.10	40
44. Chile	0.56	5.75	324.60	55.80	1630

	Literacy Rate (%)	Student/ Teacher Ratio	Number of Physicians per 1000 People	Infant Mortality Rate per 1000 Live Births	Overall HEETT Index
High-Income Countries					
1. Australia	100	17	2.00	7	4.00
2. Austria	100	11	2.00	7	4.00
3. Belgium	99	10	.23	9	4.00
4. Canada	99	15	2.22	7	4.00
5. Denmark	99	11	2.60	7	4.00
6. Finland	100	18	2.40	6	4.00
7. France	99	12	2.90	7	4.00
8. Germany	99	17	2.70	6	4.00
9. Ireland	98	27	1.60	5	4.00
10. Italy	97	12	4.76	8	4.00
11. Japan	99	21	1.64	5	4.00
12. Netherlands	99	10	2.40	6	4.00
13. New Zealand	99	19	1.40	7	4.00
14. Norway	99	6	2.00	6	4.00
15. Spain	95	21	3.60	8	4.00
16. Sweden	99	6	2.70	5	4.00
17. Switzerland	99	10	1.60	6	4.00
18. United Kingdom	99	20	2.00	7	4.00
19. United States	98	15	2.40	9	4.00
High-Income Less Developed Countries					
20. Hong Kong	77	27	1.50	6	3.23
21. Israel	92	17	1.00	9	4.00
22. Kuwait	73	15	2.00	10	3.57
23. Singapore	88	26	1.22	5	3.12
24. United Arab Emirates	68	18	1.00	19	2.50
Middle-Income Countries					
25. Albania	72	19	1.00	32	2.72
26. Algeria	57	28	0.50	55	1.46
27. Angola	42	40	1.00	65	3.00
28. Argentina	95	18	3.33	29	4.00
29. Armenia	100	8	4.00	21	4.00
30. Azerbaijan	98	10	1.60	8	4.00
31. Bahamas	90	45	2.00	55	2.43
32. Bahrain	77	50	1.00	75	2.88
33. Barbados	99	60	1.00	90	2.06
34. Belize	91	55	2.00	95	2.68
35. Bermuda	98	40	2.00	80	3.82
36. Bolivia	78	25	1.00	82	4.00
37. Botswana	72	30	0.20	35	3.45
38. Brazil	81	23	1.00	57	4.00
39. Brunei	77	50	1.00	98	2.81
40. Bulgaria	93	15	4.00	16	4.00
41. Burma	81	35	1.00	78	1.48
42. Cameroon	54	51	0.08	61	1.60
43. Cape Verde	66	43	0.50	98	3.32
44. Chile	93	25	0.50	17	4.00

Table B.1 *(continued)*

Country Group	Scaled Railroads (km)	Scaled Highways (km)	Scaled Number of Airports	Telephone per 1000 People	Electricity per capita (kwh)
45. Colombia	0.10	2.16	560.40	54.10	1050
46. Congo	0.33	5.00	64.00	7.60	135
47. Costa Rica	0.30	4.80	1157.40	89.40	1130
48. Czech Republic	0.91	5.40	202.70	192.50	6030
49. Dominican Republic	0.22	1.56	144.00	24.73	660
50. Ecuador	0.09	2.68	295.00	30.40	700
51. El Salvador	0.11	1.80	603.40	20.60	390
52. Estonia	0.64	18.65	311.83	186.51	700
53. Gabon	0.60	6.70	206.10	133.60	920
54. Georgia	0.28	6.02	168.20	119.30	2835
55. Greece	0.24	3.70	185.70	389.70	3610
56. Guatemala	0.10	4.83	1215.40	9.30	260
57. Guyana	0.25	10.40	53.00	36.70	370
58. Hungary	0.75	12.60	242.10	109.30	3000
59. Iran	0.08	2.20	62.20	35.00	710
60. Iraq	0.13	1.80	114.00	34.00	700
61. Ivory Coast	0.05	3.37	57.53	6.35	150
62. Jamaica	0.12	7.20	514.30	50.20	1090
63. Jordan	0.21	2.00	95.00	21.40	1070
64. Kazakhstan	0.84	11.02	104.30	60.00	4739
65. Korea Republic	0.07	1.41	181.70	297.60	2380
66. Latvia	0.90	21.75	357.10	36.00	2125
67. Libya	0.00	4.00	64.80	76.00	2952
68. Lithuania	2.00	6.00	167.00	100.00	3000
69. Malaysia	0.09	1.25	129.00	52.80	1610
70. Mauritius	0.00	1.63	156.20	43.40	570
71. Mexico	0.30	2.30	301.10	70.90	1300
72. Mongolia	0.74	5.26	43.50	26.60	1622
73. Morocco	0.07	2.12	59.30	10.02	317
74. Namibia	0.52	5.36	139.80	40.70	850
75. Oman	0.00	15.80	292.80	30.40	3200
76. Panama	0.09	3.30	659.00	85.30	1720
77. Papua New Guinea	0.00	4.68	400.00	17.07	400
78. Paraguay	0.20	4.33	201.00	15.44	3280
79. Peru	0.08	3.01	110.70	23.44	760
80. Philippines	0.00	2.30	128.00	12.74	420
81. Poland	0.70	9.36	119.80	105.00	3750
82. Portugal	0.30	7.00	173.00	256.50	2510
83. Puerto Rico	0.03	3.60	300.00	263.40	4260
84. Romania	0.50	3.14	175.50	985.00	2540
85. Russia	1.00	5.30	109.00	106.00	6824
86. Saudi Arabia	0.08	4.20	81.00	92.20	3690
87. Senegal	0.12	1.65	56.80	7.10	100
88. Slovak Republic	0.70	3.30	179.00	18.60	4550
89. South Africa	0.48	4.40	361.00	105.10	4100
90. Syria	0.14	2.02	179.30	37.00	830
91. Taiwan	0.22	0.95	68.00	364.00	4718
92. Thailand	0.06	1.32	50.50	12.60	760
93. Trinidad & Tobago	0.00	6.10	150.00	82.90	2680
94. Tunisia	0.25	2.06	70.70	28.00	600
95. Turkey	0.14	5.26	44.00	55.80	750
96. Turkmenistan	0.54	5.90	10.60	65.00	3079
97. Ukraine	0.44	5.30	341.90	135.00	5410

	Literacy Rate (%)	Student/ Teacher Ratio	Number of Physicians per 1000 People	Infant Mortality Rate per 1000 Live Births	Overall HEETT Index
45. Colombia	87	30	1.00	21	3.30
46. Congo	57	55	0.20	110	2.11
47. Costa Rica	93	32	1.00	14	4.00
48. Czech Republic	90	10	4.00	10	4.00
49. Dominican Republic	83	47	1.00	41	2.52
50. Ecuador	86	20	1.10	45	3.78
51. El Salvador	73	44	0.50	40	2.00
52. Estonia	100	20	5.00	13	4.00
53. Gabon	61	44	0.25	94	3.76
54. Georgia	100	8	5.90	19	4.00
55. Greece	93	20	2.00	8	4.00
56. Guatemala	55	34	1.00	62	3.60
57. Guyana	95	40	0.06	100	2.44
58. Hungary	99	12	3.33	15	4.00
59. Iran	54	31	0.33	65	1.70
60. Iraq	60	30	0.25	30	2.04
61. Ivory Coast	54	37	0.10	91	1.37
62. Jamaica	98	37	1.00	14	3.40
63. Jordan	80	24	1.30	28	2.55
64. Kazakhstan	100	15	4.00	31	4.00
65. Korea Republic	96	34	1.00	13	3.34
66. Latvia	100	8	5.00	17	4.00
67. Libya	64	20	1.00	20	2.43
68. Lithuania	100	10	4.00	16	4.00
69. Malaysia	78	20	0.50	14	2.62
70. Mauritius	61	21	1.00	18	2.56
71. Mexico	87	30	1.00	35	4.00
72. Mongolia	60	25	3.33	60	3.73
73. Morocco	50	27	0.21	57	3.27
74. Namibia	38	20	0.25	57	3.15
75. Oman	50	27	1.00	20	3.95
76. Panama	88	20	1.20	21	3.32
77. Papua New Guinea	52	31	0.08	54	3.87
78. Paraguay	90	25	1.00	36	3.63
79. Peru	85	28	1.50	52	2.48
80. Philippines	90	33	0.12	40	1.99
81. Poland	98	17	2.00	14	4.00
82. Portugal	85	14	2.50	9	4.00
83. Puerto Rico	89	10	1.00	8	4.00
84. Romania	98	17	2.00	23	4.00
85. Russia	100	10	5.00	20	4.00
86. Saudi Arabia	62	16	2.00	28	3.12
87. Senegal	38	58	0.06	68	1.15
88. Slovak Republic	80	18	4.00	13	4.00
89. South Africa	76	20	1.00	53	4.00
90. Syria	64	25	1.00	36	2.83
91. Taiwan	86	20	2.00	30	3.24
92. Thailand	93	18	0.25	26	1.90
93. Trinidad &Tobago	95	26	1.00	15	3.26
94. Tunisia	65	26	1.00	48	2.22
95. Turkey	81	29	1.00	54	2.15
96. Turkmenistan	100	10	4.00	54	4.00
97. Ukraine	100	8	4.35	18	4.00

Table B.1 *(continued)*

Country Group	Scaled Railroads (km)	Scaled Highways (km)	Scaled Number of Airports	Telephone per 1000 People	Electricity per capita (kwh)
98. Uruguay	0.90	15.70	214.80	106.10	1900
99. Uzbekistan	0.16	3.54	247.70	72.00	2300
100. Venezuela	0.03	3.90	230.80	71.60	2830

Low-Income Countries

Country Group	Scaled Railroads (km)	Scaled Highways (km)	Scaled Number of Airports	Telephone per 1000 People	Electricity per capita (kwh)
101. Afghanistan	0.00	1.27	24.00	2.00	60
102. Bangladesh	0.02	0.06	4.80	2.00	75
103. Benin	0.10	1.00	26.90	1.50	5
104. Bhutan	0.00	3.09	28.60	7.10	2203
105. Burkina Faso	0.06	1.70	85.70	0.50	40
106. Burundi	0.00	1.00	26.73	1.30	20
107. Central African Repub.	0.00	7.10	83.50	1.60	30
108. Chad	0.00	5.80	43.10	0.90	15
109. China	0.05	1.00	8.00	0.70	1630
110. Egypt	0.08	0.90	34.30	10.00	830
111. Ethiopia	0.02	0.73	45.50	1.90	10
112. Ghana	0.06	1.90	13.70	2.50	300
113. Guinea	0.00	6.10	15.00	5.00	160
114. Guinea-Bissau	0.00	3.00	271.40	2.80	30
115. Haiti	0.00	0.60	68.40	5.60	75
116. Honduras	0.15	1.70	236.00	7.00	390
117. India	0.06	3.00	12.40	5.00	340
118. Indonesia	0.04	0.60	59.60	30.00	200
119. Kenya	0.07	2.36	176.40	9.50	100
120. Lao	0.00	6.00	138.50	1.60	220
121. Lesotho	0.00	3.80	150.00	3.10	100
122. Liberia	0.17	3.50	195.00	17.40	275
123. Madagascar	0.08	3.07	146.00	4.60	35
124. Malawi	0.08	1.30	137.30	4.30	65
125. Mali	0.07	1.80	20.70	1.20	90
126. Mauritania	0.32	3.50	23.80	23.50	70
127. Mozambique	0.20	1.62	145.90	3.70	115
128. Nepal	0.00	0.34	53.60	2.43	50
129. Nicaragua	0.09	6.50	226.00	15.00	290
130. Niger	0.00	4.80	17.00	1.70	30
131. Nigeria	0.04	1.10	21.40	0.60	70
132. Pakistan	0.08	0.90	27.00	7.00	350
133. Rwanda	0.00	0.60	34.80	1.20	15
134. Sierra Leone	0.02	1.60	58.00	5.24	45
135. Somalia	0.00	3.40	28.40	1.50	5
136. Sri Lanka	0.10	4.20	26.40	6.40	200
137. Sudan	0.20	0.70	19.00	1.40	40
138. Tajikestan	0.08	5.10	87.00	100.00	2879
139. Tanzania	0.13	3.00	58.00	3.80	20
140. Togo	0.10	1.60	56.20	2.40	60
141. Uganda	0.07	1.35	41.00	0.50	30
142. Vietnam	0.00	1.40	44.80	6.00	120
143. Yemen	0.00	1.40	51.13	6.00	120
144. Zaire	0.13	3.50	76.00	5.00	160
145. Zambia	0.14	4.10	116.00	50.00	1400
146. Zimbabwe	0.25	7.80	200.00	22.80	830

	Literacy Rate (%)	Student/ Teacher Ratio	Number of Physicians per 1000 People	Infant Mortality Rate per 1000 Live Births	Overall HEETT Index
98. Uruguay	96	22	2.00	20	4.00
99. Uzbekistan	100	23	4.00	42	4.00
100. Venezuela	88	23	2.00	33	3.85
Low-Income Countries					
101. Afghanistan	29	60	0.06	120	0.63
102. Bangladesh	35	63	0.12	91	0.47
103. Benin	23	35	0.04	110	0.86
104. Bhutan	60	15	0.08	129	1.69
105. Burkina Faso	18	58	0.02	132	1.12
106. Burundi	50	66	0.02	106	0.69
107. Central African Republic	27	90	0.04	105	1.46
108. Chad	30	64	0.03	122	1.12
109. China	93	22	0.50	31	1.60
110. Egypt	48	24	0.80	57	1.45
111. Ethiopia	62	30	0.03	122	1.06
112. Ghana	60	29	0.04	81	1.05
113. Guinea	50	49	0.50	133	1.24
114. Guinea-Bissau	36	30	0.06	140	2.68
115. Haiti	53	40	0.05	60	1.11
116. Honduras	73	38	0.32	49	2.82
117. India	48	60	0.40	79	1.02
118. Indonesia	77	23	0.14	66	1.45
119. Kenya	69	31	0.10	66	2.27
120. Laos	84	28	0.23	97	2.33
121. Lesotho	59	54	0.05	46	1.92
122. Liberia	40	30	1.00	55	2.75
123. Madagascar	80	40	0.12	93	2.09
124. Malawi	22	64	0.02	134	2.04
125. Mali	32	47	0.05	130	0.82
126. Mauritania	34	47	0.06	117	1.40
127. Mozambique	33	55	0.06	162	1.84
128. Nepal	26	39	0.06	99	0.84
129. Nicaragua	57	36	0.68	56	3.07
130. Niger	28	42	0.03	123	0.93
131. Nigeria	51	39	0.05	84	0.86
132. Pakistan	35	41	0.34	95	1.34
133. Rwanda	50	58	0.03	117	0.73
134. Sierra Leone	21	34	0.06	143	1.00
135. Somalia	24	20	0.04	132	1.13
136. Sri Lanka	88	12	0.20	18	2.20
137. Sudan	27	34	0.10	99	0.87
138. Tajikestan	100	10	2.90	49	3.58
139. Tanzania	46	36	0.04	92	1.39
140. Togo	43	59	0.04	85	1.08
141. Uganda	48	20	0.11	122	1.29
142. Vietnam	38	32	0.05	100	0.99
143. Yemen	38	37	0.05	106	0.98
144. Zaire	72	20	0.05	58	1.94
145. Zambia	73	30	0.09	107	2.29
146. Zimbabwe	67	39	0.14	47	3.22

Selected, Annotated Bibliography

This bibliography is not intended to be a complete listing of the publications available on LDCs or their debt. The authors have, in their opinion, selected a representative sample of books and articles concerning this topic which should prove adequate to both scholars and practitioners. Many of the entries were selected because they contain substantial reviews of the literature which can guide the readers to more sources. Further, the bibliography contains only those items published since 1984, with particular emphasis on more current publications. The bibliography is divided into two separate sections—one for books and one for articles.

BOOKS

Cardoso, Eliana, and Ann Helwege. *Latin America's Economy: Diversity, Trends, and Conflicts.* Cambridge, Mass.: MIT Press, 1992.
>   *This book provides an economic history of Latin America before proceeding to an analysis of the region's current economic health. There is also a substantial discussion of politics of the region and economic policies.*

Claudon, Michael P., ed. *World Debt Crisis: International Lending on Trial.* Cambridge, Mass.: Ballinger, 1986.
>   *This book is a collection of studies concerning the origin of the debt crisis, appropriate economic policy responses, and international organization responses. The final section of the book contains a discussion of crisis-resolving models for international debt crises.*

Cline, William R. *International Debt: Systematic Risk and Policy Response.* Cambridge, Mass.: MIT Press, 1984.
>   *This book presents a comprehensive analysis of the factor resulting in the rescheduling of LDCs' sovereign loans until 1984. This book is focused on the economic theory of the world debt crisis as it existed in 1984.*

Cooper, Richard N. *Economic Stabilization and Debt in Developing Countries.*
    Cambridge, Mass.: MIT Press, 1992.
    *This book presents arguments that economic stabilization in developed
    countries and the world debt crisis in LDCs are not dichotomous
    problems. To obtain sustained acceptable rates of economic growth in the
    LDCs, the developed countries must maintain economic stability.*

Dornbusch, Rudiger. Stabilization, Debt, and Reform: Policy Analysis for
    Developing Countries. Englewood Cliffs, N.J.: Prentice-Hall, 1993.
    *This book provides a comprehensive discussion of policies and needed
    reform in LDCs across each region of the world. The final section of the
    book presents country studies, including Brazil and Mexico.*

Edwards, Sebastian, and Felipe Larrim. *Debt, Adjustment and Recovery: Latin
    America's Prospects for Growth and Development.* Oxford: Blackwell, 1989.
    *This book presents a recent economic history of Latin America and its
    debt crisis. It examines the possibilities for private-sector growth and
    strategies used by the governments in this region for economic
    development.*

Eichengreen, Barry, and Peter H. Lindert, eds. *The International Debt Crisis
    in Historical Perspective.* Cambridge, Mass.: MIT Press, 1989.
    *This book is a collection of studies concerning the history of international
    debt, with particular focus on those factors that contributed to the current
    world debt crisis.*

Madrid, Raul L. *Over-exposed: U.S. Banks Confront the Third World Debt
    Crisis.* Washington, D.C.: Investor Responsibility Research Center,
    1990.
    *This book presents the results of a study concerning U.S. banks'
    involvement in the world debt crisis. It presents a complete analysis of the
    U.S. banks' lending motives, risk considerations, and rescheduling
    behaviors.*

Miller, Morris. *Debt and the Environment: Converging Crises.* New York:
    United Nations Publications, 1991.
    *This book simultaneously analyzes the world debt crisis and the rising
    environmental crisis. A wide range of economic and financial
    imbalances were found to exist that require an integrated policy
    approach to resolve both problems as a simultaneous system in
    dysfunction.*

Mohr, Ernst. *Economic Theory and Sovereign International Debt.* New York:
    Academic Press, 1991.
    *This book is an analysis of the debt crisis, using theoretical economics
    rather than presenting empirical evidence. It explains the debt crisis as a
    function of standard economic rationing through markets.*

O'Cleireacain, Seamus. *Third World Debt and International Policy.* New York:
    Praeger Press, 1990.
    *This book is an examination of international political economy from the
    perspective of the world debt crisis. Causes of the debt crisis are analyzed
    in a framework of historic, political, and economic variables.*

Sachs, Jeffery D., ed. *Developing Country Debt and the World Economy.*
    Chicago: University of Chicago Press, 1989.

This book is a collection of research reports and essays concerning various aspects of the LDC debt crisis and its impact on the world economy. Several case studies are included in the book, including studies concerning Argentina, Brazil, Indonesia, South Korea, and Turkey among others.

United Nations. *World Economic Survey: 1991/92: A Reader.* New York: United Nations Publications, 1991.

This book contains articles covering a wide variety of topics. Included in this book are articles concerning the current state of the world economy, women, poverty, the end of the Cold War, and international markets.

ARTICLES

Avery, William P. "The Origins of Debt Accumulation among LDCs in the World Political Economy." *Journal of Developing Areas* 24 (4; July 1990): 503–521.

This article examines the various causes for LDCs to accumulate external debt. It focuses primarily on Latin American countries.

Baer, Werner, Joseph Perry, and Murray Simpson, eds. "Special Issue—Latin America: The Crisis of the Eighties and the Opportunities of the Nineties." *Quarterly Review of Economics and Business* 31 (3; Autumn 1991).

This special issue of the journal examines the economic problems of Latin America during the 1980s and the historical events leading to those problems. The articles also suggest future directions for progress in the region.

Berg, Gerald C. "The Effects of the External Debts of Mexico, Brazil, Argentina, Venezuela and the Philippines on the United States." *Applied Economics* 20 (7; July 1988): 939–956.

This article analyzes the effects of the external debt of several LDCs on U.S. balance of payments. The evidence suggests that the United States suffered decreases in forty of sixty-one nonservice industries in net trade.

Boehmer, Ekkehart, and William L. Megginson. "Determinants of Secondary Market Prices for Developing Country Syndicated Loans." *Journal of Finance* 45 (5; December 1990): 1517–1540.

This article reports evidence that a country's adoption of a debt-conversion program reduces its loan market prices significantly. It is also shown that loan prices depend on a country's solvency rather than liquidity variables.

Bulow, Jeremy, and Kenneth Rogoff. "Sovereign Debt: Is to Forgive to Forget?" *American Economic Review* 79 (1; March 1989): 43–50.

This article shows that reputational damage resulting from default or rescheduling is insufficient to enforce international loan contracts with small countries, as is the case with large LDCs. Sanctions must be specified in the loan contract with small countries to provide for enforcement.

Cohen, Daniel. "Low Investment and Large LDC Debt in the 1980s." *American Economic Review* 83 (3; June 1993): 437–449.

This article reports empirical evidence that a large foreign debt does not predict low investment in LDCs. However, the study did find evidence that debt service obligations crowds out investment, at a ratio of about three dollars to each dollar of debt service.

Conybeare, John C. "On Repudiation of Sovereign Debt: Sources of Stability and Risk." *Columbia Journal of World Business* 25 (1/2; Spring/Summer 1990): 46–52.
This article assumes that repayment of sovereign loans depends on a country's willingness rather than ability to repay. The author suggests that domestic politics is far more important in the repayment decision than economic measures of the ability to repay.

Fullerton, Thomas M. "Predictability of Secondary-Market Developing-Country Debt Prices." *Applied Economics* 25 (10; October 1993): 1365–1371.
This article examines the development of secondary markets for LDC debt instruments. It also reports the results of econometric study of the predictor variables for secondary-market prices for three Latin American countries.

Ganitsky, Joseph, and Gerardo Lema. "Foreign Investment through Debt–Equity Swaps." *Sloan Management Review* 29 (2; Winter 1988): 21–29.
This article examines debt–equity swaps as a strategy for LDCs to mitigate their indebtedness. The advantages of these arrangements are examined in detail.

Hartmann, Mark A., and Dara Khambata. "Emerging Stock Markets: Investment Strategies of the Future." *Columbia Journal of World Business* 28 (2; Summer 1993): 82–104.
This article examines the development of emerging stock markets in LDCs. The emerging stock markets have the potential to displace foreign indebtedness in the accumulation of capital in LDCs and have performed impressively since 1982 by more than doubling their percentage of global market equity.

Kenen, Peter B. "Organizing Debt Relief: The Need for a New Institution." *Journal of Economic Perspectives* 4 (1; Winter 1990): 7–18.
This article examines the need for an International Debt Discount Corporation (IDDC) to assist in resolving the debt crisis. The IDDC proposal is described in both structure and function.

Klein, Thomas. "Innovation in Debt Relief: The Paris Club." *Finance & Development* 29 (1; March 1992): 42–43.
This article reports that the Paris Club has been effective in assisting in severely indebted, low-income countries in restructuring debt to developed countries.

Lee, Suk Hun. "Are Credit Ratings Assigned by Bankers Based on the Willingness of LDC Borrowers to Repay?" *Journal of Developmental Economics* 40 (2; April 1993): 349–359.
This article empirically examines various measures of the willingness of LDCs to repay as explanatory variables for variations in banker credit ratings of LDCs.

Lehman, Howard P. "International Creditors and the Third World: Strategies and Policies from Baker to Brady." *Journal of Developing Areas* 28 (4; January 1994): 191–217.

This article reviews plans to mitigate the world debt crisis introduced in and continuing after the 1980s. Implications for intercreditor conflict and leverage of creditors in debt negotiations are examined.

Looney, Robert E. "The Influence of Arms Imports on Third World Debt." *Journal of Developing Areas* 23 (2; January 1989): 221–231.
This article examines the role played by military expenditures and arms imports in affecting the level of LDC indebtedness. Because military expenditures do not give rise to productive resources, it is doubtful that those countries buying arms can expand their purchases in the future.

Molz, Richard. "Privatization in Developing Countries." *Columbia Journal of World Business* 25 (1/2; Spring/Summer 1990): 17–24.
This article reports that many LDCs have embarked on ambitious programs of privatization. The privatization is motivated to enhance total economic productivity, increase national wealth, and help cope with the world debt crisis.

Nafziger, Wayne E. "Debt, Adjustment and Economic Liberalization in Africa." *Journal of Economic Issues* 27 (2; June 1993): 429–439.
This article examines the move toward liberalization of many African economies. It presents evidence that the World Bank, IMF, and creditor nations have acted as a cartel that has harmed economic growth in sub-Saharan Africa.

Rahnama-Moghadam, Mashaalah, and Hedayeh Samavati. "Predicting Debt Rescheduling by Less-Developed Countries: A Probit Model Approach." *Quarterly Review of Economics and Business* 31 (1; Spring 1991): 3–14.
This article reports empirical results indicating that five economic variables predict debt rescheduling for most LDCs.

Rockerbie, Duane W. "Explaining Interest Spreads on Sovereign Eurodollar Loans: LDCs versus DCs, 1978–84." *Applied Economics* 25 (5; May 1993): 609–616.
This article reports that spreads charged to LDCs are a function of the risk of default. The evidence also shows that there is a spread that favors developed countries because of investment return in the developed countries.

Sachs, Jeffery D. "The Debt Crisis at a Turning Point." *Challenge* 31 (3; May/June 1988): 17–26.
This article describes the problems facing debtor nations and how the creditors had managed to avoid substantial difficulties. Particular attention is paid to the inflation problems in indebted LDCs.

Sachs, Jeffery D. "A Strategy for Efficient Debt Reduction." *Journal of Economic Perspectives* 4 (1; Winter 1990): 19–29.
This article critically examines debt-reduction proposals and concludes that the International Debt Facility is likely to succeed where voluntary approaches are unlikely to succeed. The author also examines five myths associated with the International Debt Facility.

Schwartz, Anna J. "International Debts: What's Fact and What's Fiction." *Economic Inquiry* 27 (1: January 1989): 1–19.
This study suggests that the 1982 debt servicing problems in LDCs did not arise from liquidity problems. The article presents evidence that the

1982 round of rescheduling arose because the debtor LDCs did not productively use the loans.

Warner, Andrew M. "Did the Debt Crisis Cause the Investment Crisis?" *Quarterly Journal of Economics* 107 (4; November 1992): 1161–1186.
This article is an empirical examination of the relation between the declines in investment in LDCs and the world debt crisis. It suggests that in eleven out of thirteen countries, debt-related explanations of the investment declines are not supported by the evidence.

Index

ABOUT THE AUTHORS

MASHAALAH RAHNAMA-MOGHADAM is Assistant Professor of Finance in the Department of Economics and Finance at Indiana-Purdue University in Fort Wayne. Rahnama has taught at several universities and has published several articles on international debt and world debt crisis in leading business and economics journals.

HEDAYEH SAMAVATI is Associate Professor of Economics in the Department of Economics and Finance at Indiana-Purdue University in Fort Wayne. Samavati has experience teaching economics and statistics at the undergraduate and graduate levels. She has several publications in the areas of macroeconomics and international business in leading economics and business journals.

DAVID A. DILTS is Professor of Economics and Labor Relations in the Department of Economics and Finance at Indiana-Purdue University in Fort Wayne. He has authored or coauthored six books and eighty articles concerning economics and labor relations issues.

ISBN 0-89930-854-6

HARDCOVER BAR CODE